Green

MW00477657

...and

1997

LEHMAN BROTHERS

Trends in Commercial Mortgage-Backed Securities

Edited by

Frank J. Fabozzi, CFA
Adjunct Professor of Finance
School of Management
Yale University
and
Editor
Journal of Portfolio Management

Robert Paul Molay
Book Editor
IMN/Information Management Network

Published by Frank J. Fabozzi Associates

©Copyright 1998 by Frank J. Fabozzi Associates
New Hope, Pennsylvania

Cover design by Robert Paul Molay

ISBN: 1-883249-45-7

Printed in the United States of America

Table of Contents

Contributing Authors

Haejin Baek	Lehman Brothers
Walter C. Barnes	Mortgage Analytics Inc.
Clive Bull	J.P. Morgan & Co.
Donald G. Carden	O'Melveny & Myers LLP
Howard Esaki	Morgan Stanley Dean Witter
John Felletter	Capital Trust
Tricia Brady Hall	Lehman Brothers
Ann Hambly	Nomura Asset Capital Services LLC
Richard Levine	E&Y Kenneth Leventhal Real Estate Group
Phoebe J. Moreo	E&Y Kenneth Leventhal Real Estate Group
John Mulligan	Prudential Securities Inc.
Joseph Philips	Morgan Stanley Dean Witter
Laura Quigg	Sanford C. Bernstein & Co.
Loy Saguil	Prudential Securities Inc.
Scott P. Sprouse	Mortgage Analytics Inc.

Index of Advertisers

GE Capital Asset Management Inc.

Intex Solutions, Inc.

Lehman Brothers

J.P. Morgan

Prudential Securities

The Trepp Group

Wall Street Analytics

Walter C. Barnes is president of Mortgage Analytics, Inc., a firm he founded in 1993. The mission of Mortgage Analytics is to analyze commercial mortgage credit risk and develop credit-risk analysis and performance benchmarking systems.

Before founding Mortgage Analytics, Barnes was assistant director of grants and applied research for the Wisconsin Center for Urban Land Economics Research at the University of Wisconsin-Madison.

Earlier in his career, Barnes was a vice president and director of research with the Travelers Realty Investment Company. At the Travelers he developed the first quantitatively-based commercial mortgage risk analysis system.There he was responsible for analysis and research of the company's $1.2 billion real estate portfolio.

Barnes holds a bachelor of science degree from Texas A&M University and a master's degree in business administration from Southern Methodist University. He has published articles in *Mortgage Banking Magazine*, the *Journal of Real Estate Research*, the *Journal of American Real Estate and Urban Economics Association*, and *Journal of Real Estate Finance*.

Scott P. Sprouse is vice president of business development at Mortgage Analytics, Inc., in West Hartford, Conn.

Sprouse has held senior marketing positions at Securities Software & Consulting, Thomson Financial Information, Trepp & Co., Dun & Bradstreet Economic Services Inc., Wharton Econometric Forecasting Associates, and American Management Systems Inc.

He holds a bachelor of arts degree from Wesleyan University, a master of arts degree from Yale University, and a master's degree in business administration from Columbia University.

Chapter 1

Measuring Risks in the Whole-Loan Commercial Market

Walter C. Barnes
President
Mortgage Analytics, Inc.

Scott P. Sprouse
Vice President, Business Development
Mortgage Analytics, Inc.

The CMBS market has exploded for many reasons that will be mentioned in other chapters of this book. One of the most notable features of the CMBS structure is its ability to transfer risk to those most able to bear it. However, despite the credit enhancing structural features of commercial mortgage-backed securities, there is still an urgent need to understand and analyze the creditworthiness of the underlying collateral.

While American investors, by nature, tend to be optimistic — witness the creation of new markets such as CMBS — one need not go far back in time to remember the Mutual Benefit implosion or the TICOR/EPIC fiasco. We applaud the growth of the CMBS market as verification that the $1 trillion commercial real estate mortgage market may finally be ready to "eat at the grownup's table" of the fixed-income capital market. However, we feel that we would be remiss if we did not offer a few words of caution and share several insights as a guide to recognizing when problems are about to occur and how to deal with them. As poet and philosopher George Santayana phrased it, "Those who do not remember the past are condemned to repeat it." Or, on a more earthly plain, Yogi Berra observed that, "The future ain't what it used to be."

THE PERSPECTIVE OF RECENT YEARS

The roller-coaster history of the commercial mortgage market over the past 20 years illustrates the erratic nature of liquidity in that market.

One measure of liquidity is volume: Large volumes of mortgage origination suggest liquidity; smaller volumes suggest less liquidity. The correlation is not perfect, but the movement in net lending volume in the 1980s and early 1990s is consistent with a story of a very liquid commercial mortgage market in the early 1980s, a very illiquid market from 1988 to 1992, and a market from 1992 to the present in which liquidity is beginning to return. Net commercial lending activity rose steadily until 1987, dropped dramatically from 1988 through 1992, and — as shown in Exhibit 1 — began to rise from 1992 until the present.

Exhibit 1: Net Commercial Lending Activity

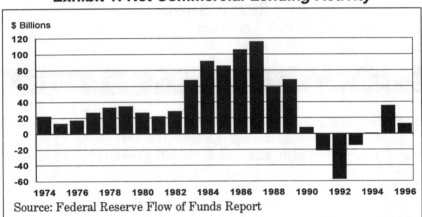

Source: Federal Reserve Flow of Funds Report

In the early years of the 1980s, a number of events drew enormous amounts of capital into that market. The 1981 tax act, with its generous passive-loss, depreciation, and capital-gains provisions, made commercial real estate very attractive as a tax shelter. The 1986 Plaza agreement, which ratcheted down the value of the dollar against the Japanese yen and most European currencies, made investments in American commercial real estate seem irresistibly inexpensive to foreigners.

The most important source of the surge in the commercial mortgage market was the deregulation of financial institutions in the early 1980s. The combination of higher levels of deposit insurance and reduced regulatory oversight gave all financial institutions in general, but savings and loans institutions in particular, the incentive to get money out the door as quickly as possible. The beneficiary of much of that money was the commercial real estate mortgage market.

The commercial market became so liquid that, by 1984, it was awash in a sea of liquidity. Interest rates on commercial loans were actually close to rates on Treasury securities of comparable maturity. Next, loan-to-value ratios rose to their highest levels in recent years. Finally, the combination of high interest rates and high LTVs led to the lowest debt-coverage ratios of recent history. The prevailing attitude of the day was that all real estate loans would be buoyed by rising collateral values. Clearly, this party could not continue.

As happens in the aftermath of most parties, the artificially induced real estate boom of the middle 1980s produced a hangover known as overbuilding. Empty office buildings, shopping centers, and condominiums began littering the landscape. The rolling real estate recession began in the Southwest and Mountain States, where energy economies gone bust exacerbated the structural problems already described. Eventually, the problems spread nationwide. The 1986 Tax Reform Act magnified the problem. It took away tax benefits emanating from the 1981 law and rendered many projects insolvent that might otherwise have remained solvent.

The consequence of these actions was a substantial rise in commercial mortgage delinquencies and foreclosures, as shown in Exhibit 2.

The regulatory agencies reacted to the real estate problem by clamping down hard on the commercial mortgage credit market. New risk-based capital rules made it more difficult for the commercial banks and life insurers to make and hold real estate loans. The Federal Institutions, Reform, and Recovery Act (FIRREA) of 1989 pretty much took S&Ls out of the commercial real estate market. FIRREA also

Exhibit 2: Commercial Mortgage Delinquencies and Foreclosures

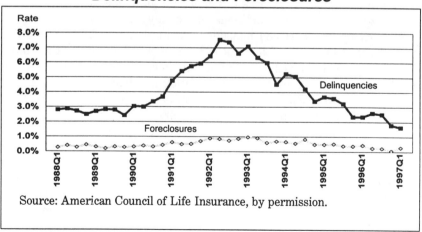

Source: American Council of Life Insurance, by permission.

required federally insured financial institutions to support their loans with appraisals drafted by certified appraisers. Both the Federal Reserve System and the National Association of Insurance Commissioners proposed tight new loan-to-value ratio rules and allocation requirements that reduced liquidity even further.

Inflationary expectations for real estate were reduced in the late 1980s because the market was convinced that the earlier price spiral had ended and because the overbuilding made it unlikely that rents would rise. As a result, loans that were poorly underwritten would no longer be bailed out by collateral appreciation. Consequently, financial institutions only made new loans that were supported by strong appraisals featuring conservative loan-to-value ratios.

So it came to be that the commercial mortgage market swung wildly from having an overabundance of liquidity in the middle 1980s to a shortage in the early 1990s. Since 1994, commercial real estate markets have rebounded sharply nationwide. Many experts think the factors are in place that could sustain this rally for several years. Nevertheless, given the cyclicality of real estate, another downturn will occur and you should be armed with better tools to anticipate and cope with it.

A CURRENT PERSPECTIVE

The perspective of history can help us focus on the current characteristics of the commercial mortgage market in terms of loan underwriting, trends in the early 1990s, current trends, documentation and control, and fixed-income asset allocation.

Loan Underwriting

The FIRREA and NAIC risk-based capital guidelines virtually dictate that regional economic conditions are a key ingredient in mortgage underwriting and portfolio management. First, many financial institutions located in areas with weak economies will have loans they must mark down. This means they might fall short of the risk-based capital guidelines and are, therefore, in no position to advance commercial real estate loans. New England makes for an obvious case in point with its 20% drop in collateral total return from 1990 to 1993.

Beyond regional economic analysis, solvency has become a concern for financial institutions when underwriting mortgages on income property. In the early 1990s, institutions seemed more concerned with current cash flows than "stabilized" net operating income. The actual cash thrown off by leases and the creditworthiness of the tenants holding those leases seemed much more important than before. At the same time, projected sales prices or reversion values derived from the "going out" capitalization rate are heavily discounted or even ignored completely during underwriting. As liquidity flows back in to market, we can see the trends from the early 90s reversing as cap rates for all property types are decreasing to levels not seen since the late 1980s.

Trends: The Early 1990s

Despite justifiable conservatism among commercial mortgage lenders, loan-to-value ratios in the early 1990s were not even close to their lowest levels historically. The reason for this was twofold: lower overall interest rates in the capital markets and a more realistic appraisal process. Falling interest rates also increased the debt-service-coverage ratio. A mortgage originated with a lower loan balance carried lower debt service payments. Debt-coverage ratios increased dramatically over the early 1990s and stood at historically high levels by 1992.

Many players in the commercial mortgage market wonder which is more informative: loan-to-value or debt coverage? Underwriters should rely on both. In any case, it is clear that financial institutions tend to keep loan-to-value ratios quite similar across property types.

Given the discussion on underwriting, this relative constancy of the loan-to-value ratio may seem paradoxical. Yet we can see the constancy (relative to the debt-coverage ratios) of the loan-to-value ratio by reviewing ACLI mortgage originations from 1970 Q4 to 1996 Q4, as seen in Exhibit 3 for the LTVs and in Exhibit 4 for the DCRs. We see that loan-to-value ratios are quite similar across the two property types (for the most part). And yet, the debt-coverage ratios for different property types have a larger coefficient of variation (the standard deviation divided by the average) than the loan-to-value ratios, as shown in Exhibit 5.

It appears that regulatory fiat will strengthen loan-to-value as the primary underwriting standard of the future. The Federal Reserve Board and the NAIC have proposed regulations that would set maximum loan-to-value ratios for a variety of property types. Should these loan-to-value regulations be codified (there is a lower chance of this happening now than several years ago, but it could still happen) , and should they be binding in the marketplace, they could place serious limitations on the flexibility of financial institutions to solve the optimal control problem involving other mortgage characteristics, such as debt coverage ratio and effective yields.

The lender uses a combination of contract interest rates and origination fees to compensate for varying levels of risk. Financial institutions offer interest rates based upon a risk-free rate of the appropriate term plus a liquidity and risk premium. (There should be a strong rela-tionship between a property type's expected delinquency rate and the interest rates lenders require to compensate for risk.) Historically, this

Exhibit 3: Loan-to-Value Ratios
Multifamily and Office Properties

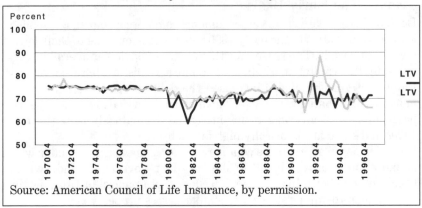

Source: American Council of Life Insurance, by permission.

Exhibit 4: Debt Coverage Ratios
Multifamily and Office Properties

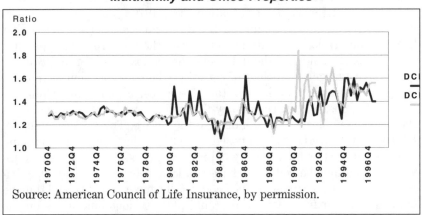

Source: American Council of Life Insurance, by permission.

Exhibit 5: Loan-to-Value versus Debt Coverage Ratios

Property Type	LTV (Avg)	LTV (Std)	CV	DCR (Avg)	DCR (Std)	CV
Apartments	71.8	3.3	0.046	1.3	0.10	0.080
Office	72.9	3.6	0.049	1.3	0.12	0.091

has been a major area of oversight in the commercial mortgage lending arena.

The average term to maturity has remained at around the 10-year mark since the end of 1982. The term to maturity refers to the time that the mortgage's outstanding loan balance is due, but not necessarily when the mortgage is amortized. Mortgages with terms to maturity of greater than five years have taken up between 40% and 60% of the market in recent years. The relationship between mortgage yields and term to maturity seems uncorrelated. This may be an artifact of the database that we are examining.

While terms to maturity have not changed much in recent years, amortization characteristics have. As recently as 1990, about 29% of commercial mortgages that ACLI members originated were interest-only with no amortization. By 1996, that number had fallen to around 5%, as shown in Exhibit 6. In 1990, 33% of all loans had no interest-only period during their life. By 1996, that number had risen to 81%.

The speed of amortization of commercial mortgages for the various property types has converged recently, as shown in Exhibit 7.

In 1990, the speed varied significantly by property type with industrial property loans carrying payments that would amortize the loans over a 29-year period, while office, apartment, and retail loans amortized over about 40 years on average. In 1996, the speed of amortization clustered around the 20- to 25-year period. Also, the average amortization periods have dropped from 1990 to 1994, but the amortization period has recently risen for apartment loans.

Exhibit 6: Amortization Characteristics

Amortization Type	% of Mortgages Originated			
	1990	1992	1994	1996
No Amortization	28.9%	15.1%	14.4%	5.3%
Partial Amortization (No I/O period)	30.0%	59.5%	66.2%	64.0%
Partial Amortization (I/O period)	38.2%	20.0%	9.0%	13.7%
Full Amortization	2.9%	5.3%	10.4%	16.9%

Exhibit 7: Amortization Speed by Property Type

Property Type	Amortization Period (Years)			
	1990	1992	1994	1996
Apartments	43	27	23	26
Office	45	24	22	23
Retail	42	27	22	21
Industrial	29	19	21	19

Current Trends

The creation and expansion of the CMBS market has brought more liquidity and lower rates to the commercial mortgage market as well as risk diversification, both through the CMBS structure and the broadened investor base. The entrance of conduits into the lending arena with banks and insurers, however, has created a boon for borrowers. In the rush to create loans for securitization, spreads are tightening and underwriting standards are weakening. LTVs are heading higher (rising into the 80% plus percentile range for selected programs). Also, the term of the loans is beginning to stretch out. There is a palpable worry that lenders are now starting to take greater risks that the next recession will surely test.

Documentation and Control

Commercial mortgage documentation generally contains a note that spells out interest and repayment provisions: the initial contract interest rate, potential adjustments to that rate, call features, the term to maturity, and amortization characteristics. The mortgage document also includes a variety of clauses for the protection of the borrower, lender, or both. These include due-on-sale clauses, subordination agreements, insurance clauses, prepayment provisions, assignment provisions, and defeasance clauses. Loans in excess of $100,000 must also be supported with appraisals by state-certified appraisers. Lenders may require rent rolls or possibly the property's actual leases.

The leases can take on a variety of forms. The length of the lease contract can range from one night (in the case of hotels) to more than 10 years (in the case of some types of industrial property). Leases can have "gross" or "net" provisions, which to a large extent determine whether the landlord or tenant bears the risk from changing expenses. Tenant improvement expenses can be borne by tenants and/or by landlords (depending upon the real estate market conditions at the time). Retail leases often contain overage or percentage rent clauses, which allow landlords to share in some portion of retail sales receipts. As the national real estate markets have softened, leases have contained concessions which give tenants periods of free rent.

Commercial mortgages impart a degree of control to the investor over the borrower's capital structure that is not present to the corporate bond investor. Most commercial mortgage documentation prohibits additional senior debt as well as severely limits or prohibits subordinated debt. For these reasons, the commercial mortgage lender is not subject to the same types of event risk as the corporate bond investor.

GLOBAL ASSET ALLOCATION

Investors in both whole loans and CMBS are beginning to examine and perceive that the commercial mortgage investments that they bring to their investment committee must compete within the global capital model. This section examines the performance characteristics of the commercial mortgage market from the perspective of the global capital markets. The performance characteristics to be examined include the risk/return premiums in the commercial mortgage market and the correlations to those of the other capital markets on a total-return basis. As yet, there is no transactions-based total-return commercial mortgage index series; therefore we will use the Berkshire/Barnes Commercial Mortgage Performance Series as a proxy for the commercial mortgage market.

To begin our examination of the commercial mortgage market from the capital market perspective, let's analyze it on both a longitudinal (over time) and a cross-sectional basis (commercial mortgage market share within the total capital market). An analysis of the corporate bond market is included along with the commercial mortgage market because commercial mortgages are often seen as corporate bond surrogates in an asset allocation framework. The commercial mortgage market grew to approximately $ 1 trillion by the end of 1996 from approximately $700 billion in 1985 — a 44.7% increase. However, the commercial mortgage markets shrunk as a percentage of the overall credit market over this time. In 1985, the commercial mortgage market was 8.43% of the overall credit market, while the percentage had fallen to 6.9% by the end of 1996. At the same time, the corporate bond market grew from $818.9 billion in 1985 to $1.399 trillion in 1996, up 70.8%. However, the corporate bond market shrunk in percentage terms to 9.6% by the end of 1996 from 9.92% of the total credit market in 1985.

How do the risk/return profiles of commercial mortgages compare with the rest of the capital markets? Exhibit 8, The Capital Market Correlation Matrix, compares commercial mortgages with other asset classes. This matrix illustrates once again the desirable characteristics of the commercial mortgage market versus the other fixed-income instruments. As an example, the correlation of commercial mortgages with the S&P 500 is 31%, while the correlation of the equity index and the corporate bond index is 40%.

Exhibit 9 illustrates the risk/return tradeoff for all of the listed asset categories. The "efficient frontier" analysis again demonstrates the desirable risk/return features of the commercial mortgage asset class.

Exhibit 8: Capital Correlation Matrix

	B/B Multi-family	B/B Retail	B/B Office	B/B Indus-trial	B/B Com-posite	Corp. Bonds	Gvmt/ Corp.	Treasury	S&P 500	RE Total	CPI
Number of Obs	76	76	76	76	76	76	76	76	76	76	76
Quarterly Return (%)	2.40	2.37	2.05	2.41	2.27	2.38	2.31	2.38	3.60	1.96	1.23
Standard Deviation (%)	2.29	2.84	2.49	2.79	2.24	5.11	4.10	6.69	7.10	1.89	0.93

	B/B Multi-family %	B/B Retail %	B/B Office %	B/B Indus-trial %	B/B Com-posite %	Corp. Bonds %	Gvmt/ Corp. %	Treasury %	S&P 500 %	RE Total %	CPI %
B/B Multifamily Index	100										
B/B Retail Index	69	100									
B/B Office Index	73	61	100								
B/B Industrial Index	71	78	69	100							
B/B Composite Index	91	81	92	81	100						
Corporate Bonds	24	10	21	20	23	100					
Gvmt/Corp	23	9	20	21	22	99	100				
Treasury	26	12	23	21	25	95	97	100			
S&P 500	33	7	33	20	31	40	38	40	100		
RE Total	-16	-12	10	-9	-7	-20	-18	-19	-7	100	
CPI	-32	-39	-35	-41	-39	-32	-29	-35	-13	49	100

Exhibit 9: Risk and Return for Commercial Mortgages A Capital Market Perspective

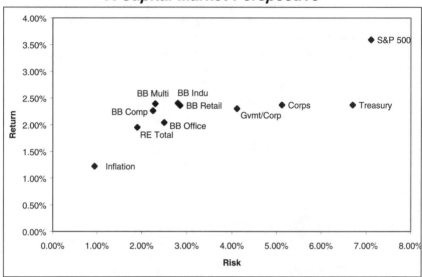

The Need for Quantitative Tools to Monitor Risk

The missing link in the commercial mortgage market and the derivative CMBS market is an industry standard commercial mortgage risk-analysis process that, among other things, can be used to assign performance-based statistical quality ratings similar to those of corporate bonds.

While the attractiveness of commercial mortgages from a yield and diversification perspective is apparent, the level of generally accepted risk analysis has not kept up with the volume and maturity of this market. The need for better risk analysis becomes even more magnified with the rapid development of the commercial mortgage derivative market — the issuance of securitizations — which now constitutes more than 10% of the $1 trillion-plus commercial mortgage market and is growing quickly.

To illustrate the point on both quality ratings and pricing, Exhibit 10 shows the pricing on commercial mortgages for two property types (office versus multifamily) for the period 1988 to 1997. Although every real estate professional knows about the very real differences in risk in the characteristics of these two property types (see Exhibit 11 for differences in delinquent loan behavior for the two property types), there has been almost no pricing differential to reflect these differences in the quality of the mortgages based on these property types.

At Mortgage Analytics, Inc., we have worked in three related areas involved with quantifying risk in the commercial mortgage market: analyzing risk down to the individual loan level, developing performance indices for different property types in different markets, and producing rigorous quality rating systems for commercial mortgages similar to those available in the corporate bond market.

We have developed an option-based mortgage model that seeks to understand the conditions that motivate a borrower to default — the probability or incidence of a credit event (delinquency, foreclosure, restructure, etc.), the loss severity of the credit event, and the timing of the credit event. For a loan or any portfolio aggregation of loans, a cred-

Exhibit 10: Interest Rates
Multifamily and Office Properties

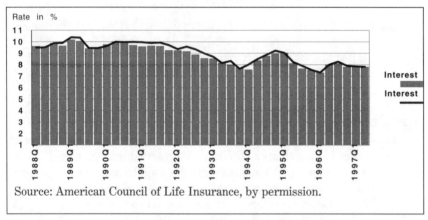

Source: American Council of Life Insurance, by permission.

Exhibit 11: Delinquency Rates
Multifamily and Office Properties

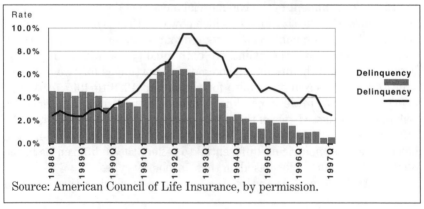

Source: American Council of Life Insurance, by permission.

it risk adjusted cash flow is produced. The difference between the contractual cash flow and the credit-risk-adjusted cash flow translates into a yield degradation of the commercial mortgage expressed in basis points.

We have developed *the Risk Analyzer®* to translate credit-loss risk into yield degradation across an entire commercial loan portfolio. *The Risk Analyzer®* allows the user to monitor risk at user-specified subset (portfolio, market, submarket, zip code, loan level). It instantaneously reflects the effect of revised market forecasts or updated credit events on loans. With this tool, the user can develop and maintain a rigorous commercial-loan-quality rating system with categories segregated by basi. point loss potential in order to:

- Identify and segregate high-risk loans.
- Value loans based on current and expected market conditions.
- Perform simulations of economic scenarios to see effects on portfolio.
- Conform to key risk-based capital lending requirements by linking loan valuation to risk factors in a credible framework.

The Berkshire Barnes Indexes for commercial loans on office, multifamily, retail, and warehouse properties were also developed at Mortgage Analytics, Inc. This family of indexes is an integral part of a trend to develop portfolio benchmarks.

Finally, the need for and movement toward more quantifiable rating systems for commercial mortgages must be acknowledged. The major advantages of a statistically based quality rating system for commercial mortgages are:

- Providing the basis for learning important lessons from performance experiences.
- Identification of the relevant factors that measure the degree of risk in a loan and consistent application and "pricing" of these factors across all mortgage loans originated by numerous underwriters and investors.
- Application both to new loans and existing loans in a consistent framework.
- Application both to individual loans and portfolios of loans.
- Providing an industry standard.

To bring us full circle, we would like to leave the reader of this book with two thoughts: We hope that participants in the commercial mortgage market will learn the lessons of its past and that this will lead to better risk monitoring, now and in the future.

C live Bull is a vice president of J.P. Morgan & Co. Prior to joining J.P. Morgan in January 1998, Bull was director of commercial mortgage finance at Smith Barney Inc. He joined Smith Barney in September 1994 with a mandate to develop commercial mortgage origination and securitization at the firm.

Earlier in his career, Bull spent eight years at PaineWebber, where he carried out several functions, eventually becoming manager of the structured finance group. His initial activities in the single-family mortgage business included structuring, negotiating, and closing PaineWebber's first agency REMICs and structuring and negotiating some of the pioneering trades of subordinate securities. In 1992 he began to focus on multifamily and commercial mortgages and, in 1993-94 set up multifamily and commercial mortgage conduits and closed several securitizations. At Smith Barney, Bull developed a fledgling multifamily mortgage conduit into a full-size commercial and multifamily conduit.

Bull holds a bachelor of arts degree in politics, philosophy, and economics from Oxford University, and a Ph.D. in economics from the University of California, Los Angeles. Prior to joining Wall Street in 1986, he was an associate professor of economics at New York University.

Chapter 2

Originating and Processing Loans In a Conduit Operation

Clive Bull
Vice President
J.P. Morgan & Co.

Commercial mortgage conduits as an industry have grown from a small-scale, exotic, cottage industry in 1993 to a major source of debt finance for commercial real estate. Employment has gone from a few dozen, in small groups around Wall Street, to several hundred — located in every major Street firm as well as major banks and finance companies across the country.

This growth on the commercial side is, in many ways, a reprise of the growth of residential mortgage conduits a decade earlier. The stimulus has been the same in both cases. Developments in the capital markets made it economically feasible to channel capital directly from the capital markets to borrowers, rather than use the traditional lending institutions. Such disintermediation makes the allocation of capital more efficient and results in a lower cost of debt to borrowers.

However, the superior efficiency of disintermediation usually runs into a practical roadblock: The mechanisms by which would-be borrowers actually borrow are owned by precisely the institutions that are to be disintermediated. For instance, in principle the owner of an apartment building in 1992 might well have been able to get better mortgage loan terms on Wall Street than from a traditional lender. But the owner would not have known that. Almost surely, everyone such an owner would have called for a loan, in particular his or her local bank or mortgage banker, would have been able to provide a loan only through the usual intermediaries. To solve this practical problem, Wall Street had to construct its own origination system — namely, the conduits.

It is something of an oddity that origination systems should be set up by the divisions of Wall Street firms specializing in capital markets, rather than retail. The focus of a capital markets division is almost exclusively large-scale trading and market-making. It is almost devoid of service-intensive businesses such as mortgage loan origination. Moreover, the cost structure of a Wall Street capital markets division is particularly unsuitable for a labor-intensive business such as loan origination.

When disintermediation is in its infancy, however, profits are large enough so that such inefficiencies are not critical. It is essential to have access to large amounts of capital that can be put at risk while a pool of loans is being built up. As competition becomes more severe, as was the case in the residential mortgage loan business, traditional intermediaries will accept the reality that loan pricing and terms will be determined by the capital markets. At that juncture, Street firms will move out of the origination process. Commercial mortgage loan originations will be performed in more suitable institutions and locations. Until that happens, however, all the conduits are continuously trying different approaches to originating and processing loans. The lessons learned from this experimentation will affect the way the conduit business is run, no matter where it is eventually housed.

ORIGINATION

Direct versus Correspondent Systems

The origination systems chosen by commercial mortgage conduits are extremely varied and in constant flux. Indeed, most conduits will, to some extent, operate a mix of origination systems simultaneously. To put some order in this apparent chaos, think of conduit origination systems as lying on a continuum stretching from the pure correspondent variety at one end to pure, direct lending at the other. In a pure correspondent system, the conduit's only roles in origination are to price loans, review underwriting and closing documents, and fund the loan. Finding borrowers, negotiating the loan, ordering third-party reports, underwriting, and closing are all in the province of the correspondent. Conversely, in a pure direct lending system the conduit itself carries out all aspects of the loan-origination process.

Very few actual conduits have ever operated at either extreme of this continuum. However, most have been much closer to one extreme than the other. It is interesting to note a clear migration over time from the correspondent model to the direct lending model. With this migration pattern in mind, the discussion of origination in this chapter begins with correspondent systems, then moves to direct lending.

Origination Through Correspondents

When Wall Street initially wanted to accumulate large commercial mortgage loans ($1 million and above) it faced multiple problems ranging from how to contact potential borrowers to the mechanics of processing and closing a loan. Given the dearth of commercial mortgage origination experience on the Street at the time, the only practical way of overcoming these problems was to enter into arrangements with mortgage bankers that had experience as correspondents for life insurance companies and pension funds. Unfortunately for the mortgage bankers, the early '90s was a period of drought because their usual funding sources were largely out of the lending business. This made some of them very anxious to work with Wall Street firms.

Mortgage bankers had a wide variety of arrangements with life companies. The correspondent generally had the right to present prospective loans to the insurer and, if the insurer liked the proposal, to underwrite the loan, close it in the insurer's name, and service it. To be a successful correspondent, the mortgage banker needed to understand the life company's likes and dislikes for types of loans and underwriting standards. By replacing the life company's loan and servicing criteria with those of the conduit, the mortgage banker could become a conduit correspondent overnight.

Naturally, things are never quite that simple. The main stumbling blocks to becoming a correspondent for a conduit were the master loan purchase agreement (MLPA) and the servicing agreement. The MLPA is needed because the conduit wishes to structure its funding of the loan at the closing table as a purchase of a loan originated by the mortgage banker.

Not being the lender has two advantages for the conduit. First, lenders may have to be licensed or, at least, qualified to do business in a particular state. The trading area within a Wall Street firm is likely to do a very bad job of what is an expensive and time-consuming business in itself: finding out what is required in each state, setting up an appropriately licensed lending entity, and maintaining such licenses. The conduit can avoid these problems by playing the role of purchaser rather than lender. The second advantage of not being a lender is that it reduces, almost by definition, the conduit's exposure to lender-liability suits. Note that both of these advantages rely on the courts or regulatory authorities not looking through the legal formality of the purchase to the underlying economics of the transaction.

While the MLPA performs a useful function for the conduit, it has been a major problem for correspondents. By virtue of being a purchase agreement, the MLPA contains extensive representations and warranties as to the loans, how they were underwritten, the collateral, and the enforceability of the loan documents.

Any material breach of these representations and warranties as they relate to a particular loan would have to be cured by the mortgage banker. Failing a cure, the mortgage banker would have to buy back the loan.

The whole notion of giving representations and warranties was alien to commercial mortgage bankers (unlike their residential cousins), because their life company correspondent relationships were not set up as sales. Not only was the concept alien, but the possibility of having to buy back a defective loan was, rightly, terrifying. For most mortgage bankers, one such repurchase was enough to bankrupt them.

Negotiations over the MLPA were often very protracted and, in many cases, the MLPA prevented good mortgage bankers becoming conduit correspondents. Although negotiations can still take time today, the MLPA will seldom get in the way of setting up a correspondent relationship. This is due to two changes.

First, the representations and warranties have been eased. Originally, they followed those used in the residential area in terms of being absolute. For instance, there was usually a representation to the effect that the mortgage was a first lien. There is very little the mortgage banker can do to check this other than rely on the title company and the title policy. By stating the flat representation, the mortgage banker is essentially acting on blind faith that the title company is right. This is not a comfortable position to be in if you are betting your mortgage banking company. This type of flat or absolute representation has now been replaced by one that allows the mortgage banker to rely on the title report, dramatically reducing the mortgage banker's exposure.

The second change has been to limit the exposure of the mortgage banker under the MLPA. This has been done in several ways, most commonly by allowing the mortgage banker to set up a very thinly capitalized shell mortgage banking entity that sells loans to the conduit. This means that the repurchase obligation becomes moot, as it is highly unlikely that the shell entity would have the net worth to carry out the repurchase. The obligation is nevertheless worth having from the conduit's point of view, because a defective loan will still cause the mortgage banker pain and loss of equity in the shell entity. From this perspective, it will still provide a positive incentive for prudent underwriting.

Servicing agreements were another source of friction with potential correspondents. Initially, these agreements were drafted as though the mortgage banker would act as a master and special servicer while the loans were owned by the conduit. The mortgage banker was was expected to advance delinquent principal and interest (P&I) payments as well as to make servicing advances. This obligation was completely alien to the mortgage bankers. Their life company servicing agreements had no such requirements.

As most mortgage bankers had no lines of credit, there was a real fear that they simply could not fund such advances if they were ever required. Even if they got over the advancing requirement, they then had to cope with the possibility of becoming a sub-servicer once the loans had been securitized. Most servicing agreements had a section that required the correspondent to accept a sub-servicing agreement from the master servicer when the loans were securitized. As neither the identity of the master servicer nor the exact terms of the sub-servicing agreement were known when the servicing agreement was being signed between the conduit and the mortgage banker, the section dealing with the mortgage banker's servicing duties upon securitization was very general and very vague. As almost no commercial mortgage bankers had experience with securitization, let alone sub-servicing in the context of a securitization, this section of the servicing document always caused problems.

Most of these issues have been resolved over time. Most conduits realized that there was really no value to them in having the mortgage banker advance delinquent P&I payments, and so removed this requirement. Similarly, the sub-servicing issue has been substantially reduced by giving the conduit the right to take back the servicing without cause, usually with payment of a release price to the mortgage banker. If a suitable sub-servicing agreement cannot be reached, the mortgage banker can walk away from the servicing and the conduit can arrange for someone else to service the loans.

The correspondent system has several attractive features. Perhaps the most important is that it holds out the promise of being able to cover the entire United States rapidly for originations while maintaining a relatively low head count at the conduit. The rapid expansion is easy to understand. If the mortgage bankers are strategically located, the negotiation of, say, MLPAs with 10 mortgage bankers will enable a conduit to have a significant presence in every major real estate market in the United States. Moreover, the conduit needs only enough staff to provide initial review and pricing of proposed loans, and a quality-control check of the full underwriting package and closing documents. Thus, a conduit with a total head count on the order of 10 professionals can rapidly be in business nationwide.

This ability to leverage up high-cost conduit staff by using correspondents is extremely attractive. As a practical matter, however, this leverage is often less than might be expected. In particular, the quality-control checks on underwriting and closing can often evolve into full-blown underwriting and closing of loans.

This evolution stems from the lack of underwriting skills at most mortgage bankers. A life company correspondent often has more experience putting an underwriting package together than in actual underwriting. Moreover, even where the correspondent did, in fact, do the underwriting, they were never at risk on the loan and so rarely developed a lender's approach to underwriting. This is in sharp contrast to, for instance, FNMA DUS mortgage bankers who are at risk on their loans and so take a lender's view of underwriting.

Similarly, on the closing side, in many cases the life company would take care of the closing documents, leaving the correspondent simply to make the loan.

Underwriting and closing documents on conduit loans are much more severe than on old-style life company and pension fund loans. It is no wonder, then, that many mortgage bankers failed to underwrite and close in a fashion that allowed the conduit to limit its role to a mere review of the packages. In reality, the conduits had to be prepared to re-underwrite loans and get very involved in the closing process.

This lack of underwriting and closing skills is still very much a concern. But it is getting slightly less common over time as the mortgage banking community has become more experienced at dealing with conduits. But familiarity with conduits has raised a further problem: Very few of the mortgage bankers that act as correspondents to conduits do so for only one conduit exclusively. This makes complete sense for the mortgage banker. Given the frequency with which conduits enter and exit the industry, plus the continual swings in competitiveness between conduits, it is only prudent for the mortgage banker to build relationships with at least two conduits. Provided the volume of loans provided is large enough to retain the attention of each conduit, the mortgage banker will definitely be better off by having multiple conduit relationships.

From the conduit's point of view, this situation raises a problem. In simplest terms, these multiple relationships make it very difficult for a conduit to determine how hard the correspondent is pushing one conduit's product as opposed to the product of a rival.

This is just one instance of the general concern about a correspondent system: It is very hard for the conduit to control — or even monitor — the way its product is being marketed. In 1993 and 1994 this concern barely mattered. There was such a dearth of lenders that marketing and competing with other conduits were secondary issues at best. Now that there is so much capital chasing borrowers, it is critical to control marketing and be competitive. In today's environment, the weakness of the correspondent system has become a much more important concern. Attempts to keep correspondents' attention by providing volume-based pricing for the loans that they sell have been somewhat successful. However, as the volume premia are usually modest, these programs do not really solve the problem.

Direct Originations

A direct origination system takes inquiry directly from borrowers or, more commonly, brokers representing borrowers. In direct origination, the conduit rather than a correspondent builds an underwriting package, underwrites the loan, and closes it. As such, the direct conduit closely resembles a bank or thrift in the way it organizes originations.

This style places a considerable head-count and cost burden on the conduit. The conduit must market to borrowers and brokers and so incur considerable advertising and marketing expenses. It must also be set up to handle a large flow of inquiry, the bulk of which will be nonproductive. The conduit must then have a staff of underwriters and loan processors to assemble the loan packages and underwrite the loans. Finally, the conduit must be licensed to close loans nationwide and have a staff capable of handling these closings.

Other than the bricks and sticks of a full branch system, the direct conduit has all the operational costs of a bank or thrift functioning on a national basis.

Given the costs involved and the time it takes to put together such an organization, it is no surprise that only one of the early conduits, Column Financial, went the direct route. Even the newer direct conduits often began life as halfway houses. To get up and running fast and to avoid the tremendous head count required, some of these early direct conduits — for example, the early Nomura conduit — had an exclusive arrangement with one mortgage banker that took all the initial inquiry and handled the underwriting and closing of the loans. In other words, the conduit outsourced most of the work.

This use of outsourcing is still a common structure today. The old Prudential/Midland conduit and the Parallel/ContiFinance conduit both devolved all of the loan origination and closing duties to the mortgage banker, while the conduit provided financing and hedging services.

Most direct conduits today have brought the origination, underwriting, and closing functions in-house, although the staff used is often on a contract basis rather than permanent head count; Merrill Lynch is one good example.

Organization has been the key problem encountered by direct conduits. The challenge has been to build an origination, underwriting, and closing system that is geographically dispersed via regional origination offices, staffed by several dozen people. Meeting this challenge requires organizational skills and a commitment to systematic, consistent performance that goes very much against the grain of Wall Street's capital markets divisions. Many horror stories associated with the early days of direct originations arose because of attempts to run such a system like a Wall Street trading desk. Most conduits have gotten through these teething troubles and are now fully functional.

A Comparison

The direct conduit is undoubtedly the most popular origination system today and has had great success in generating large volumes of loans. The reasons why this way of originating conduit loans is currently preferred to the correspondent system are threefold:

- The conduit has control over its marketing and, at the level of the individual loan, negotiations with the prospective borrower.

- Given the poor level of underwriting by many mortgage bankers, many loans are underwritten twice. Going direct removes this costly double-underwriting.

- Given the lack of attention paid to closing by most mortgage bankers, one major advantage of going direct is that the conduit takes control of this process and can speed it up.

Do these advantages spell the end of correspondent conduits? This is perhaps the wrong question to ask. A better and more relevant question is: Can such labor-intensive organizations as direct conduits survive in a high-cost environment like Wall Street? Certainly, these direct conduits are profitable at present, but profit margins have been dropping precipitously and are likely to continue to drop.

At some point, conduits with very large head counts and average costs per head well in excess of $100,000 will be driven from the market. This will leave the field open for well-capitalized mortgage bankers to run their own, low-cost direct conduits. To be in the conduit business at all at that point, a Wall Street firm will need either some true competitive advantage in originations, such as a retail brokerage system, or a low-cost operation via some form of correspondent system.

PROCESSING

Loan processing can be divided into four phases: initial sizing and pricing, underwriting, closing, and quality control and cleanup. Underwriting receives the lion's share of attention in most organizations. But a good case can be made for initial sizing and closing being at least as important.

Initial Sizing and Pricing

All conduits start with the same kind of initial information package. This will include some historical property financials, a rent roll, a description of the property, a description of the borrower, and a loan request. The question is: What to do with this information?

There are three goals in dealing with this package. First of all, the response must be quick. A one-day turnaround is expected; anything much beyond three days is going to lose the conduit the deal and the correspondent. Second, the response needs to be accurate. There is no surer way to ruin a correspondent or borrower relationship than to size and price a loan initially, then cut back the loan or raise the spread after underwriting is complete, when no adverse material information has emerged in the underwriting process. Finally, the process must be cheap on a per-closed-loan basis.

The cost issue drives much of the design of the initial sizing and pricing process. In a direct conduit there will be a relatively large flow of inquiry from borrowers and brokers. Many of them will have little or no idea about the conduit's underwriting requirements. Or they will have the germ of an idea, but are just throwing the loan request out and seeing what sticks. In this situation the fraction of initial inquiries that result in a closed loan is likely to be very small. In turn, this means that the process for handling initial inquiries has to be very low-cost.

This cost restriction implies some form of analyst-and-spreadsheet process. An analyst with no real estate training is given a spreadsheet that will size loans on different property types and will also include a pricing matrix for loans. The analyst's job is to take the preliminary information supplied, make it fit the spreadsheet, and then generate a quote. If enough analysts are put to work, this system will have a short response time and relatively low cost. Of course, it will also generate a large number of erroneous quotes, because the real estate and/or the loan request does not match those for which the spreadsheets were designed. The analyst, being untrained in real estate, may not recognize the errors.

At the other extreme is the underwriter/trader process. Here, the initial inquiry comes directly to an underwriter who reviews the information and sizes a loan. The underwriter then consults a trader for pricing, if the loan is not plain-vanilla. This process will give very accurate quotes, but takes time and is inherently expensive. In fact, it is only really feasible if the initial inquiry itself is prescreened. A correspondent system has the advantage over a direct system in that the correspondent should be screening inquiry before passing it on to the conduit.

In fact, both direct and correspondent conduits use a mixture of these approaches to initial sizing and pricing. A direct conduit will have a mechanism for flagging certain inquiry as requiring more attention. Size of loan request is a common and very sensible criterion for routing the inquiry through an underwriter rather than an analyst. Property type is also often used. Multifamily properties lend themselves to the analyst-and-spreadsheet method, whereas skilled-care nursing homes do not. Conversely, many correspondent conduits will often delegate much of the sizing and pricing process to analysts for certain classes of loans. The underwriter in such cases simply oversees the process and maintains quality control.

Underwriting

Underwriting begins with the accumulation of an underwriting package. In a correspondent system the package is put together by the correspondent. This is a very time-consuming task that can have serious impact on the relationship with the borrower. It is important to remember that the information requirements for a conduit loan far exceed those traditionally required by lenders, notably banks and thrifts. There is, therefore, often a real sense of disbelief and shock when a new correspondent or a first-time conduit borrower faces a conduit information request checklist.

The borrower typically will believe that the conduit cannot possibly require all this information. The borrower will consequently send only part of it and firmly expect that the loan will be made promptly. It is therefore critical both for the relationship with the borrower and for the speed of loan origination to disabuse the borrower quickly of this notion.

Once the package is received for underwriting in a correspondent system, theoretically the underwriter will simply carry out a quality control check. Is the underwriting package complete? Are the third-party reports acceptable? Does the correspondent's underwriting memo satisfactorily explain the loan and why it should be made? In a direct system, the underwriter must truly underwrite the loan. This underwriting process is in many ways very similar to that at a traditional lender: In both cases, the underwriter is trying to assess the riskiness of the loan.

However, conduit underwriting has a twist. After establishing the risk factors in the loan, the next task is to assess whether the loan is marketable to rating agencies and subordinate-securities buyers. Suppose, for instance, that estimates have been made on an office building for lease rollover, likely tenant improvements, leasing commissions, and the likelihood of lease extensions. Is there a need for a TI and LC escrow? If so, how big in order to make the loan marketable?

In some conduits, marketability is treated as an underwriting issue and is dealt with by the underwriter. In others, marketability is viewed as being the responsibility of a deal manager or credit committee. The underwriter's task is then simply to point out the issues and provide the facts.

Both approaches have merit. The latter approach means that the underwriters can be pure real estate underwriters and need no rating agency knowledge or securitization experience. This type of underwriter is relatively cheap and plentiful. Moreover, in this approach only the credit committee need be up to speed on the latest rating agency and subordinate security buyer preferences.

The disadvantage of this approach becomes apparent when it is necessary to negotiate with the borrower. Mitigating loan credit risk will adversely affect the borrower. As the borrower has other financing options, there will be a negotiation over mitigating these risks that cannot be carried out by a credit committee. An underwriter who understands marketability issues is very well placed to conduct these negotiations quickly and effectively.

Closing

Having underwritten a loan and issued a commitment letter, the next step is to close the loan. Again, in a correspondent system this is largely the province of the correspondent. Part of the process is, in principle, straightforward, for example title and survey, and the correspondent can handle this well. A tougher issue is negotiating the loan documents. Obviously, the correspondent will have to obtain the conduit's permission for any changes in the documents. Lacking a very clear concept of what is or is not negotiable, the correspondent or his attorney can easily become a messenger — simply transmitting borrower's requests to the conduit and relaying back the conduit's responses. Needless to say, having such an intermediary does not speed up or lower costs of the closing process.

In a direct system, the conduit runs the closing process. Negotiating the loan documents is easier in this case. However, maintaining consistency of loan documents can be harder. In the correspondent system, the conduit will usually have one review counsel that will approve every set of loan documents. The availability of this counsel makes it relatively easy to ensure that all loans closed use the same standard documents and that negotiated changes are consistent with the level of risk a conduit finds acceptable. Consistency is harder for a direct conduit to maintain because it will typically use different law firms to close loans in different geographical areas, or even different firms for different property types. It is very difficult to ensure that all these firms are using the same standard documents and are negotiating those documents in the same way.

Post Closing

Conduit loans are, by definition, originated in order to be sold or, more often, securitized. For this reason, the true cost of operating a conduit should include the costs of delivering the closed loans to a buyer or into a trust. These costs can be quite substantial, particularly in terms of human resources. Moreover, these costs tend to occur precisely when the personnel resources of the conduit are already being used to capacity - namely, at securitization. It is therefore very important to reduce the cost of delivering loans to a trust and to spread the costs out over time, rather than have them concentrated at the time of delivery.

One seemingly trivial but regularly overlooked aspect of delivering loans is that the loan file, usually held by a custodial bank, should be complete. The typical problems with a loan file revolve around having certified copies rather than originals of the recorded documents, and title policy binders rather than original policies. These documents all dribble in randomly after closing, but often do not get to the custodian. Instead, they end up sitting in the closing attorney's or the conduit's offices. Unfortunately, these deficiencies usually come to light only shortly before a securitization, when time and spare manpower are both in short supply. To avoid this, a simple tracking system — together with a clear allocation of responsibilities among the conduit's staff — can ensure that the custodial exceptions report can be kept short.

A second, and more serious, source of delivery problems is errors in the closed loan documents. Unlike most large traditional lenders, most conduits do not have a formal quality-control process. Instead, they rely on the closing attorney and the custodian.

Many errors can get through this system. Examples are note dates and maturity dates that do not get updated when the closing on a loan is delayed. These errors are readily fixed if they are caught shortly after closing. But if they are missed they can be very hard to fix quickly shortly before securitization. It is also worthwhile remembering that if the documents are corrected, someone must check that the correction was done correctly. For example: Were all the relevant dates changed? Did the borrower sign or initial the changes as required for legal acceptability?

Perhaps the largest post-closing issues relate to data. The rating process calls on the conduit to deliver vast amounts of updated, accurate data to the rating agencies — which condense it down to three letters and a plus or minus sign. Delivering the data can be a nightmare unless they have been accumulated and scrubbed right from the date the loan was closed.

Data on the loan and its underwriting should be entered into a database very soon after the loan is closed. At that early stage, the accuracy of these data should be checked. This process is a valuable quality-control tool. While most errors in the database for a newly closed loan will have been caused by faulty input, some of the mistakes will accurately reflect errors in the loan.

Finally, the data that change over time, notably the financial information, need to be collected and entered into the database.

Ann Hambly is president and chief executive officer of Nomura Asset Capital Services LLC. Nomura made a strategic decision in October 1997 to form its own servicing group, thereby retaining control of the loan throughout its entire life cycle. As of third-quarter 1998, the NACS servicing portfolio is expected to be over $10 billion, making it one of the largest servicers for CMBS.

Prior to this position, Hambly was chief executive officer of GE Capital Asset Management Corp. GECAM's portfolio at the time of Hambly's departure was approximately $14 billion; $4 of that total was garnered by Hambly during her first year at GECAM as marketing director. Prior to joining GECAM in late 1995 she was director of marketing and operations for Bank of America in California.

Hambly has over 20 years of experience in the commercial servicing industry. She was chair of the Real Estate Capital Resource Association (RECRA) in 1996, is currently a governor on the board of directors of the Commercial Securitization and Secondary Market Association (CSSA), and is chair of its post-issuance committee. Hambly is also on the board of directors of the Multi-Family Housing Institute.

She has been a contributing author for many industry publications, and is a featured speaker at industry conferences.
Hambly attended the graduate school of the University of Southern California.

Chapter 3

Master Servicer, Special Servicer, and Trustee

Ann Hambly
President and Chief Executive Officer
Nomura Asset Capital Services LLC

The master servicer, special servicer, and trustee play important and distinct roles in a securitization. This chapter defines the roles and explain the functions of each.

DEFINITIONS

Master Servicer

There is only one master servicer in each securitization. The master servicer must be rated by the same agencies that rate the securitization itself. Because the master servicer performs the advancing, as described later in this chapter, the master servicing company (or its parent company) must also have a long-term debt rating by the agency that rates the securitization. The master servicer has overall responsibility to ensure that the loans are serviced in accordance with the standard of servicing spelled out in the particular pooling and servicing agreement that governs the securitization.

In conduits today, there are usually multiple sub-servicers. Although the differences in the duties of a sub-servicer and master servicer are described later in this chapter, it is important to note that the master servicer retains all liability to the trust for the servicing activities. Exhibit 1 lists the top five as of yearend 1996, based on amount of new business won in 1996. Approximately 75% of all commercial mort-

Exhibit 1: Leading Master Servicers for CMBS Issues

		Market Share (%)
1	Midland Loan Services	18.3
2	Amresco	16.5
3	GMAC Commercial Mortgage	7.6
4	Boatmen's National Mortgage	7.2
5	GE Capital	7.2

gage-backed securities are serviced by five to 10 master servicers.

Sub-Servicer

There can be multiple sub-servicers in each securitization. The sub-servicers usually are the same entities that originate the loans that become securitized. The sub-servicers are often mortgage banking companies, life companies, banks, etc. After originating a loan they retain the daily servicing by becoming the sub-servicer for those loans. sub-servicers do not need to obtain a rating and they have no responsibility for advancing.

Special Servicer

There is also only one special servicer in each securitization. The special servicer is appointed at the beginning of the securitization, although the work often does not start until loans begin to default. The special servicer is responsible for maximizing the returns (or, in some cases, minimizing the losses) to the certificate holders. Oftentimes, the special servicer is the very entity that owns the lowest tranches of certificates. The lowest tranche owner likes to have the special servicing responsibility so that it can be "in charge of its own destiny" or manage any loans that become delinquent. Approximately 75% of the securities in the CMBS industry are specially serviced by five to 10 special servicers.

Exhibit 2 shows the top five special servicers in the CMBS industry (based on new basics volume for 1996) as of year-end 1996.

Exhibit 2: Leading Special Servicers for CMBS Issues

		Deals Won in 1996
1	Lennar Partners	9.0
2	Amresco	7.5
3	Criimi Mae	7.0
4	Banc One Management	2.5
5	Midland Loan Services	3.0

Trustees

There is only one trustee for each securitization. The trustee holds legal title to the underlying security collateral for the benefit of the security holders. The trustee acts as a liaison between the master servicer and the certificate holders. The trustee is usually the backup advancer to the master servicer, which means that the trustee will be liable for advancing to the certificate holders if the master servicer ever defaults and/or does not advance. That is why the trustee has input into the selection of the master servicer for a securitization. The trustee must be comfortable that the master servicer is financially capable of advancing throughout the life of the securitization. The leading trustees for CMBS issues, that dominate the industry today, are State Street Bank, LaSalle National Bank, and Bankers Trust.

FUNCTIONS PERFORMED

Master Servicer

The master servicer plays a different role in securitizations for which there are subservicers than with securitizations for which there are no sub-servicers.

First, let's describe the functions performed by the master servicer when there are sub-servicers in the securitization. In this scenario, the master servicer is responsible for three basic functions:

- Reporting to the trust.
- Advancing.
- Oversight and liability of the sub-servicers.

First and foremost of these responsibilities is ensuring that the sub-servicers are continually servicing the loans in accordance with the prescribed servicing standard in the pooling and servicing agreement for that securitization. This is done in many different ways. The degree of oversight performed by the master servicer over the sub-servicer is, in many ways, determined by the degree of comfort the master servicer has with that particular sub-servicer. Sub-servicers that are new to the industry may be more closely monitored than long-term, proven performers.

The master servicer collects monthly loan performance reports and loan payments from the subservicers. These reports are consolidated into one standard report that is sent to the trustee on the remittance date prescribed in the pooling and servicing agreement. Typically, the subservicers are required to submit their reports to the master servicer a few days prior to the remittance date, giving the master servicer adequate time to prepare the consolidated report. The master servicer must remit to the trustee the total amount due to the certificate holders — the "scheduled payment" — regardless of how much is collected from the borrowers — the "actual payment." The difference between the two amounts is called the advance amount. The master servicer must make sure that the amount advanced per loan is never in excess of the value of the underlying real estate, so that the advanced amount will be recoverable to the master servicer at the eventual reinstatement of the delinquent loan or sale of the property.

Subservicer In this arrangement, the subservicer has the primary contact with the borrower and performs the basic functions often associated with a servicer of any loans. These functions include:

- Monthly billing and payment collection.
- Interest rate adjustments.
- Payment and monitoring of property taxes and insurance.
- UCCs.
- Basic reporting to the master servicer.

The sub-servicer remits to the master servicer only the actual payments collected from its borrowers. Again, there are usually multiple subservicers in a securitization reporting to one master servicer.

In a securitization for which there are no sub-servicers, the master servicer retains all the functions of a normal master servicer in addition to all the functions of the sub-servicers.

Special Servicer

When a loan becomes delinquent, the special servicer is responsible for returning it to performing status — via modification, restructure, or serious collection efforts — or else foreclosing the property and selling it. The special servicer must always consider the returns to the certificate holders when deciding which course of action to take. An analysis prior to any action determines the net amount the certificate holders would receive if the property were foreclosed and sold immediately. A similar analysis is performed when the loan is modified and the borrower continues to manage the property in hope that it will eventually return to performing status.

Whichever scenario is likely to return the most amount of money to the certificate holders is usually selected. Timing is critical, as all advances made to the certificate holders during the delinquency will affect the ultimate return they receive. In either scenario, the special servicer cannot give undue consideration to any class of certificate holders; all classes, or tranches, must be treated equally. This can require a fine balancing act when the special servicer owns some of the certificates — usually the lowest class, or tranche.

Although fees are discussed later in this chapter, it is important to note here that the special servicer collects fees only during the period that it is actually managing a problem loan.

During the time that the special servicer is managing the problem loan, the master servicer and/or subservicers retain all day-to-day servicing and reporting responsibilities; however, they cease all direct communication with the borrower. For obvious reasons, the special servicer becomes the main contact with the borrower during the time it is servicing the loan. Suppose, for example, that the master servicer or subservicer needs to pay property taxes — and sufficient funds are not in the borrower's escrow account — during the period that a loan is being worked out by the special servicer. The master servicer cannot advance for this tax payment without the consent of the special servicer. In essence, the special servicer becomes the controller of all regular servicing functions during the time that a loan is being worked out.

All reporting to the trustee continues to be done by the master servicer. Therefore, enhanced reporting becomes necessary from the special servicer to the master servicer.

TRUSTEE

The trustee is primarily responsible for reporting and paying of proceeds to the certificate holders. The trustee takes the total amount remitted to it by the master servicer for all scheduled loan payments and appropriately calculates the distribution to each certificate holder based on class of certificate and the "waterfall" of funds prescribed in the pooling and servicing agreement.

The trustee is responsible only for the funds due to each certificate holder, not for the accuracy of related reports. The trustee relies entirely on the master servicer for the accuracy of the reporting to the certificate holders.

The trustee is usually also the custodian of the original documents for each loan in the securitization. As custodian, the trustee is responsible for properly housing and controlling all original collateral documents for each loan in the securitization.

FEES

All servicing fees are computed based on the outstanding principal balance of the loan(s).

Typical Master Servicer Fees

The first part of this section addresses specific servicing fees; the second part addresses various ways that the servicers make their income. Much of this income is derived from other than straight servicing fees.

In the early REMIC securitization days (late 1980s and early 1990s), the typical master servicing fee was 25-30 basis points. (A basis point is one one-hundredth of one percent.) As competition heightened, the fees slowly tightened to where they are today: 0 to 5 basis points for the average securitization. This is typically referred to as "fee for service" pricing.

In today's market, the master servicer often has to "pay" for the servicing in the form of an excess servicing strip or an interest-only (IO) strip (referred to as "purchase servicing"). This is determined in the following way: Let's say that the master sevicer would have needed to charge two basis points to service the transaction and make appropriate returns, yet the underwriter has set aside 12 basis points as the servicing spread; the master servicer would need to pay for the additional 10 basis points.

The amount of up-front cash that the master servicer pays for this 10 basis point excess-servicing strip is determined by taking the 10 basis point cash flow for the life of the securitization and applying a net-present-value discount to the calculation. This is often done for a variety of reasons.

One main reason is that the rating agencies gain more comfort that a servicer will perform its duties to the prescribed servicing standard if it has an up-front investment that it must recoup during the transaction. A classic case of "putting your money where your mouth is." In other words, if the servicer is sure that it can perform its duties, then there is little risk that it will not get its money back. If, on the other hand, the servicer defaults, the servicer loses its up-front investment and a replacement servicer can easily be found for 12 basis points.

Another factor to be considered is whether the underwriter can garnish a higher return for the excess-servicing strip or for an IO strip to a certificate holder. Often, both methods are "shopped" until the highest return is determined.

Master servicers are often asked to bid on a transaction both ways: fee-for-service and purchase servicing. This method leaves open the underwriter's options. On fee-for-service, the lowest bidder usually wins; on purchase servicing, the highest purchase price wins. Of course, there are many other factors involved in selecting a servicer. These will be discussed later in this chapter.

Typical subservicer Fees

Subservicer fees are usually higher than the master servicer fees. They are generally negotiated directly with the underwriter when the subservicer makes arrangements to place its loans into the securitization or when the subservicer decides to originate loans for the underwriter. Both arrangements are common in a conduit.

Typical subservicer fees are five to 12 basis points. They are less competitive and more diverse due to direct negotiation with the underwriter and the lack of bidding.

As mentioned earlier, the master and subservicers often make income in a variety of ways other than straight servicing fees. Some of the most common types of additional income for the servicer are:

- P&I — float on the money held for remittance to the trustee.
- T&I — Float on the tax and insurance money.
- Ancillary fees for lateness, assumption, modification, etc.
- Refinance income on maturing loans.

Of course, the recipient of these fees varies with each securitization. The prudent servicer will attempt to negotiate at least some of these fees into the transaction. Often, these fees are split between the master and subservicer and, of course, the float income goes to the party actually holding the funds. This additional income often far outweighs the straight servicing fees on the transaction.

Special Servicer Fees

Since the special servicer is often the lowest class of certificate holders and thereby, "pays itself the special servicing fees," there is great flexibility in the amount the special servicer can charge. The industry does seem to have an acceptable fee range of 25-50 basis points. Again, this fee is paid to the special servicer only during the time that it actually manages the problem loan.

To explain the concept of "paying itself the special servicing fees," let's use a typical loan in foreclosure and a typical waterfall of cash to certificate holders, as shown in Exhibit 3.

Since the special servicer collects its fees only during the time that it is managing a problem loan, the special servicer often is entitled to a "standby" fee, usually around one basis point.

The special servicer also often collects a fee upon disposition of the property. This disposition fee varies per transaction but is typically 25-100 basis points of the disposed amount of the real estate.

Exhibit 3: Special Servicer Fees

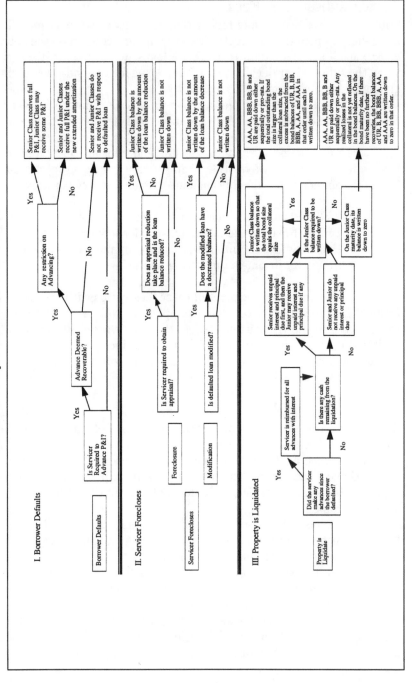

Trustee

In the early REMIC transactions, the trustee would usually earn two to three basis points. Today the trustees are usually paid less than one basis point.

FLOW OF INFORMATION

To better understand the various roles and responsibilities of each entity in a securitization, Exhibit 4 reflects the flow of cash in a typical securitization.

Exhibit 4: Flow of Cash in a Typical Securitization

Borrower's Payment   Master/Sub-Servicer   Trustee

Available Cash

Senior Bond Holders

Mezzanine Bond Holders

Unrated Subordinate Bond Holders

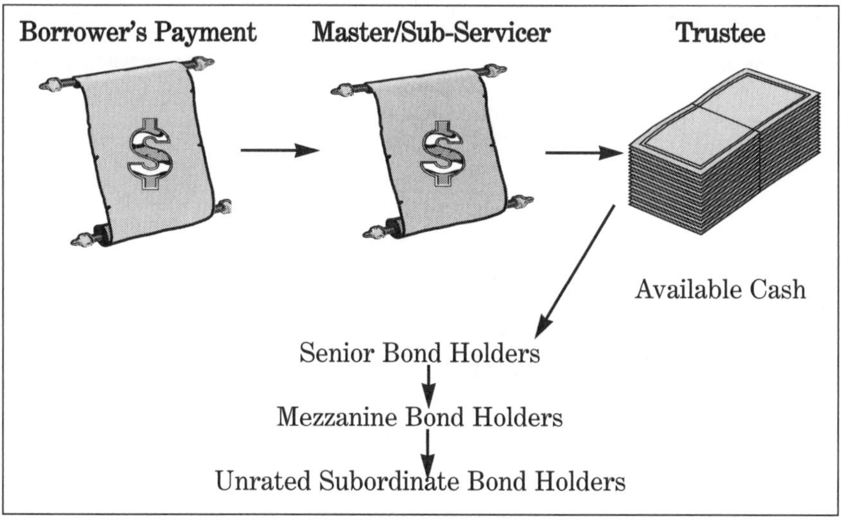

Another illustration that helps define the roles and responsibilities of each entity in a securitization is Exhibit 5, showing the flow of information.

Notice that each entity has a specific role in the dissemination of information. It is important that this flow of information be correctly documented in the pooling and servicing agreement and that each party fully understand its role.

The dissemination of information is one of the most important roles of the master servicer and trustee in a securitization. The certificate holders must be able to get reliable, detailed, and timely information regarding their investment. Many legal issues surrounding the dissemination of information on securitizations have not been fully resolved. However, it is improper and foolish for servicers merely not to provide important information to certificate holders in a securitization.

Exhibit 5: Flow of Information in a Typical Securitization

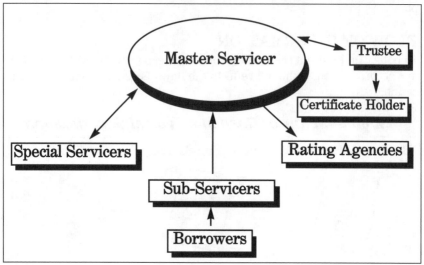

Qualification of a Master Servicer

This section is in no way intended to describe fully all requirements of the master servicer. Each rating agency provides a detailed booklet outlining the requirements to be a rated servicer. This section will discuss the most common and perceived important requirements.

Financial Strength Due to the fact that the master servicer is required to advance payments to the certificate holders, the minimum rating agency requirement is that the master servicer must have a long-term debt rating at least equal to the second-highest class, or tranche, of certificates in the security. Example: If the highest-rated certificates in the securitization are A, then the master servicer must have a long-term debt rating of AA.

Ratings The master servicer is required to be rated by the rating agency or agencies rating the specific transaction. Three of the four agencies — Duff & Phelps, Fitch, and Standard & Poor's — periodically publish a list of all rated servicers. The fourth, Moody's, does not publish a list of rated servicers.

In order to become rated, the master servicer must engage the rating agency to perform a review of the servicer's operations. The rating agencies charge approximately $20,000-$30,000 for this review. The reviews must be done annually and the fees paid annually.

The ratings listed in Exhibit 6 are given by each of the three agencies that publish results.

Generally, the highest rating is not given the first time a rating agency reviews a servicing operation, as the agencies like to see sustained performance in servicing securitizations. The ratings are viewed in the industry as sort of a "Good Housekeeping Stamp of Approval."

Exhibit 6: Ratings for Master Servicer/Special Servicer

Rating Agency	Master Servicer	Special Servicer
Fitch	Acceptable	Superior
	Unacceptable	Above average
		Average
		Below Average
		Weak
Standard & Poor's	Strong	Strong
	Above Average	Above Average
	Average	Average
	Below Average	Below Average
	Weak	Weak
Duff & Phelps	SA-1	SA-1
	SA-2	SA-2
	SA-3 (Average)	SA-3 (Average)
	SA-4	SA-4
	SA-5	SA-5

Sound Computer Systems The master servicer must have the flexibility to provide data in a variety of formats. Although there is no mandate to have a specific type of software, there are a few highly acceptable/recognized CMBS servicing systems in the industry today. The master servicer must be able to respond quickly to the ever-changing and growing demand for information in the CMBS industry.

Proactive Asset Management The master servicer must do more than collect and report monthly payments. The master servicer is actually engaged by the trust to oversee the assets. This means that the master servicer must proactively monitor the performance of each asset. This is done through annual site inspections of the property, review of operating data of the property, etc. The master servicer should not only collect, analyze, and report these data, but must be aware of trends in the market and must be able to report this information globally to the certificate holders in a usable format. Master servicers unwilling to perform this function in the industry today are being left in the dust by the many servicers who understand the importance to certificate holders.

Low Cost of Servicing With the tightening of servicing fees, a servicer must have a large infrastructure and, thereby, economies of scale, and hopefully low servicing cost per loan. The most recent Mortgage Banking Assocation survey of operations servicing over $1 billion in loans was approximately $1,200 per loan. To win the servicing on a new securitization today, the cost must be well below $1,200 per loan. Therefore, the servicers are faced with keeping the costs of servicing low without compromising the quality of service.

SERVICING TRENDS IN THE MARKET

Consolidation of Servicers

As demands continue to increase today and fees continue to be squeezed, many servicers are forced to decide whether they will continue to be key players. Many are deciding to sell their portfolios to other servicers who are interested in growing their CMBS servicing portfolios. It is anticipated that by the year 2000 there will be only a handful of large, low-cost servicers for the ever-growing CMBS market, as described in a report by Fitch Investors Services:

> "As the CMBS market continues to evolve, so, too, will the roles of master and special servicers continue to be further refined. More shakeout in the master servicing segment can be expected as the larger players use their financial muscle to maneuver themselves into more dominant positions. The special servicing industry, meanwhile, is likely to see additional alliances formed between special servicers and financial partners seeking to invest in subordinate debt securities. However, it will be difficult for new entrants to join the increasingly exclusive circle of highly rated, proven special servicers. Servicing fees will continue to be driven by the market, as servicers endeavor to pare their operating costs to better compete in the marketplace. Again, the larger companies will demonstrate their mettle in operating in such an environment. The technology for delivering information to investors will be utilized to make information more

accessible, as both proprietary services and the Internet gain wider acceptance."[1]

More Intense Reporting

The certificate holders need access to information that could affect the likelihood of receiving their full investment back prior to losing money. Imagine investing $1 million, then calling to check on your investment and being told that information is not available. When your $1 million is gone, you would then, of course, be notified. This absence of reporting would not be satisfactory to most investors. Hence, as the market matures, certificate holders are expecting higher quality of information on the underlying collateral.

The typical monthly report submitted to the trustee by the master servicer consists of detailed information at the loan level as well as property performance.

The industry has made great strides in standardizing the reporting formats. One of the most common standard reporting formats that incorporates both loan-level and property-level information is the CSSA 100, developed in 1996 by the Commercial Securitization and Secondary Market Association.

---

[1]*Commercial Mortgage Servicers in the Spotlight*, Fitch Investors Services: Feb. 5, 1996.

Tricia Brady Hall, who joined Lehman Brothers in 1987, is a vice president and manager of the CMBS surveillance department.

Hall tracks the post-closing performance for all commercial, multifamily, and single-asset mortgage-backed securities transactions. She manages all servicing and trustee-related issues pertaining to commercial MBS and, when appropriate, acts as the operating adviser.

Hall is responsible for the production of Lehman Brothers CMBS monthly performance report, which summarizes the collateral performance for 28 multi-asset, 16 single-asset, and 27 RTC/FDIC securitizations.

She is an active member of the CSSA post-issuance disclosure committee working to standardize reporting and information flow on commercial MBS transactions.

Hall is a member of the 1997 *Institutional Investor*-ranked Third Team for commercial mortgage-backed research, along with teammate Haejin Baek.

She holds a bachelor of science degree in computer science from Marist College in Poughkeepsie, N.Y., and a master's degree in business administration from Pace University in New York City.

Chapter 4

Surveillance and Collateral Reporting

Tricia Brady Hall
Vice President
Lehman Brothers

Commercial mortgage-backed securities, due to the nature of the underlying collateral and the size of the individual loans, require the tracking of more information than most other securitized products. From 1985 to 1990, CMBS transactions were not backed by a large number of loans; the overall market was securitizing only $2 billion to $4 billion per year compared with the $30 billion securitized in 1996 and the $40+ billion expected in 1997. In 1991, the Resolution Trust Corporation transactions changed the CMBS market and paved the way for the deals done today. The industry learned from the mistakes made on those early transactions that had little information provided and no special servicers.

While today's market continues to grow and learn, it has improved as compared with its early years and is still evolving. Information standards have developed and surveillance and collateral reporting are accepted as necessary for the industry's survival. CMBS surveillance involves the understanding of the bonds' cash flow as well as the monitoring of the credit quality of the loans underlying the bonds.

Historically, it has been difficult to track down and collect current information on CMBS transactions. Today, most CMBS underwriters, trustees, and servicers have addressed this issue. Information dissemination is dependent on the documentation for each deal that specifies who is authorized to receive the information.

THE NEED FOR SURVEILLANCE

The degree of surveillance and collateral reporting required depends on the type of bond an investor wishes to purchase. The type of deal securitized will also dictate the scope of surveillance that is appropriate. The level of surveillance is determined by each bondholder and the class held as an investment. A B-class holder needs more surveillance than a triple-A holder, but less than the holder of the most subordinate class. The type of securitized deal will also dictate the level of surveillance that is needed — and possible.

Types of CMBS Transaction

Conduit Conduit transactions involve the securitization of newly originated mortgage loans that are financed and underwritten through a Wall Street firm, with many different originators. The loans are generally well diversified geographically and by property type. The average loan size ranges from $2 million to $40 million and each deal generally has 100-300 loans. This type of transaction needs a convenient method to monitor delinquencies and changes in debt service on all loans. Most conduit transactions require the borrowers to submit financial statements quarterly or monthly.

Large Loan Large loan transactions involve the securitization of newly originated or modified loans, loans having higher debt-service-coverage ratios, and may include loans secured by multiple properties. There are usually one to 10 loans and the size of these loans is $50 million to $350 million, but there could be from one to 100 properties per loan. These properties are often cross-collateralized. Surveillance on the property level is necessary, but often a comfort level is derived from adequate coverage and an institutional borrower.

Agency Agency transactions involving commercial mortgage loans are backed by the Federal National Mortgage Association (Fannie Mae) and the Federal Home Loan Mortgage Corporation (Freddie Mac). Ownership of these bonds is similar to owning triple-A-rated CMBS, with Fannie Mae and Freddie Mac guaranteeing a par payoff.

Existing Performing Existing performing deals contain seasoned mortgage loans not originated with securitization in mind. This can mean limited information provided by the borrower, which can also limit the ability to do surveillance. Payment history is critical to evaluate performance. The servicer can play an important role in these transactions by responding quickly to a delinquent borrower and not allowing a borrower to slip behind in monthly payments. In many cases, the borrower is not required to submit financial statements. It is therefore critical for the servicer to collect financial statements diligently from each borrower, where possible.

Single Property Generally, single-property securitizations are collateralized by either a large office building or a regional mall. Surveillance is based on the operating statement and rent roll received either annually or quarterly from the borrower.

Single Borrower Single-borrower transactions involve the securitization of mortgage loans backed by properties all of which are owned by the same borrower. Surveillance will depend on the comfort level with the borrower and the properties that have been securitized. Often, properties are crossed within the transaction.

REIT Transactions collateralized by mortgage loan properties owned by a particular REIT are usually similar to a single-borrower deal. The surveillance will depend on the comfort level with the REIT and the properties that have been securitized.

Lease Backed A lease-backed transaction is similar to a corporate bond because the securitization is based on the lease agreement and the credit of the tenant leasing the property. Often, in the event that the tenant moves out of the property, such a tenant usually agrees to pay rent until the lease expires.

The last four transaction types listed in Exhibit 1 — nonperforming, international, Re-REMIC, and FASIT — represent a small percentage of the CMBS market. Because of the uniqueness of these transactions, the surveillance levels vary deal by deal.

Exhibit 1: Types of Transactions in 1997

Product Code	Number of Deals	Amount ($Millions)	% of Total
Conduit	24	21,934	49.5
Large Loan	6	6,250	14.12
Agency	9	2,635	6.0
Existing Performing	12	2,900	6.6
Single Property	10	1,336	3.0
Single Borrower/Non-REIT	6	1,600	3.6
REIT	5	1,020	2.3
Lease-Backed	16	1,079	2.4
Nonperforming	2	557	1.3
International	13	3,557	8.0
Re-REMIC	2	963	2.1
FASIT	1	439	1.0
Total:	106	44,269	100.0

Source: *Commercial Mortgage Alert*, Hoboken, N.J., by permission.

STANDARDIZATION OF INFORMATION

Monitoring a transaction in the past had been difficult due to the lack of standardization in the commercial real estate lending market. Unlike the residential MBS market, where Fannie Mae and Freddie Mac dictate reporting standards, no group in the CMBS market — until recently — had the power to set reporting requirements. Since 1990, Fannie Mae and Freddie Mac have had some influence over requirements on multifamily loans. It was not until 1992, when mortgage loans were originated for CMBS and rated by the rating agencies, that information requirements necessary to track the financial status of a property began to appear on all commercial loans..

Because the conduits needed an exit strategy for all property types, they turned to securitization. As shown in Exhibit 2, it is easy to see how the growth of conduit programs and, therefore, indirectly, the growth of rating agencies, began to influence lending in commercial real estate.

Conduit loans generally require, under loan documents, quarterly and, in some cases, monthly financial statements as well as current rent rolls. The borrower must provide information to avoid being placed in technical default. Without current property-level information, the lender and the rating agencies are blind to the borrower's status, and everything will appear to be fine until there is a payment default.

Exhibit 2: The Growth of Conduit Programs In Commercial Real Estate

Year	Amount ($Millions)	% Conduit	% Agency
1985-1989	12,839	None	None
1990	4,829	None	2.8
1991	8,197	None	None
1992	13,997	0.6	None
1993	17,475	2.1	3.7
1994	20,331	10.5	8.4
1995	18,971	29.5	7.5
1996	29,889	42.7	6.7
1997	44,269	50.0	6.0

Source: *Commercial Mortgage Alert*, Hoboken, N.J., by permission.

Securitizations closed prior to 1994 did not require the borrowers to send property-level information, as is the case today. But this lack of information, coupled with a downturn in the real estate cycle, taught the industry the lesson of standardization the hard way. In order for the CMBS secondary market to survive, information dissemination was critical. In 1994 the first noticeable changes began to appear in the statement delivered monthly to certificateholders and in the CMBS offering document with the inclusion of more detailed collateral tables and a list of all, or most, properties loan by loan.

LaSalle National Bank was the first trustee to design a certificate holder statement that gave collateral information, delinquency and payment history, along with the bond information. Lehman Brothers began working with LaSalle in 1994; SASCO 1994-C1 was the first transaction to use LaSalle National Bank's new certificateholder's report and to attach supplemental reports disclosing information on delinquent and REO properties, historical losses. and modifications.

CSSA Designs a Standard Information Package

The Commercial Real Estate Secondary Market and Securitization Association (CSSA) is an "...organization focused on the development and enlargement of secondary marketing opportunities for creators and/or holders of commercial real estate assets." This organization was founded in 1993 to help shape the CMBS market. In 1996 the CSSA post-disclosure committee created two file layouts to be used as industry standards for proper deal surveillance; both files are for loan-level information. The post-disclosure committee took the first step toward addressing the CMBS industry's need to develop standards.

The original loan setup file should be provided by the underwriter in the offering document and distributed by the trustee after the initial offering. Then, monthly, a periodic loan update file is produced by the master servicer and distributed by the trustee.

Each layout was designed by a representative group of investors, servicers, trustees, underwriters, and rating agencies. They provide a template to report loan-by-loan information on a CMBS transaction. This information is essential for the continued rapid growth and liquidity within the secondary market. Standardization provides investors and rating agencies with reliable information to determine the probability of timely interest and principal payments on a CMBS investment.

Reports described in Exhibit 3, also presented by the CSSA post-issuance committee, are designed to facilitate the move toward greater disclosure of historical losses, modifications, and financial information. The standard operating statement for each property compares the information in the year in which the deal was underwritten with the last two full years and the year to date. An operating statement is prepared and updated by the party responsible for analyzing the financial statements.

This standardized statement allows surveillance on an individual property level as necessary.

Exhibit 3: Supplemental Reporting

Debt Service Reports	
Level 1 Comparative Financial *monthly*	*Compares debt-service coverage, NOI, and revenue fiscal-year-end with underwriting.information. This report, which is in spread sheet format, with one line per property, is used to target loans for a closer look.*
Level 2 Operating Statement *quarterly*	*Summarizes and compares the property's current financial information with underwriting information as well as year-to-date data. Shows revenue and standard expense line items. Answers detailed questions about the properties.*
Level 3 NOI Adjustment Worksheet *annually*	*Normalizes the operating statement numbers, showing any adjustments the responsible party made to normalize. This worksheet explains the difference between the borrower's statement and the operating statement.*

In 1997, the CSSA post-issuance committee added a property file to the CSSA standardized reporting package. The property file is necessary when a securitization includes loans secured by multiple properties. It facilitates surveillance of deals at the property level.

Entering 1998, the CSSA reporting package contains a mixture of old and new standards. Some portions of this package are referred to as reports, others as files. The difference between reports and files lies in their usage. While reports are submitted and read on printed sheets (hard copy), the files are intended for use exclusively within a computer data base. The standard package consists of surveillance reports, loan files, and a property file.

Surveillance The surveillance portion is subdivided into three types of reports: property financial statement, status, and historical. Property financial statements include the comparative financial report, operating statement, and NOI adjustment worksheet. Status reports include information on delinquent loans, REO, and the loans on a servicer's watch list. Historical reports provide information on modifications and liquidations. Some further details of these reports are shown in Exhibit 4.

Exhibit 4: *Status and Historical Information*

Status Reports	
Watch List *monthly*	*Prepared by the servicer to list all loans that are in jeopardy of becoming specially serviced.*
Delinquency Status *monthly*	*Shows all loans specially serviced, delinquent (30, 60, 90+ days), or in foreclosure. Contains summary information and comments. Spread-sheet format. One line per loan.*
REO Status *monthly*	*Shows all loans REO properties. Contains summary information and comments. Spread-sheet format, with one line per REO property.*
Historical Modification and Liquidation Reports	
Historical Loan Modification *monthly*	*Lists all loans that have been modified. Shows real losses and estimated interest loss as well as any changes made to terms of the loan, such as rate, loan balance and maturity date.*
Historical Liquidation *monthly*	*Lists all loans that have been liquidated with a realized loss. This is usually in the form of an REO sale, discounted payoff, or note sale.*

Loan File The loan file provided at issuance contains all the information as of closing. For each successive month, an update file provides current balance, rate, maturity date, and other items as appropriate.

Property File The CSSA property file provided at closing comprises all information related to the property, such as location, type, DSCR, NOI, and revenue. This file, updated with changes in DSCR, NOI, occupancy, allocated loan amounts, and other items, is to be provided each month on the respective remittance day.

The complete CSSA standard information package contains the following reports:

1. Comparative financial.
2. Operating statement.
3. NOI adjustment worksheet.
4. Watch list.
5. Delinquency status.
6. REO status.
7. Historical loan modification.
8. Historical liquidation.

Under files, this package includes:

1. CSSA loan setup.
2. CSSA loan periodic update (servicer).
3. CSSA property (servicer).

NORMALIZATION OF FINANCIAL INFORMATION

Most servicers normalize financial information internally but do not report the normalized numbers to investors unless the transaction documents require them to do so. The methodology described in this section is a sample of a servicer-adjusted or normalized NOI, which facilitates a meaningful comparison of a property's ongoing performance with performance at the time of original underwriting. The actual normalization methodology may vary by transaction, depending upon the requirements of the transaction document. Debt-service coverage numbers are normalized once a year when the servicer receives the annual financial statement for a property. The items enumerated in this section highlight some of the major categories that require adjustment; however, the servicer is expected to use discretion in making any necessary adjustments. During the normalization process, the servicer responsible for reporting the financial information will not re-underwrite the loan but, rather, will apply some basic rules:

• Assume a property management fee of at least 3% to 5%. Usually 5% is an accurate estimate; however, on larger properties, 3% or 4% may be sufficient. (For normalizing NOI do not use a management fee which is less than that which was used for the underwriting).

- Remove capital expenses from any above-the-line categories (such as extraordinary repairs and maintenance). Put these expenses below the line in capital expenses.
- Include annual property taxes due, excluding any delinquent taxes or credits from prior years which would cause the number to be higher or lower.
- Exclude nonrecurring extraordinary income, such as tax refunds, lease buyouts, or income received for a period other than the year in question. If past-due rent for a prior year was paid and recorded in the current year, it should be deleted and footnoted.
- Care should be used when reflecting percentage/overage rents to ensure that these rents relate to the appropriate period and that the numbers are supported by tenant sales information.
- Remove any legal fees or consulting fees not pertaining to the operation of the property, such as fees for the closing of a loan restructure.
- Analyze income and expenses by reviewing the variances by category. For significant variances it is necessary to investigate with the borrower and make appropriate adjustments and/or footnote the reason for the difference. For example, electricity expenses went down because a major tenant vacated.
- The debt service should be an actual amount the borrower paid as per the servicer. If the servicer does not have a full year of payments available, a full-year amount should be estimated by using the information available.

The servicer should use the NOI adjustment worksheets to document the adjustments made to arrive at normalized NOI. Footnotes should be included as necessary to guide the reader through the analysis. These adjustment worksheets will then represent the backup for the property's operating statement analysis, which will contain a historical record of the previous three years' normalized financial statements and a comparison with the original underwriting.

Normalization facilitates the comparison of debt-service coverage on loans from year to year as well as from securitization. Today's CMBS investors expect normalized debt-service coverage numbers as part of the standard reporting package shown in Exhibit 3. Investors should always ask if the information they are given is normalized.

Reporting

Debt service, status, and historical modification and liquidation reports are recognized as standard supplements to the monthly certificateholders' statement. They are available on almost all Lehman Brothers securitizations and have been adopted as a standard by many other underwriters, as well. The reports are not always part of the standard package given to certificate holders and must be specifically requested from the trustee.

Information Providers

The information providers for any CMBS are the underwriter, trustee, master servicer, and special servicer. Their ability to gather information at the front end will affect an investor's ability to monitor a transaction. The underwriter originally provides all the necessary information within the prospectus, or private placement memorandum (PPM), which should include a diskette. The diskette should include all the information shown in the prospectus or PPM, as well as a CSSA setup file layout. The underwriter also establishes the guidelines for the deal in the trust agreement or the pooling and servicing agreement. These agreements will dictate which party is responsible for various reporting requirements as well as who is allowed to see the reporting.

Trustee Usually the trustee receives a file from the master servicer but in some cases the trustee may also receive a file from the special servicer. The file contains all the information the trustee needs to calculate the bond payments and report to certificateholders. This file should be in the CSSA periodic update file layout. In the past the master servicer provided the necessary data in various formats. The trustee is usually the provider of files and reports such as the certificateholders and rating agencies. Most trustees provide files via a bulletin board or internet, and reports by mail, internet, or fax.

Master Servicer Master servicers usually collect all payments and are required to advance payments on delinquent loans. Often they are also responsible for collecting and reporting financial statement information. Many master servicers maintain a web site or other method for distributing the information required.

Special Servicer Special servicers are normally responsible for the loans with issues. Usually these issues are the loans that are 60-plus days delinquent or loans that the master servicer has identified as having a specific problem that needs special-servicer attention. In some transactions the analysis of the statements is the responsibility of the special servicer. Some special servicers view this as a function they should perform especially in those instances in which they are also the owner of the lowest bond holder. By reviewing the financial statements and performing the property inspections required by a transaction a special servicer can monitor its own investment.

The special servicer is an important player in any CMBS transaction, especially if it begins to have delinquency problems. It is important for the special servicer to have an interest in the nonrated bonds, as it provides an additional incentive to minimize losses.

Sub-Servicer The role of the sub-servicer most often appears in conduit transactions. The sub-servicer is usually the originator of the loan who may perform some of the master-servicer's functions, such as collecting payments or financial statements. This added layer of servicing usually exists when the originator has a relationship with the borrower which the originator hopes to maintain. This established relationship can be helpful in obtaining statements from the borrower and dealing with issues.

WHERE TO FIND THE INFORMATION

Information on CMBS transactions is usually available but is not always readily accessible. On each transaction, the servicer and the trustee have different methods of providing the information. This variety is beneficial because servicers are competing with trustees to provide the best information, yet detrimental because it may be confusing to the investor. The information provided can be different for each transaction, even when managed by the same servicer. One of the more consistent providers of information is Midland Loan Services, which incorporates current standards on old and new deals. Some servicers are in the process of developing or using the internet to distribute information on newer deals. This is most effective when debt service information is provided on each property in a transaction. Such information, difficult to distribute by the trustee and hard to maintain by the investor, becomes easily accessible and manageable through the internet or an electronic dial-up system. Exhibit 5 shows some details about access to information. The information in this exhibit is always evolving, as servicers and trustees improve the ability to distribute information. Over time, the servicers and trustees should evolve and incorporate new standards for older deals.

Even in a situation where the originator, the master servicer, and trustee are using current standards, the process for receiving this infor-

Trustee		
CSSA Loan File CSSA Property File	Certificate- Holder Reports	For all other information call the administrator
Bulletin Board (Download File)	Fax System	Internet
Bankers Trust Chase LaSalle Norwest State Street	LaSalle Norwest State Street	LaSalle State Street

Servicer		
Dial Up System	Internet	Must call for additional information
Midland	AMRESCO** BOMCC** First Union Midland	Bankers Trust* Bank of America GE GMAC Mellon Pacific Mutual

* Purchased by Mellon   ** Only have some deals on internet

mation is different on each transaction. It is important to query the underwriter, trustee, and servicer about what information is available on a specific transaction and how to access it. Newer securitizations generally should describe the reporting process in the prospectus or ppm but on older deals items may have changed or not been clearly described in the prospectus or ppm. Servicers and trustees are constantly working to update their technology and provide more information. That is why it is important to inquire constantly about information developments in order to keep up with what is available.

An educated investor who is tracking new developments can have more information than others. Investors will interpret information they have and may draw different conclusions; while up-to-date information may be available to all, not everyone will use it. In the end, bonds may trade differently than might be indicated by the information provided because not everyone analyzes the same amount of information to make a decision. The main reason for this variance is that the pursuit of information can be very time-consuming. The rating on a bond and the credit support may provide enough of a cushion so that the information is not necessary. Where one person may be satisfied with a certificateholder's report, someone else may want all or part of the CSSA standard information package.

The prospectus should be the road map to information that is available. It should include the CSSA loan setup file on diskette so that everyone can begin with the same information. It should also describe the reports available and who is responsible for providing them.

USING THE INFORMATION FOR SURVEILLANCE

Every transaction has individual requirements but the surveillance should be approached by reviewing the credit support, delinquencies and debt-service coverage, and collateral review.

At the time the bonds are created, the credit support is determined by the rating agencies. The level of credit support necessary for each bond class depends on the rating of the bonds and the quality of the loans and underlying properties that are to be securitized. The amount of credit support required increases as the quality declines. Other factors that affect credit support are environmental issues, debt-service coverage, and loan-to-value ratios, as well as concentration issues. Concentration issues include property location, property type, and borrower concentration analysis. Certificateholder reports on deals originated after 1994 will show collateral reporting to get an understanding of most deals. Reports do not usually show credit support, but it can be easily calculated.

The credit support levels at origination and current levels shown in Exhibit 6 represent the SASCO 1996-CFL or Confederation Life transaction. The current credit support levels are calculated for the A classes, which are rated triple-A, by adding the bond balances below (class B to class J), and dividing the total bond balance. This process continues for each class until the last class, which has no credit support.

It is important to keep watch on the credit support because changes in the numbers can affect the way investors and rating agencies view the bonds. Credit support levels that rise high enough above the original credit support levels might indicate that an upgrade would be appropriate. Similarly, a drop in credit support levels below the original levels might indicate the possibility of a downgrade. Credit support levels are only one part of the information that the rating agencies review to conduct their surveillance.

Exhibit 6: SASCO 1996-CFL
as of July 25, 1997 Remittance

Class	Current Rating Fitch/ S&P	Original Size ($000's)	Current Size ($000's)	Current % of Deal	Desc	Credit Enhancement Original	Current
A-1A	Retired	149,769	0	0.00	Fix	41.00	N/A
A-1B	AAA/AAA	196,000	24,551	1.58	Fix	41.00	50.53
A-1C	AAA/AAA	441,000	441,000	28.30	Fix	41.00	50.53
A-2A	AAA/AAA	171,098	130,234	8.36	Fix	41.00	50.53
A-2B	AAA/AAA	175,000	175,000	11.23	Fix	41.00	50.53
X-1	AAA/NR	1,574,016*	1,252,838*	N/A	I/O	N/A	N/A
X-1A	AAA/NR	1,151,591*	830,372*	N/A	I/O	N/A	N/A
X-2	AAA/NR	346,098*	305,312*	N/A	I/O	N/A	N/A
X-2A	AAA/NR	346,098*	305,234*	N/A	I/O	N/A	N/A
B	AAA/AA	96,006	96,006	6.16	Fix	36.00	44.37
C	AA/A	134,408	134,408	8.63	Fix	29.00	35.74
D	A/BBB	134,408	134,408	8.63	Fix	22.00	27.11
E	BBB/BB+	96,006	96,006	6.16	Fix	17.00	20.95
F	BB+/BB	57,603	57,603	3.70	Fix	14.00	17.26
G	B/B	96,006	96,006	6.16	Fix	9.00	11.09
H	B-/B-	48,003	48,003	3.08	Fix	6.50	8.01
I	CCC/CCC	67,204	67,204	4.31	Fix	3.00	3.70
J	Non-Rated	57,603	57,651	3.70	Fix	0.00	0.00
P	Non-Rated	6,427**	6,258**	0.40	Fix	N/A	N/A
Total:		1,920,113	1,558,079	100.00			

 * Notional balance
 ** Not included in total balance and not used to calculate credit support

Delinquencies and Debt Service Coverage

Delinquencies and debt-service-coverage ratios can also indicate how a deal is performing. The interest of an investor in these numbers will depend on the bond class that he or she owns. On the one hand, a triple-A-rated bondholder will review how a deal is performing with minimal concern if the delinquencies are below 8%-10% and the overall weighted average debt service coverage is close to origination. On the other hand, the holder of a nonrated bond will be concerned about every delinquent loan and any decline in debt-service coverage. This is because the losses are taken in reverse order and the nonrated class is the first to take any losses.

Performing surveillance on a deal is dependent on the monthly information provided by the trustee and servicers. The underwriter can dictate what information can be disclosed to various parties. The deals done in 1996 and 1997 have shown tremendous improvement over the earlier deals. Information disclosure has evolved and will continue to evolve to facilitate the growth of the industry. As standards are developed, it is important for the older deals to use the latest standards when appropriate. This obviously does not occur on all transactions and can be a challenge for an investor to figure out what information is available on each deal. Surveillance on deals is only as good as the information provided.

Delinquencies

The first look at delinquencies is on the trustee's certificateholder's report but this typically describes only the number of loans, scheduled balance, and the percentage for the five delinquency categories: 30-day, 60-day, and 90-day, loans in foreclosure, and properties that are REO and owned by the trust. The question that needs to be answered revolves around losses: Will there be losses based on the loans that are having delinquency problems and the properties that are REO? It makes sense to review the REO properties first, then the loans in foreclosure, and then the 90-plus days delinquent. The loans that are 30 and 60 days delinquent should be reviewed, but may not be long-term issues and often disappear without any loss to the trust. Two reports are needed to understand what type of losses to expect.

Status Reports The status reports in Exhibit 4 are concerned with loans that are delinquent and REO. These reports should show the location and the balance owed to the trust as well as any advances and expenses accumulated and, when added together, indicate total exposure on each loan. If given an idea about the expected sales price or value of the property, an investor can determine if losses will be incurred on each loan. If a deal uses the appraisal reduction feature, this report will disclose the amount of loss expected on any one loan and how much has been recognized by the appraisal reduction. An expected sale date of the property is also helpful because this will indicate the timing of the loss needed to accurately predict future cash flow.

Borrower's Financial Reporting Financial reports are needed to evaluate the debt-service coverage ratio, net operating income, and revenue for each property. Using this information, a judgment regarding losses can be made on all properties in the portfolio. The comparative financial report allows the investor to quickly review the debt-service-coverage column of the report and highlight loans for closer review. This report also allows the investor to compare the latest year's information with the prior year and the original underwriter's numbers published in the prospectus or ppm. The rating agencies also use the comparative financial report to judge how the deal is performing compared with the original rating and their last review.

The loans in question then require a closer look, and this is when the operating statement is used. This report compares the underwriting number with that of the past two years and also gives detail so that changes to the NOI and DSCR can be explained or questioned.

Exhibit 7 shows the comparative financial status report. Exhibits 8, 9, and 10 show the operating statement analysis report.

Collateral Reporting

This information has been given to investors as part of the certificate-holder's report and is usually in the form of tables that describe the attributes of a portfolio. Typical attributes are the states, types of properties, and ranges for many of the numerical characteristics (current balance, rate, ARM fields, maturity date, etc.) Real estate is cyclical, and understanding the particular characteristics of real estate underlying the mortgage loans can be a deciding factor when purchasing CMBS bonds. Investors may not be interested in bonds if they are adverse to specific collateral characteristics. Having an understanding of the collateral characteristics can help investors make investment decisions within the portfolio.

If a catastrophic event occurs in a particular region, the investor may want to take a look at state and city to judge his or her exposure to the situation. This can be accomplished by looking up the collateral tables in the certificateholders report or downloading the CSSA loan and property file from the trustee's bulletin board or internet.

The needs of investors when monitoring CMBS are likely to differ. The obvious approach is to understand the bonds' cash flow and the credit issues behind the bonds. How this is accomplished is dependent on the strategy of the individual. There are various formats of information and one or all of these can be used to understand a transaction:

- Prospectus or private-placement memorandum.
- Electronic file provided by the trustee (CSSA loan and property file).
- Certificateholder's statement.
- Supplemental financial, status, and historical reports.
- All electronic information found on the internet or Bloomberg.

Exhibit 7: Comparative Financial Status Report

Commercial Mortgage Trust, Series 199x-C1

S4	S57	S58	P7	P8	S72	S69	S70	S65	S66	P65	P64	P61	P59	P58	P57	P52	P54	P56	P72	P73	P66	P68	P70	P2
					Original Underwriting Information — Basis Year					2nd Preceding Annual Operating Information — as of ___				Preceding Annual Operating Information — as of ___					Trailing Financial or YTD Information — Month Reported Actual					Net Change — Preceding & Basis
Prospectus ID	City	State	Last Property Inspect Date yy/mm	Scheduled Loan Balance	Paid Thru Date	Annual Debt Service	Financial Info as of Date yy/mm	% Occ	Total Revenue	NOI	(1) DSCR	Financial Info as of Date yy/mm	% Occ	Total Revenue	NOI	(1) DSCR	Financial Info as of Date yy/mm	% Occ	Total Revenue	NOI	(1) DSCR	FS Start Date yy/mm	FS End Date yy/mm	Total Revenue	NOI	% DSC R	% Occ	% Total Revenue	(1) DSC R

List all properties currently in deal with or without information largest to smallest loan

| Total: | | | | $ | | $ | WA | $ | $ | WA | WA | $ | $ | WA | WA | $ | $ | WA | WA | $ | $ | WA | WA | WA | $ | $ | WA | WA | WA | WA |

Financial Information:

	Received				Required		
	Loans #	%	Balance $	%	Loans #	%	Balance $	%

Current Full Year:

Current Full Yr. received with DSC <1:

Prior Full Year:

Prior Full Yr. received with DSC <1:

(1) DSCR should match to Operating Statement and is normally calculated using NOI / Debt Service.

(2) Net change should compare the latest year to the underwriting year

Exhibit 8: Operating Statement Analysis Report, Part 1

PROPERTY OVERVIEW

- LB Control Number
- Current Balance/Paid to Date
- Property Name
- Property Type
- Property Address, City, State
- Net Rentable Square Feet
- Year Built/Year Renovated

	Underwriting	1993	1994	1995	YTD
Year of Operations					
Occupancy Rate *					
Average Rental Rate					

* Occupancy rates are year-end.

INCOME:

- Number of Mos. Annualized
- Period Ended

		Prior Year		Current Yr.		No. of Mos.		
Statement Classification	Underwriting Base Line	1993 Normalized	1994 Normalized	1995 Normalized	1996 YTD** as of / /96	1995-Base Variance	1995-1994 Variance	
Rental Income (Category 1)								
Rental Income (Category 2)								
Rental Income (Category 3)								
Pass Through/Escalations								
Other Income								
Effective Gross Income	$0.00	$0.00	$0.00	$0.00	$0.00	%	%	

Normalized - Full year Financial statements that have been reviewed by the underwriter or Servicer
** Servicer will not be expected to "Normalize" these YTD numbers.

Exhibit 9: Operating Statement Analysis Report, Part 2

					%	%
OPERATING EXPENSES:						
Real Estate Taxes						
Property Insurance						
Utilities						
Repairs and Maintenance						
Management Fees						
Payroll & Benefits Expense						
Advertising & Marketing						
Professional Fees						
Other Expenses						
Ground Rent						
Total Operating Expenses	$0.00	$0.00	$0.00	$0.00		
Operating Expense Ratio						
Net Operating Income	$0.00	$0.00	$0.00	$0.00		
Leasing Commissions						
Tenant Improvements						
Replacement Reserve						
Total Capital Items	$0.00	$0.00	$0.00	$0.00	$0.00	
N.O.I. After Capital Items	$0.00	$0.00	$0.00			
Debt Service (per Servicer)	$0.00	$0.00	$0.00			
Cash Flow after debt service	$0.00	$0.00	$0.00			

Exhibit 10: Operating Statement Analysis Report, Part 3

(1) DSCR: (NOI/Debt Service)

DSCR: (after reserves\Cap exp.)

Source of financial Data:

The years shown will roll always shownning a three year history. 1995 is the current year financials; 1994 is theprior year financials.

This report may vary depending on the property type and because of the way information may vary in each borrower's statement.

Rental income needs to be broken down whenever possible differently for each property type as follows:

    Retail: 1) Base Rent
                 2) Percentage rents on overflow.

    Hotel: 1) Room Revenue
                 2) Food/Beverage.

    Nursing
    Homes: 1) Private
                 2) Medicaid
                 3) Medicare

Income: Comment
Expense: Comment
Capital items: Comment

(1) Used in the Comparatove Financial Status Report.

Once an investor has the available information on a transaction, the first concern is basic bond performance. Reviewing the current delinquencies and credit enhancement can provide a sense of the immediate situation. A closer look at the financial information can give an overall sense of the transaction and allow the investor to compare at-securitization figures with the most recent information. It can also be helpful to review the historical performance of the transaction since issuance.

Laura Quigg joined Sanford C. Bernstein & Co., Inc., in September 1997 as a senior portfolio manager responsible for commercial real estate fixed-income investments.

At the time she wrote this chapter, Quigg was a vice president inthe taxable credit research department at J.P. Morgan & Co., specializing in corporate bonds issued by REITs, commercial mortgage-backed securities, and other real estate fixed-income securities. Her research focused on market analysis and investment strategy, as well as the structural and credit aspects of CMBS and unsecured REIT bonds.

Prior to joining J.P. Morgan, Quigg was in the mortgage strategies group at Lehman Brothers, where she focused on commercial MBS and asset-backed securities.

From 1990 to 1992, she was an assistant professor of finance at the University of Illinois at Urbana-Champaign, teaching and conducting research on real estate and real estate finance. Quigg holds a bachelor of arts degree in economics from Georgetown University, a master's degree in economics and in international affairs from Columbia University, and a Ph.D. in finance from the University of California-Berkeley.

Chapter 5

Default Risk in CMBS Bond Classes

Laura Quigg
Senior Portfolio Manager
Sanford C. Bernstein & Co., Inc.

The main risk of most commercial mortgage-backed securities (CMBS) is credit risk. CMBS differ from single-family mortgage-backed securities (SMBS) in this fundamental respect, as the latter are primarily driven by prepayment or interest rate risk. CMBS are relatively less exposed to prepayment risk because prepayment is expensive and often prohibited for commercial borrowers. For homeowners, however, prepayment is almost always permitted and comparatively cheap. CMBS are more exposed to default risk because defaults are more prevalent and less predictable on the commercial side than for homeowners. Unlike SMBS, the majority of CMBS are nonagency; that is, not guaranteed by Ginnie Mae, Fannie Mae, or Freddie Mac.

VULNERABILITY
Default risk affects CMBS in different ways. Subordinate classes absorb losses first and are therefore generally most vulnerable to defaults. Interest-only (IO) class investors, however, are also at risk to default because any reduction in their notional principal balance represents a loss of interest income without any compensating prepayment penalties.[1]

Mezzanine-class investors are generally well protected against any principal losses, but they need to analyze default risk in order to understand their exposure to extension risk, which is the risk that balloon loans will not be able to pay off their principal balance at maturity (or hyperamortizing loans will not pay off at the expected maturity).

Finally, even senior-class investors are affected by default risk. CMBS with lower quality collateral have greater cash-flow risk, since defaults appear as prepayments with no penalty to these classes. Senior classes may also be exposed to extension risk. In addition, CMBS with

---

[1]Perversely, for IOs tied to more senior classes, in the event of default the IO buyer prefers higher rather than lower losses because higher losses mean that the notional balance is not reduced as much.

more default risk have more ratings risk because there is more uncertainty about future losses for these transactions. That is the case because, even though rating agencies should set higher credit support levels to protect against expected losses and are likely to be conservative, the range around those expected losses may be quite large. We've seen significantly more rating changes for CMBS with distressed loans and poor-quality information than for CMBS with higher-quality collateral and information.

CREDIT PERFORMANCE

To date, the credit performance for CMBS has been very strong. Compared with the corporate market, CMBS have been subject to very few rating actions and, unlike the corporate market, upgrades have outweighed downgrades over the past several years. Most downgrades have been limited to a small number of transactions, many with features that have been improved upon in modern CMBS.

We estimate that approximately $3.6 billion CMBS were downgraded and $5.2 billion upgraded from 1991 through year-end 1997, giving a ratio of downgrades to upgrades of about 0.73 based on the original principal balance of the bond classes. As the majority of CMBS outstanding are rated AAA and cannot be upgraded, this performance is very strong.

However, given the robust economy, short history, and changing character of the CMBS market, entering 1998 we do not expect this strong performance to be sustained. We are at the high point in the cycle for most property types and regions, with still strong demand and lagging supply in most submarkets. As a result, commercial mortgage defaults are at historically low rates. Therefore, we must hypothesize and extrapolate from various information sources that might shed some light on future performance.

SOURCES

A number of sources are available to understand CMBS default risk. Most data come courtesy of the life insurance industry, which includes American Council of Life Insurance (ACLI) quarterly surveys of life insurer commercial mortgage performance as well as a number of studies that track commercial mortgage portfolio performance over time. We also have information from CMBS performance in cases where most of the loans being tracked are from the older, RTC-type CMBS, backed with loans from failed thrifts, most of which were issued by the Resolution Trust Corporation (RTC).

Applicability to CMBS

Most of the information on commercial mortgage performance is focused on life insurance-type loans or, from outstanding CMBS, loans made in the late 1980s and early 1990s by failing S&Ls. This information will, of course, be most useful in understanding the default risk of CMBS that securitize life insurance company portfolios or other relatively high-quality assets and, at the other end of the spectrum, RTC-type CMBS.

Information based on failing S&Ls is not as directly reliable for understanding the majority of today's CMBS, which are issued through conduit-type arrangements, typically composed largely of $1 million-$15 million mortgages on B and C quality multifamily and retail (anchored and unanchored community shopping centers) properties. Even though these loans are "thrift" quality, they differ from those in the RTC-type transactions in that they are originated with today's underwriting standards (giving no credit for future income growth, for example) and are subject to the scrutiny of the underwriters, rating agencies, and investors.

Conduit pools also differ from life insurance company portfolios because life company loans tend be larger and on higher-quality properties with a greater concentration of office and hotels loans and larger retail properties, including more regional malls. Large-loan conduit collateral looks more like insurance company product, but quality and size vary within a wide range. Insurance companies also tend to focus on larger markets, missing many smaller cities.

In most cases, we would expect better performance from a life insurance company-type of mortgage than for a conduit-type mortgage. We think higher-quality properties should retain their value better, and larger, better-capitalized borrowers should be less vulnerable to short-term cash-flow problems (although more profit-oriented borrowers may default more ruthlessly). Also, life insurance loans underwritten for the company's own portfolio are probably higher quality than those underwritten with only a short-term horizon in mind.

Finally, we think many of the costs of working out a life company loan may be understated, since the process is handled internally rather than using the arms-length pricing as on a CMBS. An offsetting factor, however, is that compared with most CMBS, insurance company portfolios tend to have a higher concentration of office and hotel loans, which default with greater frequency and severity. All of the insurance company studies which track the performance of multiple portfolios over time do not control for this property type differential since the information is not available on performance for the different property types. Therefore, we think the results of those studies only modestly understate default risk relative to conduit type CMBS.

ACLI Surveys

The most detailed information on commercial mortgage performance comes from the ACLI surveys.[2] Each quarter, ACLI surveys its members (accounting for the majority of life insurers), which report the number and percentage of their mortgage loan portfolios that are delinquent, restructured, in the process of foreclosure, or foreclosed in any given quarter. The information is very useful in that it is the only source we have currently with a breakdown by property type and region, and for which we can see a trend over time. Its main deficiency is that each survey represents a snapshot, giving the percentage of loans in a portfolio that are delinquent, etc. What we don't see is the timing or accumulation of defaults which are necessary to determine summary or cumulative effects on a pool like one in a CMBS.

Portfolio Studies

The second main source of information consists of a number of studies that examine life insurance company portfolios, including Barnes and Giliberto;[3] Ciochetti;[4] Ciochetti and Riddiough;[5] Wechsler, Forst, and Lederman[6] of Fitch Investors Service; and Snyderman,[7] and Vandell, et al.[8]

Ciochetti; Wechsler, Forst and Lederman; and Snyderman track

[2]American Council of Life Insurance, "Commercial Mortgage Loan Performance." *Investment Bulletin*, quarterly.

[3]Walter Barnes and S. Michael Giliberto, "A Model for Assessing Commercial Mortgage Risk-Based Capital Factors." Monograph (1994).

[4]Brian A. Ciochetti, "Loss Characteristics of Commercial Mortgage Foreclosures." *Real Estate Finance* (Spring 1997): 53-69.

[5]Brian A. Ciochetti and Timothy J. Riddiough, "Foreclosure Loss and the Foreclosure Process: An Examination of Commercial Mortgage Performance." Monograph (1997).

[6]Ron J. Wechsler, Janet P. Forst, and Harvey M. Lederman, "Commercial Mortgage Stress Test." Fitch Investors Service, L.P. (June 8, 1992).

[7]Mark P. Snyderman, "Commercial Mortgages: Default Occurrence and Estimated Yield Impact," *Journal of Portfolio Management* (Fall 1991): 82-87, and "Update on Commercial Mortgage Defaults." *Real Estate Finance* (Summer 1994): 22-32.

[8]Kerry D. Vandell, Walter Barnes, David Hartzell, Dennis Kraft, and William Wendt, "Commercial Mortgage Defaults: Proportional Hazards Estimation Using Individual Loan Histories." *AREUEA Journal* vol. 21 (1993): 451-480.

multiple portfolios over time, providing useful information about the cumulative effects of default, the timing of the transition from performing to delinquent to various stages of default, and loss severities that result from different types of default. Barnes and Giliberto use similar data, but for a different purpose — to determine appropriate risk-based capital requirements for insurance company regulation.

Limited Information

Unfortunately, the data used in this research contain limited information about each mortgage. Most of the data are provided from life insurance company annual statements filed with state regulatory agencies. In these statements, companies are required to report mortgage holdings as of their year-end status: active, 90 days delinquent, in process of foreclosure, or foreclosed.

Included in the schedule are:

- Mortgage number (which permits tracking of an individual mortgage over time).
- State in which the loan was originated.
- Year of loan origination.
- Mortgage book value.
- Items capitalized during the year.
- Principal payments received on the loan during the year.
- Increase and decrease during the year.
- Value transferred to real estate.
- Real estate number.

As already noted, the property type is not known. Overall, life insurance company portfolios consist of about 40%-50% office buildings, 15%-25% retail, about 10% industrial, 10%-20% multifamily, and about 15% other properties (mostly hotel).

Two studies used data from one insurance company, benefiting from very good loan-level detail and thereby avoiding the pitfalls of the other studies. However, it may be difficult to generalize to a broader universe of commercial mortgages based on these results. In an early study, Vandell et al. estimated a model of default, and found that the current loan-to-value (LTV) is a key determinant of a borrower's propensity to default. Ciochetti and Riddiough track 480 defaulted loans from one insurance company originated from 1974 to 1990 and tracked from 1985 to 1995, providing new insights into the timing and costs of foreclosure.

Outstanding CMBS

The other source of information we have comes from performance of outstanding CMBS. Much of the information is scattered, appearing in the remittance reports and rating agency writeups that monitor individual transactions. The main summary pieces are from Fitch Investors Service. The rating agency's most recent research, Dillon and Belanger,[9] reports performance of 22 transactions it rates.

Most of the data in this study consist of loans in RTC or RTC-type pools, not surprisingly since the CMBS market was dominated by the RTC and other seasoned pools from 1991 to 1993, and these transactions experienced the majority of defaults. The loans were mostly originated with loose lending conditions, lived through very tough economic times, and were overleveraged but performing (the study includes no nonperforming CMBS) at the time of securitization. Also, very little information was available at securitization, so the ratings were assigned based on a number of generally conservative assumptions.

In this chapter, we report the findings of the Dillon and Belanger which we consider to be the most reliable and robust. Generally, we recommend using the results as near to the worst case. As discussed in Quigg[10], the main obstacle to drawing conclusions based on this study is that all of the analysis reported was done by looking at the affect of a single variable (DSCR, property type, etc.) on defaults and losses (univariate regression). This type of analysis may lead to distorted results because the impact of one variable may really be attributable to another, correlated variable. In addition, the data set is unique in a way which is likely to skew the results; it consists of often at least mildly distressed loans underwritten by failing thrifts, which were performing at the nadir of the real estate recession, and tracks their performance through improving market conditions.

A ROLE FOR CORPORATE DEFAULT RATES

Another way to look at default risk is to assume that ratings truly do mean the same thing for CMBS as for corporates and look at corporate default rates. According to Standard and Poor's[11], since 1981, the average cumulative default rate over 15 years is 4.26% for triple-B rated securi-

---

[9]Pamela Dillon and Donald S. Belanger, "Trends in Commercial Mortgage Default Rates and Loss Severity." Fitch Investors Service, L.P. (November 11, 1996).

[10]Laura Quigg, "Analyzing CMBS Performance — A Discussion of the Fitch Study." J.P. Morgan Securities Inc. (January 6, 1997).

[11]Standard and Poor's "Ratings Performance 1996." (February 1997).

ties, 17.62% for double-Bs, and 27.72% for single-Bs. Details are shown in Exhibit 1, based on data compiled by Standard & Poor's.

Exhibit 1: Average Cumulative 15-Year Default Rates

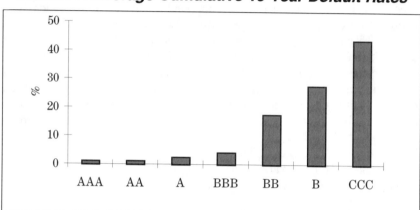

Typical credit support in a conduit-type CMBS is about 13% at the BBB level, 7% at the BB level, and 2% at the B level. Assuming a loss severity of 50%, these credit support levels mean that 28% of the time the rating agencies expect defaults to exceed 4% (resulting in a default for the single-B class), 18% of the time they expect defaults to exceed 14%, and 4% of the time they expect them to exceed 26%. Of course, the exact timing of these defaults would greatly affect the yields on lower rated CMBS.

BENCHMARK FINDINGS

These studies report a few general findings that serve as useful benchmarks for assessing CMBS default risk. In Snyderman's latter study of 10,955 loans of eight life insurance company portfolios originated from 1972 to 1986 and tracked through 1991, he found a 13.8% cumulative default rate and 18.3% projected lifetime default rate. Wechsler, Forst and Lederman of Fitch replicated Snyderman's earlier study and arrived at approximately the same figures. To estimate cumulative rates of default, Fitch tracked 1,524 loans in 11 insurance company loan portfolios originated from 1984 to 1987 through the end of 1991, and found default rates that averaged 14%. However, the rating agency reports that the actual default rate was probably closer to 20%, since certain loans in the data set were not counted as defaults because they were either restructured or sold to a subsidiary before they defaulted.

The studies do not incorporate defaults experienced in the two years after 1991, which were hard times for commercial real estate. Fitch projected that total defaults in its sample would reach 30%. Because Fitch believed the climate in the early 1990s represented an A-type recession, it originally set credit support for A-rated securities high enough to protect against its estimated 30% default rate.

Fitch also required credit-support benchmarks to protect against default rates of approximately 24% for a BBB rating, 30% for A, 40% for AA, and 50%-56% for AAA. Fitch also estimated a loss factor of 40%-50% of the loan amount on defaulted loans for typical pools, higher for AAA classes. Multiplying the default rates × the assumed loan severities, Fitch arrived at benchmark credit support requirements of 25%-28% for a AAA rating, 18%-20% for a AA rating, 13%-15% for an A rating, and 11%-12% for a BBB rating. These levels are calculated assuming that a pool consists of fixed-rate loans on high-quality, diversified property types and locations, with DSCRs between 1.15 and 1.25.

A Closer Look at the ACLI Surveys

The ACLI surveys show greater detail than these cumulative default studies. The data from ACLI show that delinquencies peaked in the second quarter of 1992 for all property types except multifamily, which peaked in the fourth quarter of 1991, as detailed in Exhibit 2.

Exhibit 2: Delinquency Rates
In Life Insurance Company Portfolios

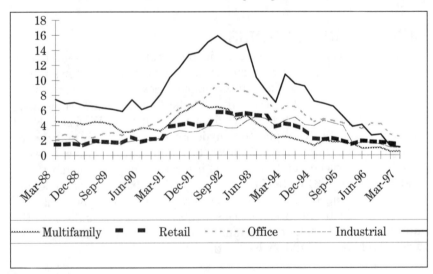

At their worst, nearly 16% of the life insurers' mortgage loans on hotel properties were delinquent, 9.5% on office buildings, 7.1% on multi-family properties, 5.8% on retail properties, and 5.2% on industrial properties. Since that time, delinquencies declined consistently and by the second quarter of 1997 declined to historically low levels — about 2.5% for office properties, 1.4% for retail, 1% for industrial and hotel, and 0.5% for multifamily.

The ACLI delinquency numbers represent the percentage of life insurance company portfolios which are currently delinquent. However, many of these loans cure or are otherwise restructured, which is much less costly than foreclosure. Most of the life insurance studies indicate that about half of the loans that become delinquent ultimately go into foreclosure, as shown in Exhibit 3.

Exhibit 3: Annual Rates of Completed Foreclosures

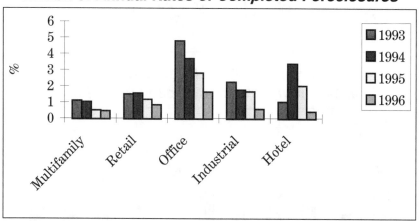

Annual rates of completed foreclosures peaked at about 3.2% in 1992 and 1993; in 1996, the rate was about 1.0% Exhibit 4, based on ACLI data, provides details on these annual rates.

We would expect a similar cure and restructure rate for CMBS where the servicers have the same incentive to maximize the present value of the collateral, unless flexibility is hampered, which may lead to a higher percentage of loans that go into foreclosure (but these may be foreclosed faster).

Ciochetti found a similar decline in his study of 2,290 foreclosed loans in 14 life insurance company portfolios, which he tracked from 1986 to 1995. In this data set, foreclosures peaked in 1992 and 1993, but fell significantly in 1994 and 1995, as shown in Exhibit 5.

Exhibit 4: Annual Rates of Completed Foreclosures In Life Insurance Portfolios

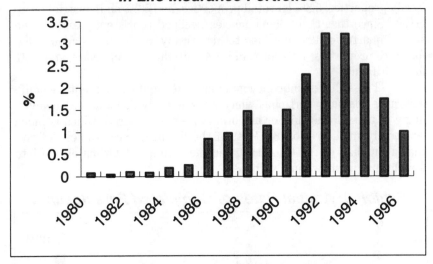

Exhibit 5: Foreclosed Loans In 14 Life Insurance Company Portfolios

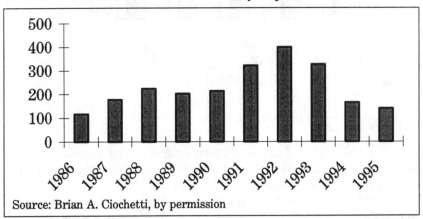

Source: Brian A. Ciochetti, by permission

PROPERTY TYPES

Different property types vary widely in their default performance, reflecting degrees of risk and volatility in each type's income and values. The ACLI data provide the most detail on delinquency rates for the different property types, as seen earlier in Exhibit 2. For the last 10 years, average delinquency rates in the life insurers' portfolios have been about

3% for retail and industrial; 3.5% for multifamily, 5% for office properties, and about 8% for office properties. Up until about 1993, retail properties experienced the lowest delinquency rates. However, more recently multifamily delinquency rates were lowest. Industrial properties have had the most stability, with delinquency rates that peaked at just over 5% at their worst. Office and hotel properties experienced more severe delinquency rates, with peaks of 9.5% and 15.9%, respectively.

Using the NCREIF Index

These trends mirror trends for values and total returns of each of these property types, which bottomed in mid-1992 as shown in Exhibit 6. According to the National Council of Real Estate Investment Fiduciaries Index, apartment, retail, warehouse properties have been more stable, with income and values less severely affected by the recession than office and R&D/office properties. NCREIF does not track hotel property values, but other sources show greater declines than seen in other property types. A number of studies, including Snyderman and Barnes and Giliberto, found defaults and property values to be significantly inversely related.

The performance of each of these property types is consistent with our logic of how they should perform, given fundamental characteristics which make rents and values more or less risky. In our view, the property types are ordered from most to least stable as follows: regional

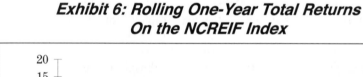

Exhibit 6: Rolling One-Year Total Returns On the NCREIF Index

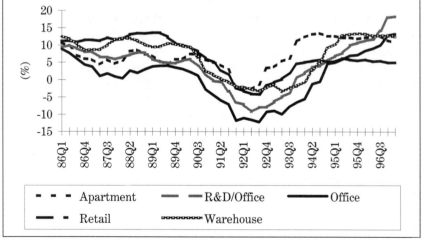

mall (dominant, well located, and well anchored), multifamily, anchored community shopping center, industrial/warehouse, unanchored community shopping center, office building, and, finally, hotel.

Regional Malls Regional malls with good locations and strong anchors are generally considered the least risky property type, because a mall requires a large tract of land and anchor tenants which give them a near-monopoly position in the market. However, weaker regional malls are vulnerable to a difficult retail market and shifting consumer tastes, and may require growing capital expenditure in order just to keep up.

Other Retail Sectors Other retail sectors vary considerably. Overall, retail properties have been on a downward but fairly stable trend due to new store formats and growth to accommodate those new formats. Well-located centers with a supermarket and/or drug store anchor should be relatively stable. Centers with a general-purpose discounter anchor such as Wal-Mart or Kmart may also be strong, depending on the quality and performance of that retailer (sales performance is usually a good gauge). Unanchored retail properties are riskier, since there is no anchor to serve as a regular draw for customers; but, usually, these properties are small and each represents a minor part of a CMBS pool.

Power Centers/Factory Outlets Power centers and factory outlet centers are more problematic, as the properties themselves are large and may be among the larger loans in a CMBS. Power centers are shopping centers with "big box" retailers such as PetSmart, Staples, HomeBase, or Circuit City as anchors, none of which is likely to draw customers on a regular basis. This is also a relatively new sector, and there is likely to be some consolidation among stores. However, we think that a well underwritten loan on a center with a good location and a variety of the more solid retail tenants can be a strong asset.

Factory outlet centers are relatively more risky, mostly because they are almost always located in out-of-the-way places so as not to compete with department stores and other distributers of the merchandise. Therefore, the center's value depends less on the value of the real estate and more on the operator and the franchise created by putting together a particularly strong group of tenants.

Multifamily Apartments Multifamily apartments derive their stability from their usually well diversified tenant base, which represents many economic and demographic groups. Although apartments can be vulnerable to new supply, the shorter time to build (typically one to two years) and homogeneity helps moderate these supply swings. Older apartment buildings are viewed as more risky because the need for more capital expenditures creates uncertainty. The multifamily market hit its peak during 1995-1996, and a few markets are moderately overbuilt. However, there are still good fundamental supply and demand characteristics which make mortgages on multifamily properties attractive and relatively stable.

Manufactured Home Communities Manufactured home communities may be more stable than multifamily if well occupied, because high costs of moving create low turnover which, together with low capital-expenditure needs, yield a stable income profile.

Self Storage Self-storage properties are generally about as risky as industrial/warehouse properties. There are risks because the sector is so new, but these are somewhat offset by the diversification of the tenant base. Better-quality facilities will have more professional management.

Industrial/Warehouse Industrial/warehouse properties are more risky because lease terms are short (three to five years) and each property is usually occupied by only a few tenants. However, turnover costs are relatively low because industrial/warehouse space is usually fairly basic and utilitarian, requiring little investment in tenant improvements. Reserves to cover re-leasing costs can mitigate some of the turnover risks. Industrial properties are also vulnerable to overbuilding because barriers to entry for new supply are very low. However, the property type's short construction time (six to nine months), homogeneity, and flexibility mean that the market can provide good feedback — which makes supply swings less severe.

Office Properties Like industrial, office properties are usually occupied by an undiversified tenant base and can be vulnerable to oversupply. In addition, re-leasing costs may be quite high (which reserves can mitigate), lease terms longer (providing some protection, but making such properties vulnerable to above-market rents), and the lead time for construction is longer (creating deeper cycles). Stronger properties are those with a good location, a good tenant roster, and little or no deferred maintenance. Currently, the office market is doing very well, especially the suburban office market and several downtown markets as well. With very little new construction since 1992, demand should exceed supply for many years to come.

Hotel Properties Hotel properties are relatively risky because income and expenses are hard to predict and manage with daily guest turnover, making strong management very critical. This sector is currently on a very positive trend and it is important to look at recent performance with a critical eye to understand the longer-term trends.

Health Care Nursing homes can be very stable if well operated. They benefit from growing demand as the population ages, coupled with limitations on supply imposed by state regulations. The experience of nursing home lenders has shown this to be a stable, low-delinquency sector, although there is some longer-term exposure to reimbursement risk.

Underwriting
Strong underwriting can, of course, compensate for many of these risks. More risky properties should have higher debt coverage ratios, lower loan-to-value ratios, and shorter amortization schedules. Better-quality loans will also have reserves to cover taxes, insurance, capital expenditure needs and re-leasing costs (for properties with term leases — retail, office, and industrial). Loans should be underwritten with strong coverage after incorporating expenses such as management fees and replacement reserves. Cross-collateralization also helps alleviate exposure to particular properties. Finally, default risk should be lower with high-quality management and a stronger, better-capitalized borrower.

DATA ON LOSS SEVERITY
It is important to estimate losses in the event a loan defaults and is foreclosed or restructured. We are starting to accumulate information on loss severities, mostly based on the experience of the life insurance industry and outstanding CMBS. The severity of loss should equal the property sale proceeds plus property revenue, less principal owed upon default, foregone interest, and expenses.

Studies that examine life insurance company experience give loss severities in the range of 25% to 36% in aggregate. In his study of eight life insurance company portfolios, Snyderman estimated loss severities of 36% of the original loan balance for foreclosed loans. He then assumed that losses for restructured loans would be about half, or 18%. In his study of 2,290 foreclosed loans from 14 life insurance company portfolios, Ciochetti found losses of 31%. For the recovered property value, Ciochetti used the value of the property as that value recorded when the loan was transferred to the real estate portfolio. In their study of 480 defaulted mortgage loans from one insurance company, Ciochetti and

Riddiough found loss severities of 26.7%, using the same methodology for determining property value.

We think these are useful data, but that the experience of CMBS backed by newly originated loans may be different. We would expect the life insurance company experience to understate losses relative to typical conduit product, because life company expenses may be underreported and higher-quality properties are likely to hold their value better. An off-setting factor is that more of life insurance company portfolios is invested in mortgages on office and hotel properties, which have experienced more volatile price swings. This factor should lead to more serious losses than mortgages on apartment and retail properties.

ACLI Findings

The ACLI surveys in 1994-1996 indicate a much lower loss severity for multifamily properties (10%) than for any of the other property types, followed by retail (22%), industrial (24%), office (30%), and hotel (35%). These figures, shown in Exhibit 7, do not include accrued interest.

Exhibit 7: Principal Losses Incurred On Properties Foreclosed

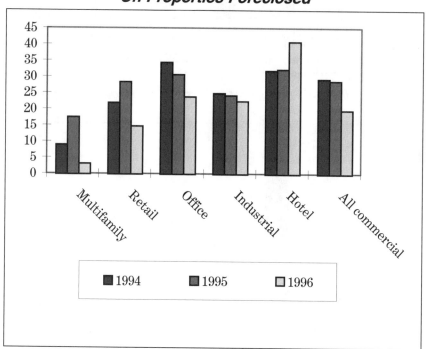

This ranking is consistent with that found by Ciochetti and Riddiough in their study of a single company, as detailed in Exhibit 8. They also found that industrial and apartment properties spent a relatively short time in foreclosure, and hotel properties spent a relatively long time, accounting for some of the differentials in loss recoveries shown in Exhibit 9.

Exhibit 8: Recovery Rates by Property Type

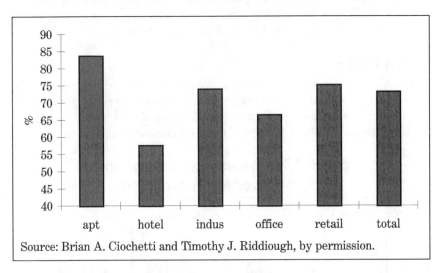

Source: Brian A. Ciochetti and Timothy J. Riddiough, by permission.

Exhibit 9: Foreclosure Time by Property Type

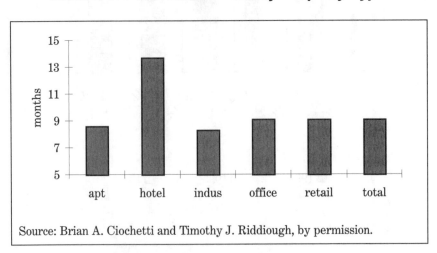

Source: Brian A. Ciochetti and Timothy J. Riddiough, by permission.

As Monitored by Fitch

The other major source of information on loss severities is the Dillon and Belanger study of older CMBS monitored by Fitch, which reported an average severity of 36.9% of the loan balance at securitization. This loss severity is approximately in line with that found in other studies — slightly higher than in a few studies of life insurance company loan performance, but lower than in a few other studies of RTC and agency loans.

We would expect higher loss severity with these loans than the life company loans, since the property and underwriting quality were generally worse — 477 of the 547 loss observations are on loans in RTC transactions. However, most of the life company studies cover longer periods of time. The loans in this study were resolved in a fairly mild economic climate, but many were originated in the middle and late 1980s, and went through a very difficult economy in the late 1980s and early 1990s. According to data from the ACLI, as shown in Exhibit 2, loan defaults peaked in early 1992.

Many of the loans in these CMBS were significantly overleveraged at the time of securitization, which the rating agencies factored into mostly very high credit support levels. These loans were originated by failed thrifts with generally weak underwriting standards and an incentive to lend aggressively due to deposit insurance and a lack of checks and balances on their underwriting.

We agree with Fitch that the conduit industry is primarily filling the void left by the thrift industry and has some of the same incentives to be aggressive given the competitive lending environment. However, we believe the scrutiny of the rating agencies, investors, and (in some cases) the investment banks that hold the loans for a period of time, severely restrict lenders' ability to shield poor underwriting practices.

Significant Differences

CMBS loans differ fundamentally from insurance company loans because there is better tracking of the actual costs of default in CMBS. The loss rate on insurance company loans may be understated to the extent that the insurance companies loaned to facilitate the sale of foreclosed properties. Other costs may be understated as well, such as interest on advances, the loss in property value, and the costs of restructuring a loan.

Since the servicers and trustees in a CMBS are compensated at arm's length, we get a much more accurate accounting of the true costs of default and foreclosure. The Fitch study found that the average loss due to property value was 32.5%, advanced interest was 8.7%, and property protection expenses were 2.0%, resulting in a total loss severity of 43.2%.

Partial amortization reduced this cost, giving a 36.9% loss rate based on the loan balance at securitization.

However, certain structural characteristics may have affected the average loss rates. In particular, CMBS which limit servicer flexibility and which lack a special servicer with the expertise to work out problem loans have experienced higher-than-average loss rates. With little or no servicer flexibility, the servicer has few options to work with the borrower to maximize the value of the loan as it deteriorates. Many of the rating agencies have reported exceptionally poor recovery rates for CMBS which lack servicer flexibility.

Appraisal Adjustment

A feature in CMBS which we believe will reduce losses is the now standard appraisal adjustment, which limits servicer advancing to the most subordinate class(es) by requiring the servicer to begin writing down delinquent loans based on the property's appraised value, before any losses are realized. Several CMBS with poorer servicing procedures have experienced very high loss severities because servicer advances were not limited and became very costly. It is still too early to measure the impact of the appraisal adjustment or other efforts to curtail advances.

Timing/Foreclosure Laws

Another factor which is important for analyzing CMBS is the time that it takes to foreclose, since most CMBS require servicer advancing during the foreclosure process, as long as these advances are deemed recoverable. Generally, the longer the time to foreclose, the higher the loss severity. Snyderman found 3.5 years between initial default and final disposition. Ciochetti and Ciochetti and Riddiough each found time of about one year between delinquency and end of foreclosure process, which does not include disposition. As discussed earlier in this chapter, the latter study found a shorter process for multifamily and industrial properties, and a longer one for hotels. We would expect that the delinquency and foreclosure process for each CMBS will depend on a number of factors, including servicer expertise, incentives for servicer to sell versus hold, economic climate (servicer may decide to wait to sell), and property strengths and weaknesses.

Both Ciochetti and Ciochetti and Riddiough found that the most important factor to affect the timing of foreclosures and, therefore, loss severities, is whether the mortgage is in a state which requires judicial foreclosure, or allows for a power of sale (POS) process. Judicial foreclosure is significantly slower, and therefore more expensive. In judicial foreclosure, the lender must convince the court to issue a judgment against the borrower and then obtain a court order authorizing the sale of the property. POS typically occurs in states which allow the deed to be held in trust by a third party. This process grants the lender the right to sell the property without a court order, as long as the trustee is convinced that the rights of both parties are satisfied. Exhibit 10 gives the predominant method of foreclosure in each state.

Ciochetti found overall gross recovery of 81.8%, which, net of

Exhibit 10: Predominant Foreclosure Method by State

Power of Sale

Alabama	New Hampshire
Alaska	New Mexico
Arizona	North Carolina
Arkansas	Oklahoma
California	Oregon
Colorado	Rhode Island
District of Columbia	South Dakota
Georgia	Tennessee
Hawaii	Texas
Idaho	Utah
Iowa	Virginia
Maine	Washington
Maryland	West Virginia
Massachusetts	Wyoming
MIchigan	
Minnesota	
Mississippi	
Montana	
Nebraska	
Nevada	

Judicial

Connecticut	New York
Delaware	North Dakota
Florida	Ohio
Illinois	Pennsylvania
Indiana	South Carolina
Kansas	Wisconsin
Kentucky	
Louisiana	
New Jersey	

accrued interest of 10.1% gives a net recovery of 69.4%. In POS states, gross recoveries were slightly higher at 82.6%, but accrued interest was lower at 9.0% giving net recoveries of 71.6%. By comparison, in judicial foreclosure states gross recoveries were 79.6%, accrued interest was 12.7%, and net recoveries were 63.7%.

Ciochetti and Riddiough found that judicial foreclosure took 2.5 months longer than POS foreclosure: 10.8 months for judicial, 8.4 months for POS. As expected, they found lower recoveries of 69.6% for judicial versus 74.9% for POS.

LOAN AGE

Another significant factor in evaluating CMBS performance is the age of the loan when default occurs. Most data support the notion that defaults are likely to be low at first, especially for well underwritten loans with good reserves to cover foreseeable expenses and potential income interruptions, and then spike up and peak in years four to six. Actual default experience will, of course, depend significantly on the economy of the time. At the peak period for defaults, most of the problems that are likely to occur already have, amortization begins to reduce the principal balance, and income rises relative to debt service, causing defaults to drop off significantly.

CMBS usually require servicer advancing of principal and interest payments through foreclosure, as long as such advances are deemed recoverable. Therefore, we think analysts should assume low defaults for the first six months to a year, with servicer advancing for the next nine to 12 months during the process of foreclosure; altogether defaults would not affect certificate classes for at least 15 months to two years. They should also allow defaults to decline by years six or seven, treating balloon defaults as a separate issue.

Both Snyderman and Ciochetti found default experience of life insurance company loans to support this view. Snyderman found that defaults rose quickly to about 1.5% by the first year and peaked in years two to five. Ciochetti found very little foreclosure activity in the first two years, but defaults rose steeply and peaked by year five. Over half (53.9%) of the foreclosures occurred in years three to seven.

About 60% of foreclosure activity occurred within six years of loan origination, and 80% within 10 years. Ciochetti also found higher recoveries for loans which default in first few years, as shown in Exhibit 11. Ciochetti and Riddiough also found loan age to be negatively related to foreclosure time period as older loans spent less time in foreclosure.

Exhibit 11: Net Loss Recovery by Loan Age

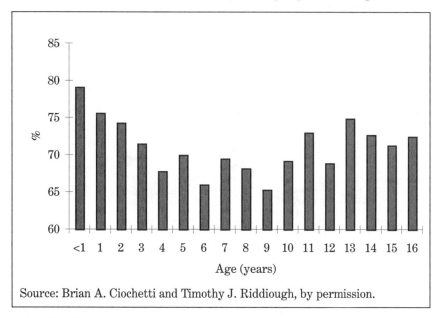

Source: Brian A. Ciochetti and Timothy J. Riddiough, by permission.

DIVERSIFICATION

CMBS default risk is also affected by diversification. CMBS with better diversification have less exposure to economic events that affect particular regions or property types. Most of the benefits come from geographic diversification, since regional recessions are more common than national recessions, and national recessions tend to affect regions differently. Also, supply cycles vary, depending on economic growth, zoning restrictions and land constraints, and capital availability.

Geographic Diversification

Exhibit 12 shows how defaults vary by region in Ciochetti's study of foreclosed loans in 14 life insurance company portfolios. These data may be somewhat misleading since we don't have information on each region's share of the company's total portfolio, but nevertheless we feel the results are instructive to understand the benefits of diversification. The Southwest (mostly Texas) accounted for most of the foreclosed loans between 1986 and 1991, but foreclosures dropped off to only 6.5% of total foreclosed loans by 1995. The Northeast moved in the opposite direction. From 1986 through 1989, only six loans had been foreclosed in this region. Rising costs of living, however, and economic weakness in the early '90s

Exhibit 12: Foreclosed Loans by Region 1986-1995

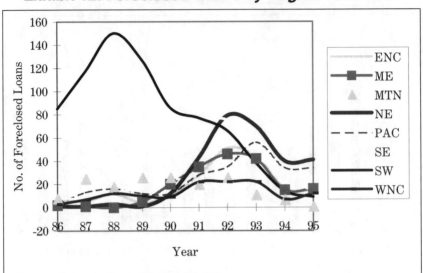

Source: Brian A. Ciochetti, by permission.

caused that number to peak at 79 foreclosed loans by 1992, the highest for any region that year. Since 1992, the Northeast has led all regions in total foreclosed loans per year.

These trends should be combined with our knowledge of how loans with different seasoning default. Based on the experience in the life insurance company industry, the most vulnerable geographically diversified pool was one with loans originated in 1984 or 1985, such that they are a few years old (the age when most defaults occur) when the Texas recession accounted for peak default rates. A geographically diversified pool would consist of fewer than 20% or 25% Texas/Southwest assets, so the pool as a whole would remain still little affected by this worst-case scenario. By the time the recession caused default rates to rise in the other regions, the loans would be more seasoned and less at risk of default.

Diversification of Property Type The benefits of property type diversification are not quite as great, since the performance of different property types tends to be more highly correlated than that of properties in different locations. We think of multifamily as being diversified in and of itself, since tenants come from all different economic and demographic backgrounds, so that a 100% multifamily CMBS can still be considered well diversified.

For the other property types, however, we think there is a benefit to mixing them, because it gives a greater variety in the tenant base and other factors which affect property performance. Exhibits 2 and 6 show delinquencies and total returns for the different property types. In the recession of the early 1990s, multifamily properties were the first to perform poorly, but were also the first to recover; industrial and retail properties were second to decline, but retail is still on a slow growth track; office and hotel declined more severely but are now on a very positive trend.

DEBT SERVICE COVERAGE RATIO

One of the most important pieces of information in assessing default risk is the debt service coverage ratio (DSCR), which is the property's net operating income or net cash flow divided by the debt service (regular principal and interest payments) on the mortgage which encumbers the property. The closer the DSCR is to one, the more risk there is that property income may fail to cover the mortgage payments. Some of this risk can be alleviated by reserves which cover periods when income is interrupted (due, for example, to a major lease turnover) or expenses are unusually high (as is the case with capital improvements).

At origination, DSCR should be higher (at least 1.4x or 1.5x) for properties with more variability to their income, such as hotels, factory outlet centers, or office buildings without net-leased-credit tenants. Properties with greater income stability, such as multifamily, manufactured home communities, regional mall, or anchored retail, can support a lower DSCR (as low as 1.2x).

A few of the studies support the importance of DSCR as a predictor of default. The studies which track multiple life insurance company portfolios over time do not have data on DSCRs, and therefore do not add to our knowledge about this variable. In the Fitch study of outstanding CMBS, Dillion and Belanger found that loans with lower DSCRs experienced higher rates of default and more severe losses, as shown in Exhibit 13 and Exhibit 14. Ciochetti and Riddiough analyze distressed loans from a single life insurance company and therefore are not in a position to assess determinants of default. However, the study further supports what one might expect that loans with lower DSCR experienced more severe losses.

LOAN TO VALUE RATIO AS AN ALTERNATIVE

In theory, the loan-to-value (LTV) ratio should be a more important predictor of default than the DSCR, because a borrower should only default when value of the property is less than the value of the loan. Even if the

Exhibit 13: Average Annual Default Rate by DSCR

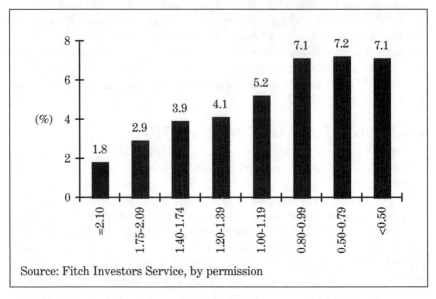

Source: Fitch Investors Service, by permission

Exhibit 14: Severity of Loss by DSCR

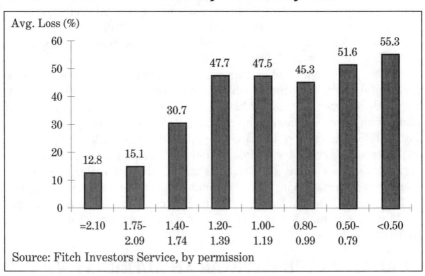

Source: Fitch Investors Service, by permission

DSCR falls below one, as long as the borrower can sell the property for more than the loan is worth, he or she should not default. In theory, a mortgage has an embedded put option that gives the borrower the right to put (sell) the property back to the lender.

However, this theory has many shortcomings in execution. First, value is a difficult concept to get a handle on, and appraised values may deviate significantly from sales prices in a distressed market. Appraisals involve a number of assumptions, the capitalization rate in particular, which makes them less useful as predictors of default. Second, real estate is usually illiquid and borrowers may lack the wherewithal to carry a property during times when net income drops off. Therefore, rating agencies and most investors weight DSCR more heavily than LTV to predict default. For example, Dillon and Belanger of Fitch indicated that they thought LTV should be an important factor in predicting defaults, but unreliable or unavailable data for the CMBS in their study made it impossible to examine the effects of LTV.

Several studies which have examined the relationships between defaults and property values have obtained meaningful results. Vandell,[12] Vandell, et.al., and Barnes and Giliberto all find that there is a statistically significant relationship between default and contemporaneous LTV (CLTV), where they estimate CLTV using the NCREIF index. Snyderman also found an inverse relationship between default rate and cumulative property value changes, and higher loss severities when property values declined.

Secondary Financing or Preferred Equity

Investors should evaluate the DSCR and LTV accounting for current and potential secondary financing or preferred equity positions, since the more equity the borrower has in a property or partnership, the less likely he or she is to default. However, if the lender/equityholder with that intermediate position is strong and well capitalized, with a reputation for identifying value, it reflects positively on the asset.

THE SIZE FACTOR

Little conclusive has been said about the effect of loan size on defaults, and, as a result, the rating agencies do not explicitly adjust for loan size in rating CMBS. One viewpoint is that large loans should perform better than small ones because they are more likely to be professionally managed, highly scrutinized, and better able to attract institutional financing and higher-quality tenants. However, a contrary argument can be made that small borrowers are less likely to be ruthless in their default strategy and carry a negative-cash-flow loan longer (very small loans are often

---

[12]Kerry D. Vandell, "Predicting Commercial Mortgage Foreclosure Experience." *AREUEA Journal* vol. 20 (1992): 55-88.

at recourse to the borrower) and may find refinancing easier.

We would argue that the market for loans under $1 million is fairly underserved and those in the range of $1 million-$15 million generally have the broadest access to financing. Financing availability for loans over $15 million has at times been fairly volatile, and is broadest for higher-quality properties in primary markets that are attractive to insurance companies. With the development of the large-loan conduit, we expect access to financing to be improved for a broader class of assets, but we have yet to see what happens to capital availability in this market in an economic downturn.

Dillon and Belanger of Fitch found mostly inconclusive results regarding loan size. Although larger loans (over $1 million) defaulted more often than smaller loans, the results are weak enough that any conclusions would be premature. Loan size also did not have a statistically significant influence on loss rates.

Ciochetti found that larger loans had lower recoveries, due both to lower gross recoveries and higher accrued interest; foreclosure costs go down with loan size (offsetting) on a percentage basis.

Although it is important to understand any concentration of risk, our view is that larger loans receive a disproportionate amount of scrutiny in CMBS compared with the small loans. We recommend that both the rating agencies and investors analyze a sample of both small and large loans in order to develop a more balanced understanding of the collateral.

PROPERTY QUALITY

The rating agencies generally assume that higher quality properties have lower default risk. The rationale for this argument is that higher quality properties hold their value better, have higher quality and better capitalized borrowers, benefit from a more liquid resale and financing environment, and are less likely to be overwhelmed by deferred maintenance problems. An offsetting factor is that higher-quality loans are typically underwritten more aggressively, with lower DSCRs and fewer reserves.

BORROWER QUALITY

CMBS investors and the rating agencies are beginning to consider borrower quality to play a more significant role. Since mortgages are generally nonrecourse for small and medium-size loans, information about the borrower is typically not provided and borrower quality is unknown. However, CMBS investors will pay a higher price for better-quality borrowers and the trend has been for more thorough discussion of borrowers which account for a concentration of loans in a CMBS.

FLOATING- VERSUS FIXED-RATE LOANS

We expect floating-rate loans to experience a higher rate of default than fixed-rate loans, because the former may be subject to the stress of a rising mortgage payment. However, since floating-rate loans are marked to market, we would expect them to default less at the balloon date as compared to fixed rate loans.

In their study of CMBS monitored by Fitch, Dillon and Belanger found significantly higher defaults and loss severities for floating rate compared with fixed-rate loans, despite what they describe as a period of relatively stable and low interest rates. We suspect that this variable may be correlated with another determinant of default, adding to the apparent significance of the results. The average annual default rate in the 1996 study was 6.7% for balloon loans and 2.4% for fully amortizing loans. The severity of loss was 31.1% for the fixed-interest loan rate and 41.2% for floating-rate, with no information about whether these defaults are balloon or nonballoon.

FULLY AMORTIZING VERSUS BALLOON LOANS

We expect balloon loans to default with greater frequency compared with fully amortizing loans, but to experience lower loss severities in the event of default. If a borrower fails to make the balloon payment on schedule, the loan is in default. Balloon defaults are more likely than defaults on outstanding loans because a property may support the current debt service but not a new loan as large as the balance on the old loan.

Repayment of the principal at the balloon maturity date normally requires the borrower to obtain refinancing. If the current LTV is more than 75% or 80% or DSCR is less than $1.2 \times$ or $1.3 \times$ (depending on the property and lending environment), the property owner may have to put equity into the property. However, we also expect higher recoveries for balloon loans since the circumstances are likely to be less dire. If the loan has performed up to that point it is probably supporting the debt service but not a refinancing at full proceeds. Dillon and Belanger of Fitch report results in support of these theories, with balloon loans defaulting in greater frequency but with lower severities. The average annual default rate by loan type was 6.7% for balloon loans compared with 2.4% for fully amortizing. The average severity of loss by loan type was 30.1% for balloon, 51.3% for fully amortizing.

SERVICING

The rating agencies generally take the view that servicer flexibility is a positive feature. We concur with this view, because we think that credit losses will be lower when the borrower can continue to run the property, rather than being forced into default. This logic is supported by life insurance company experience — according to ACLI, for companies managing their own portfolios, only a small percentage of delinquent mortgages are foreclosed; many more are restructured. Also, among the few CMBS that have been downgraded are several issued prior to 1993 which lack servicer flexibility. These CMBS have experienced very high credit losses (60% or more for multifamily properties), in part because the servicer was hamstrung into foreclosing properties in a bad market (Southern California).

Hyperamortization

A number of other servicing features have been put in place which have not truly been tested. One is the hyperamortizing feature, in which mortgages are fully amortizing, but as of an expected maturity — the anticipated repayment date or ARD (what would be the balloon date) — the mortgage interest rate typically rises by two percentage points and all income from the property is funneled into a lockbox and used to pay down the mortgage balance. This is the kind of procedure which a servicer would institute if balloon payment is not made. On the one hand, a hyperamortizing mortgage which is not paid off at the expected maturity is not in default and, therefore, is not subject to as much stress as a regular balloon loan. However, the servicing procedures for working out that loan are less flexible than in most CMBS. From that perspective, we view them as potentially more stressful for the borrower. We have not seen how this feature works in practice.

Extension

Another feature is the extension adviser and limits on extension of balloon loans. Because these features limit servicer flexibility, they also increase default risk, in our view. However, senior-class investors are likely to prefer them since they provide a check on the extension appetites of subordinate-class investors.

PREPAYMENT PENALTIES

High prepayment penalties or lockouts may increase default risk, as borrowers may choose to default in order to get out of a loan without paying the penalties or in violation of a lockout provision. Also, in a competitive lending environment, prepayment is one of many negotiated items (besides price, proceeds, and reserves), and investors should question why a borrower would accept onerous provisions of any kind.

John Mulligan is a first vice president and head of trading in commercial mortgage-backed securities at Prudential Securities Inc.

From 1986 through 1992, Mulligan worked at Prudential Insurance in various capacities, including commercial mortgage loan underwriting, workouts, and the buying and selling of CMBS.

Earlier in his career, he spent three years as head of commercial mortgage research at Donaldson, Lufkin & Jenrette.

Mulligan holds a bachelor of arts degree in economics from Brown University and a master's degree in management from Northwestern University.

Chapter 6

Relative Value in the CMBS Market

John Mulligan
First Vice President, CMBS Trading
Prudential Securities Inc.

Since the true inception of commercial mortgage-backed securities in 1991,[1] investors have enjoyed an appealing return profile driven by attractive credit performance and an unparalleled degree of spread tightening. Exhibit 1 highlights this performance.

Investors in the earliest bonds were lured by spreads that were frequently two to three times those available from comparable fixed-income alternatives such as corporate bonds or agency mortgage pass-throughs and collateralized mortgage obligations. Since those early days, improvements in credit fundamentals, information and analytical availability, and liquidity have greatly reduced the yields available on CMBS. As a result, fixed-income portfolio managers must evaluate CMBS investment opportunities more closely. Investors use relative-value analysis to determine the desirability of any investment, CMBS included, versus competing alternatives.

INVESTOR OBJECTIVES
The value of a security is shaped by the objectives of the investor. Investor objectives are determined by performance measures. In the CMBS market, as in many fixed-income sectors, the two main types of investors are total-rate-of-return money managers and liability-matching portfolio managers. Although some distinctions are starting to blur, performance measurements of the two investor types often differ.

Total Rate of Return
Total-rate-of-return money managers are usually compensated based upon the amount of assets under management and, sometimes, directly upon the quarterly or annual total rate of return that their portfolios gen-

---

[1]The year that the Resolution Trust Corporation began its multifamily-mortgage-backed issuance. Assorted private-label CMBS had been issued in the 1980s, but the size of the market was insignificant.

	AAA 5 year	AAA 10 year	AA 10 year	A 10 year	BBB 10 year	BBB- 10 year
1993						
December	115	125	135	155	230	335
1994						
March	110	120	130	160	225	335
June	110	120	130	160	225	335
September	105	115	125	160	225	330
December	90	110	115	150	225	330
1995						
March	80	105	115	140	210	330
June	80	105	115	130	190	330
September	80	100	110	140	190	330
December	80	100	110	130	175	315
1996						
March	80	93	105	120	165	195
June	75	90	100	105	140	190
Sepember	62	83	95	105	130	165
December	53	70	80	90	110	150
1997						
March	50	66	75	85	105	135
June	48	62	67	75	88	115

erate. Whether or not this latter measure is explicit, it is always implicit in the sense that strong performance will generally result in more assets under management. Total-rate-of-return managers track their performance based not only upon income return and realized capital returns from the sale of assets, but also from unrealized capital returns measured by periodic "marks to market" obtained from the dealer community. As such, they are most interested in bonds for which prices can appreciate more than their performance benchmarks. While strong income return is important, total-rate-of-return investors are unlikely to sacrifice price movement to get it. Investors of this type are typically constrained as to the credit rating and the durations of the assets in which they invest, as set forth in investment guidelines through which they have marketed their services to clients.

Liability Matching

Liability-matching portfolio managers, such as investment departments at banks and insurance companies, are more frequently compensated on income generation and their ability to match accurately their firm's liability profile with assets. These managers are generally less influenced by interim mark-to-market valuations. They are frequently constrained by predetermined portfolio weightings that might, for example, limit the percentage of mortgage products in the portfolio to a set percentage. Also, the tax implications of asset sales are a more significant factor for liability-matching managers than they are for total-rate-of-return managers.

Key Attributes of Bond Value

Without regard to these differences, virtually all fixed-income investors analyze several key attributes of a bond when assessing its value, these attributes come together to determine an estimate of risk-adjusted return.

Creditworthiness The first analysis attribute is the creditworthiness of the source of repayment of principal. While investors certainly take guidance from the rating agencies, many also perform their own credit analysis to determine the degree of repayment risk. Obviously, lower-rated bonds demand greater attention to credit detail than triple-A-rated paper.

Cash Flow Structure The second bond attribute reviewed is the structure of the cash flows, including coupon, maturity date, the period over which principal will be repaid, and call features. This analysis helps the manager assess the degree of duration drift or average life variability, as well as the bond's ability to appreciate in price.

Liquidity Once these attributes have been assessed, investors gauge the liquidity of the proposed investment, frequently described in terms of a bid/offer price spread.

Appropriateness of Pricing Finally, with all of the other attributes reviewed, a manager can assess the appropriateness of the pricing of the asset. The weight that each attribute will be given in the investment decision will be driven, as mentioned earlier, by the objective of the investor.

This chapter describes and assesses these fixed-income asset attributes for CMBS and competing fixed-income alternatives, determines the appropriate competing assets for benchmarking comparisons, and makes some relative-value conclusions. Although the broad CMBS market consists of both private-label and agency-guaranteed paper, the discussion in this chapter focuses exclusively on the more diverse private-label market.

COMPETITION FOR CMBS:
ATTRIBUTES OF THE FIXED-INCOME UNIVERSE

Aside from the general level of interest rates (a systematic risk), there are essentially only two risks associated with bonds — credit risk and cash-flow timing risk. Noncallable U.S. Treasury notes are perceived to be free of either of these risks and are therefore the most expensive (lowest yielding) bonds that investors can purchase. In order to take either type of risk, investors must be offered additional yield over Treasuries as compensation.

Credit Risk

Credit risk is most often described in terms of ratings assigned to bonds by nationally recognized statistical rating agencies. Corporate bonds, some mortgage-backed securities, and asset-backed securities carry such ratings. Bonds rated BBB- or above are considered to be investment grade, while bonds with lower ratings are considered to be high-yield or "junk" credits.

A large segment for which credit risk is not described in terms of ratings is the agency market, named for the agencies of the federal government that guarantee the principal and interest payments of these securities. The major agency participants in the fixed-income market are the Government National Mortgage Association (GNMA or Ginnie Mae), the Federal National Mortgage Association (FNMA or Fannie Mae), and the Federal Home Loan Mortgage Corporation (FHLMC or Freddie Mac). Because of their direct line of credit from the U.S. Treasury, GNMA securities are perceived to be free of credit risk. FNMA and FHLMC have the implicit backing of the government and are, therefore, perceived to be virtually free of credit risk. All three agencies guarantee principal and interest payments of mortgages secured by single-family and multifamily housing. FNMA and FHLMC also issue the form of corporate debt known as debentures.

Cash-Flow Timing Risk

Cash-flow timing risk is frequently described as duration drift or average life variability. It can take the form of prepayments, which shorten the duration and average life of a bond, or extension, which does the opposite.

Timing risk is most commonly associated with mortgage securities, although Treasuries, corporate bonds, and agency debentures that have call features are also in this category. This type of risk is prominently displayed by single-family mortgage securities, such as GNMA or FNMA pass-through certificates. This risk arises from the ability of home owners to prepay their mortgages at any time, without penalty.

To address this concern, the market prices these bonds — which are usually scheduled to amortize fully over 30 years — assuming that a certain level of prepayments will occur in the pool. To the extent that these prepayment estimates are overstated, the bonds have a longer average life than originally anticipated and are said to have extended.

Collateralized mortgage obligations (CMOs) were created with the goal of limiting the amount of timing risk in mortgage securities. In a CMO, the cash flows from the underlying mortgages are used to create bonds with a variety of payment priorities. Some of these bonds, such as planned amortization classes (PACs), are structured so that they receive prepayments only in high-prepayment-speed environments, thereby reducing the degree of average life variability. To accomplish this goal, structurers must create a bond or bonds which receive the prepayments that would otherwise have been received by the PAC. These so-called companion bonds serve as prepayment shock absorbers in a CMO. Because the prepayment risk of all of the underlying mortgages is concentrated in these bonds, they actually have more cash flow timing risk than the underlying mortgages.

Unanticipated or Delayed Principal Payments

While the impact of credit deterioration or principal loss on a bond's value is apparent, the impact of unanticipated or delayed principal payments is less obvious. From the perspective of an insurance company portfolio manager, duration drift can bring about situations in which liabilities come due and assets are not maturing in time to pay them off. This is called asset/liability mismatch, which is generally not desirable. From a total-rate-of-return fund manager's perspective, the influence of structure on relative value comes entirely in the capital component of total return.

Convexity

A bond's structure can in some ways be summarized by a mathematical term known as convexity. Convexity compares a bond's price changes in rising and falling Treasury markets. For example, positively convex bonds will experience greater price appreciation in a rising (price) Treasury market than they will experience price deterioration in a falling Treasury market. Because U.S. Treasury securities are a benchmark against which most fixed-income managers are compared, it is important to know how an alternative bond's price will behave in various interest rate environments. All else being equal, positively convex bonds are more valuable to investors than negatively convex bonds. Callability and creditworthiness strongly influence convexity.

Intuitively, one knows that it would be unwise to pay more than par for a bond that — with 100% certainty — will be called at par the next day. It would be similarly unwise to pay more than the recovery value for a bond that — again, with 100% certainty — will default the following day. In falling rate environments, investors do not generally want their capital returned prematurely. If this risk is present, they will demand more spread as compensation. The higher the dollar price of the purchased bond, the more painful will be the early return of principal, via either prepayment or default recovery. So, in order for the price of a bond to rise at a rate similar to Treasuries, the bond must prove to investors its limited exposure to default and prepayment risk.

It is perhaps helpful to think of the fixed-income universe as a continuum as it relates to cash-flow timing risk or structure, with the most tightly structured assets (the least timing risk) on the far left and progressively more variable structures as one heads to the right. The far left side would consist of U.S. Treasury notes, corporate bonds, and non-callable agency debentures. The right side would consist of single-family mortgage products, such as GNMA and conventional mortgage pass-through securities, and less-stable classes of CMOs such as companion bonds. Assuming equal credit risk, liquidity, and duration, bonds on the left side of our continuum will be more highly valued by the marketplace than those on the right. Our first task in assessing the relative value of CMBS is defining its place on the continuum.

PRIVATE LABEL CMBS

CMBS Bond Structure

Investors in all structured fixed-income products, including CMBS, must undertake two levels of analysis. The first stage is typically a review of the collateral or the underlying commercial mortgage loans; the second is an assessment of the bond structure. The work for a CMBS buyer is far more heavily weighted toward collateral review because, to date, CMBS bond structures have been quite similar and fairly simplistic.

Senior Subs Virtually all CMBS transactions are structured as senior-subordinated straight sequential pay deals. The senior-subordinated structure refers to the fact that the bonds created from a pool of mortgages are ranked in priority of loss absorption. In this structure, all of the bonds with an inferior credit rating to a given bond serve as credit support or loss "shock absorbers" for that bond. A typical trust will issue bonds with ratings ranging from triple-A all the way down to bonds deemed so risky as to be unworthy of a rating by the rating agencies. Losses incurred on *any* loans in a pool reduce the principal balance of the the lowest-rated bond in the pool.

Straight Sequential Pay Straight sequential pay refers to the fact that all principal received during each collection period, whether scheduled or unscheduled, is distributed to the senior-most (usually triple-A-rated) bond until it is retired. In addition to reducing the risk of repayment by shortening the higher-rated bonds, this structure also has the desirable feature of generating increased credit support over time. That is, the ratio of more highly rated debt to total mortgage debt gradually increases over time (assuming the level of losses incurred in the pool is lower than the amount of debt being repaid). Further, this structure has the desirable impact of creating bonds (other than the current pay bond) with very tight principal windows. These are desirable bonds due to their ability to "roll down the curve" and appreciate in price.

Because the AAA-rated portion of a CMBS deal is typically large (frequently 70% of the total debt issued), deal structurers frequently time-tranche these bonds into at least two classes. For example, Class A1 receives all scheduled and unscheduled principal until it is retired, and only then does Class A2 receive principal. In a common structure, A1 would have a five-year average life while A2 would have an average life of 10 years. Exhibit 2 shows a typical structure of a CMBS transaction. Because both A1 and A2 are AAA-rated securities, they receive interest and absorb any losses on a pro rata basis. In order to keep the dollar prices of the senior bonds in a CMBS transaction close to par (100% of the face amount of the bonds), an interest-only (IO) strip is frequently created and sold in addition to the regular principal and interest bonds.

Although bond structures have been generally homogeneous, collateral types have been varied. A significant pricing distinction among CMBS is frequently based on the source of the commercial mortgages comprising a pool. The two main sources for a pool have been newly originated loans and purchases of seasoned loan portfolios. We will detail the distinctive characteristics of each and tie these into the relative-value analysis of the bonds that these loans support.

Exhibit 2: Structural Picture of MRAC 1996-C2

Class	Fitch/ Moody's Ratings	Approx. % of Total	Approx. % Credit Support	Average Life	New Issue Spread
A-1	AAA/Aaa	28.5	30.5	5.5	+53
A-2	AAA/Aaa	41.0	30.5	9.7	+70
B	AA/AA2	6.0	24.5	10.0	+80
C	A/A2	5.5	19.0	10.0	+90
D	BBB/Baa2	4.5	14.5	10.8	+110
E	BBB-/NR	1.5	13.0	11.8	+150
F	BB+/NR	3.0	10.0	11.9	—
G	BB/NR	2.5	7.5	12.1	—
H	BB-/NR	1.0	6.5	12.1	—
J	B/NR	2.5	4.0	13.0	—
K	B-/NR	1.5	2.5	14.9	—
L-1 (Principal Only)	NR —	2.5 —	— —	16.3 —	—
L-2 (Interest Only)	Unrated	—	—	16.3	—
A-EC* (Interest Only Strip)	AAA/Aaa	NA	30.5	9.1	—

*Excess interest on all classes except L-1.

NEW ORIGINATIONS

Many types of private-label CMBS transactions comprise newly originated loans. For the first several years of the market's existence, deals backed by seasoned portfolios predominated. As the real estate market has recovered and interest rates have fallen, however, fewer and fewer portfolio lenders have been willing to sell seasoned loans. Simultaneously, Wall Street loan origination machines have become more efficient, resulting in a major swing in the composition of the market. New origination deal types include single-asset, single-borrower, multiborrower, credit lease, and conduit. Each of these deal types has unique attributes chiefly related to how the loans are combined into pools. But they share the characteristics of strong call protection and the presence of complete and current underwriting information which are present in virtually all newly originated loans.

Call Protection

Call protection comes in several forms, including hard lockout, or stiff prepayment penalties that serve as a deterrent to the borrower. Treasury make-whole (yield maintenance) is a common form of prepayment penalty that requires the borrower to accompany any prepayment with a premium which, when reinvested by the loan owner in Treasuries for the remaining term of the loan (had it not been prepaid), would exactly recreate the lost yield on the prepaid loan. Fixed-percentage prepayment penalties are also common, and require the prepaying borrower to pay a premium equal to a set precentage of the balance being prepaid. Many newly originated loans are protected by yield maintenance or a combination of lockout and yield maintenance for at least 85% of their term. Fixed penalties frequently start after the expiration of a lockout or yield-maintenance period and frequently remain in place until six months prior to maturity of the loan.

Standard Underwriting Packages

As distinct from many seasoned loans that end up as collateral for CMBS, loans being originated for securitization in today's market have complete underwriting packages (using fairly uniform standards) containing current information. This permits investors, underwriters and the rating agencies to make a more complete assessment of the credit risks associated with a particular loan.

Because of these attributes, CMBS backed by newly originated loans have limited cash-flow variability. This fact is demonstrated in Exhibit 3, which compares the yield profile of a triple-A-rated conduit

Exhibit 3: CMBS Versus Agency PAC

	Price	CPR O	10	15	25	35	50
AAA CMBS							
MLMI 96 - C2 A3	101 - 0+						
Yield		6.846	6.846	6.846	6.846	6.846	6.847
Average Life (Years)		8.9	8.9	8.9	8.9	8.8	8.8
Spread		+58/C	+58/C	+58/C	+58/C	+58/C	+58/C
Agency PAC							
FHR 1455 H	100 - 28						
Yield		6.978	6.929	6.929	6.851	6.757	6.58
Average Life (Years)		15.4	9.3	9.3	5.7	3.9	2.5
Spread		+61/C	+66/C	+66/C	+67/C	+67/C	+62/C

bond MLMI 1996-C2 A3 to an agency CMO, assuming a combination of high prepayment speeds and 1% annual defaults (with 25% loss severity). Thinking back to the fixed-income continuum, the strong credit and call protection combine with the tight principal window structure of CMBS bonds to place CMBS backed by newly originated loans firmly on the left side. That is, most CMBS backed by newly originated loans have less structural risk than other types of mortgage-related assets and, hence, are more comparable to corporate bonds and agency debentures.

Price Comparisons

Now that we have more precisely defined the universe of comparable types of bonds, we turn to price comparisons. Exhibit 4 highlights conduit CMBS against other convex assets. For comparison, Treasury spreads are shown for A-rated and BBB-rated corporate bonds issued by industrial firms, agency debentures, certain types of asset-backed securities, and well structured PACs from agency-guaranteed CMOs. Par dollar prices are assumed for all of the securities presented.

Exhibit 4: Market Spreads as of June 30, 1997

CMBS			Agency Debentures		Agency CMOs		ABS	Industrial Corporates	
AAA	5 yr	48	5 yr	14	5 yr PAC	44	5 yr 31 credit cards	5 yr single-A	41
			5/NC 3 yr	29					
AAA	10 yr	62	10 yr	20	10 yr PAC	55			
			10/NC 5 yr	57					
AA	10 yr	67							
A	10 yr	75						10 yr single A	62
BBB	10 yr	88						10 yr BBB	80
BB	10 yr	185							

As shown in Exhibit 4, the variously rated classes of CMBS offer consistent opportunities for investors to pick up spread (income return) versus similarly rated and well structured bonds of like average life. With 10-year average life AAA-rated CMBS, investors can trade even spread to corporate bonds rated two full rating categories lower. The spread pickup is even more significant versus bullet agency debentures, with AAA 10-year CMBS offering a 42 basis point improvement. Incredibly, investors can even pick up five basis points versus 10-year agency debentures with only five years of call protection, that is, far more average life variability. Although a conduit transaction is used in this example, the story would be similar for other types of CMBS deals comprising newly originated loans. The following section provides a brief description of each of these types of transactions.

Transaction Types

Single Asset These are the simplest of all CMBS deals. They are backed by a single loan on an individual property, frequently of some notoriety. Typically, the properties are large enough to support over $100 million of debt, such as regional or super-regional malls and large office properties. The loans do not generally represent more than 60% to 65% of the value of the property, and even the last loan dollar is typically rated no lower than BBB or BBB-. Because of the concentrated nature of the risk in a single-asset deal, most rating agencies will rate the senior-most bonds no better than three letter grades better than the lowest rated bonds, resulting in many AA-rated senior-most bonds from these deals. Investors are mixed in their opinion of these bonds, with real estate experts favoring them while bond experts usually shun the concentration. For those confident in the underwriting, the AA-rated senior-most bonds represent excellent relative value. These bonds have AAA-rated loan-to-value ratios and debt service coverage ratios and can be purchased at AA-rated spreads.

Conduit The most common "new origination" transactions in today's market are the so-called conduit deals, which accounted for approximately 30% of the $30 billion of CMBS issuance in 1996. Securities created from conduit-originated loans are backed by a relatively large number (frequently 100 to 150) of relatively small loans (generally $3 million to $7 million). The loans are originated either directly by investment banks or by third-party lenders that take their collateral to Wall Street to be securitized.

In addition to strong call protection and complete underwriting information, conduit loan pools have great diversification by loan size, borrower, asset type, geographic location, and — to a lesser extent — maturity date.

The loans are most frequently 10-year balloon loans on 25- or 30-year amortization schedules, although five-year, seven-year and 15-year terms to maturity are also present in many conduit loan pools. Conduits were expected to represent the largest source of CMBS in 1997, and most active market participants anticipate that they will hold this top position in the years ahead.

Single Borrower/Multiborrower The single-borrower deal is typically backed by a single, cross-collateralized, cross-defaulted loan on a portfolio of properties owned and operated by a single entity. Owner/operators that have used this method of financing include privately held companies as well as publicly traded real estate investment trusts, or REITs. Frequently, these deals have been characterized by additional concentrations in either property type or geographic location, or both.

Offsetting some of these potential credit concerns are tighter constraints on the borrower, such as the requirement that properties be owned by special purpose entities (a mitigant to bankruptcy risk) and lockbox mechanisms that insure that rents make their way to the bondholders. The performance of the properties is also easier to monitor than conduit deals, as large single borrowers almost always comply with requirements to provide updated financial statements.

As is the case with single-asset deals, the investor community is somewhat split as to the value of single-borrower deals. Those with real estate backgrounds welcome the chance for thorough due diligence and embrace these deals, while those with more traditional fixed-incom backgrounds generally avoid the concentrated risk.

The rating agencies generally employ the same rating methodology as they do with single-asset deals.

Historically, an owner needing $100 million or more of financing could do his own standalone CMBS deal. Today, borrowers of this size and even larger are frequently pooled together to form multiborrower deals. The Mega-Deal concept from Nomura is a common example of the format. These transactions are simply an aggregation of single borrowers, and have the characteristics described above.

Credit Tenant Lease These transactions are characterized by a strong reliance on the credit rating of the lessee, as opposed to the value of the real estate — which is the case with most other CMBS deals. The underlying mortgage loan is usually fully amortizing over a period of 15 to 20 years based on the rental stream of the credit tenant. The leases are structured as triple net leases, requiring the tenant to pay all of the expenses associated with owning and operating the property.

The bonds are usually time tranched, so that shorter average life bonds can be created. The bonds generally have the same rating as the corporate credit of the tenant. Although they are the same credit, the bonds trade at a discount of 15 to 40 basis points to the unsecured debt of the tenant. This is due to the fact that if the tenant declares bankruptcy and rejects the lease as part of a restructuring, the CMBS bondholders may receive only a fraction of the remaining payments (up to three years or 15%) scheduled under the lease, although they can also foreclose on the property.

Liquidity

The final aspect of our relative-value analysis is a comparison of liquidity. When the CMBS market started, a major component of the premium required by investors related to its very poor liquidity. The poor liquidity stemmed from several factors. First, the investor base was small. As with any new product, it took some time for investors to learn enough about it to get comfortable. Second, ongoing information on the credit performance of the collateral was limited to nonexistent. Third, simple analytics such as price-yield tables were not widely available and more detailed analyses on defaults and prepayments were even more scarce. Finally, because of the second and third issues, few dealers were in a position to make markets in bonds underwritten by other dealers.

Since 1995, virtually all of these issues have been remedied. While early transactions were distributed to 10 to 15 investors, today's CMBS deals are usually distributed among 40 to 50 investors. Participants include all investor types from hedge funds to commercial banks. Information flow has improved dramatically through the creation of on-line servicing systems which display updated debt-service coverage ratios on each underlying loan and provide detailed descriptions of the status of problem assets. The rating agencies also provide updated subordination levels for bonds and pool delinquency statistics on a monthly basis via the widely available Bloomberg system. More detailed analytics — such as loan-level defaults and prepayments, including yield maintenance premiums — are now being provided by third-party firms which are accessible over the Internet.

These developments have made dealers eager to trade each other's bonds. Since many investors are still in a net add position for CMBS, dealer inventories have remained rather light. In a press to boost inventories, dealers have resorted to making very tight markets (two to three basis points) for investment-grade CMBS, frequently having to pay the offered side from the last trade to buy bonds. As such, liquidity in the CMBS market is now comparable to that found in the corporate bond and agency debenture market, and only slightly weaker than that of the asset-backed and agency mortgage pass-through market.

SEASONED LOAN POOLS

Seasoned loan pools have represented the largest single category of CMBS issuance in each year of the market's existence. Much of this can be attributed to the heavy issuance by the Resolution Trust Corporation as it disposed of commercial mortgage assets acquired from failed thrift institutions. Additional seasoned pool issuance has come from banks and life insurance companys as these entities either repositioned their portfolios of commercial mortgages or exited them entirely. The largest CMBS deal completed to date is the $1.9 billion liquidation via securitization of the Confederation Life portfolio.

While there is nothing inherently bad about seasoned commercial mortgages, several attributes common to most of these loan pools make them trade cheaper than CMBS backed by newly originated loans. The first attribute of note is that many of the loans in the seasoned pools have more limited call protection than that found on today's loans.

Second, none of these loans was underwritten with rating agency standards in mind. While this isn't always terrible, many of the standards used were inferior to those of today. For example, many lenders underwrote using net operating income in the mid 1980s versus the net-cash-flow standard imposed by the agencies today. Many loans in the mid to late 1980s were also underwritten on speculatively developed and partially leased properties, using a net-operating-income figure that could be realized when (and if) the building reached a stabilized occupancy. As we now know in hindsight, many properties never did achieve stabilized occupancy in the late 1980s and early 1990s.

Third, even if prudent underwriting was done, many of the loans in seasoned pools were originated at the height of the real estate market in 1986-1988, suggesting that many are overleveraged and may not be able to refinance at their balloon date. All of these features combine to introduce greater average life variability than is found in newly originated CMBS and, in many cases, negative convexity. In order to represent value, CMBS backed by seasoned loans must generally offer more spread than CMBS backed by newly originated loans. The amount of additional spread required is dictated by the perceived credit quality of the collateral and the degree of call protection remaining on the pool.

One offsetting positive for bonds backed by seasoned loans is a higher likelihood of being upgraded by the rating agencies. The reason for this has been the ability of these pools, due to a combination of shorter maturity dates and weaker call protection, to build up overcollateralization or increased subordination more rapidly relative to credit support amounts required at new issue.

For example, assume the rating agencies required 33% subordination to achieve a triple-A rating and 29% subordination to achieve a double-A rating for a seasoned loan pool at the date of initial securitization. Rapid paydown of the AAA-rated bond can cause the percentage of total remaining CMBS rated lower than AA to grow to 33%. At this point, the rating agencies will likely consider the AA-rated bond as a candidate for an upgrade to AAA. Clearly, this is a positive for the investor holding this bond, since AAA-rated bonds are more valuable in the market than AA-rated paper. In seasoned loan pools, investors must weigh this potential against the negative implications of average life variability to determine value.

CONCLUSION

This chapter has defined the risk characteristics of both CMBS and competing products and made pricing and liquidity comparisons to determine relative value. We have made Treasury spread comparisons between CMBS and like assets from the rest of the bond universe and found that CMBS indeed offers investors income enhancing opportunities without sacraficing convexity. Finally, we determined that any liquidity give-up investors are required to absorb in order to achieve this extra income is at worst minimal relative to the spread that they are earning. We have been able to conclude that, at today's market levels, CMBS does indeed represent a valuable investment alternative for fixed-income money managers. Some big-picture issues further solidify this conclusion.

First, because of the slow underwriting and accumulation period for the loans and the lengthy rating agency diligence process, there is a natural annual cap on the supply of CMBS. This should be a comfort to investors when compared with sectors like the corporate bond market, where lower interest rates can instantly double or triple the weekly new issue calendar.

Second, regulatory changes have favored CMBS and will likely continue to do so. For example, ongoing discusssions with the Department of Labor may result in the extension of ERISA eligibility to CMBS bonds rated BBB and higher, which would permit broader participation by pension fund money mangers. Finally, with the economic recovery continuing strong, credit fundamental for the national real estate markets are good. Construction, although up from the lows of the early 1990s, is still moderate and appears to be rationally following demand.

With supply and demand in relative equilibrium and credit fundamentals strong, we would expect that CMBS continue to represent value in the fixed-income universe for some time to come.

John P. Felletter, CFA, is director with Capital Trust, based in New York City.

Felletter is responsible for portfolio management and credit surveillance. He has over 15 years of real estate experience, with positions in lending, mortgage banking, portfolio management, and troubled-debt management. He was involved in the issuance and management of the SKW I securitized transaction, one of the first securitizations of nonperforming debt.

Felletter is a member of the executive committee of the Commercial Mortgage Secondary Market and Securitization Association, and heads the CSSA's education committee. Additionally, he is a member of the American Real Estate Society and the Mortgage Bankers Association.

Felletter has attained the Chartered Financial Analyst designation, and previously was licensed as a Series 7 General Securities Registered Representative, and Series 24 General Securities Principal.

He holds a bachelor of science degree from Central Connecticut State University, a master of science degree in management from the University of Southern California, and a diploma in real estate investment analysis from New York University.

The author thanks Christopher Wilkos, vice president of Phoenix Home Life, and Rodney Pelletier, associate director of Fitch Investors, for help in preparing this chapter.

Chapter 7

Insurance Company Involvement
In the CMBS Industry

John Felletter
Director
Capital Trust

This chapter presents various ways in which an insurance company may be involved with CMBS. The primary role to be discussed is that of the insurance company as an investor in CMBS. To help provide a framework for evaluating the impact of CMBS investment on an insurer, the chapter provides details on a rating agency's view. Included is a demonstration of the comparative impact on insurance company risk-based capital (RBC) and liquidity resulting from investment in CMBS versus whole loans.

This chapter then addresses the impact of securitizing an existing pool of mortgage loans, the use of a securitization model for portfolio benchmarking and valuation, certain operational issues and cost considerations that might impact the decision to invest in either CMBS or whole loans, the potential role for an insurer as an originator or issuer of CMBS, and the use of a FASIT vehicle for ongoing investment.

OVERVIEW

Commercial mortgage-backed securities are bonds backed by pools of commercial mortgage loans. The pools are of two primary types: those consisting of assets that have been held for some time in an existing mortgage portfolio (seasoned pools) and those consisting of loans that were originated specifically for securitization (conduit pools). The cash flow resulting from the payment of interest and principal on the mortgage loans is the source of repayment for the bonds. The discrete cash flow provided by each individual loan is aggregated into an homogeneous cash-flow stream, which is then reallocated (tranched) into claims representing various levels of seniority and, accordingly, various gradations of credit risk. There are also strip tranches known as interest-only (IO) and principal-only (PO). The relative credit strength of each tranche is largely driven by the level of bonds that are junior in claim to the bond in question. This subordination level is a primary determinant of the credit rating of the bonds.

The quantitative factors that determine the tranching levels are debt-service coverage (DSC) and the loan-to-value (LTV) ratio provided by the underlying loans. Due to the impact on default likelihood, the DSC is generally given the greater weighting, although rating agencies will vary somewhat in their approach. Also, in low interest rate environments, the LTV may become the critical test as lower interest rates inflate DSC ratios on all loans.

Qualitative factors that impact subordination levels are the collateral underlying the mortgage loans, diversification by property type and geography, average loan size, size of the pool, reserve requirements, prepayment prohibitions, the nature of the borrowing entity, and the rating of the ultimate loan servicers. Exhibit 1, based on data compiled by Phoenix Realty and outside sources,[1] demonstrates a simplistic breakout of the tranches of a prototype CMBS issuance.

Exhibit 1: Breakout of Tranches in a CMBS Prototype

Rating	% of Offering	% of Subordination	DSC	LTV	Spread over Treasuries
AAA	72.9	27.1	2.35	46.9	70
AA	5.0	22.1	2.20	50.1	85
A	5.0	17.1	2.10	53.1	95
BBB	5.0	12.1	1.92	57.6	130
BBB–	2.3	9.8	—	—	155
BB	5.3	4.6	1.78	62.2	230
B	2.8	1.8	1.72	64.4	450
Unrated	1.8	0.0	1.70	65.1	1,100

CMBS Investors

Through early 1998 there continued to be a strong appetite within the investment community for all classes of CMBS investment. Investors in the senior tranches typically include pension funds and insurance companies, with more risk-tolerant buyers focusing on the mid-level tranches. The noninvestment-grade tranches are typically purchased by real estate investment firms, which usually act as special servicers for the portfolio.

---

[1]Howard Esaki and Lisa Schroer, *The CMBS Research Weekly*, Morgan Stanley Dean Witter, March 2, 1998, and *Commercial Mortgage Alert*, Harrison Scott Publications, Hoboken, N.J., March 2, 1998; both by permission.

(The special servicer manages the underlying mortgages at such time as they become delinquent or otherwise present a high level of risk of default or loss.) These investors, also known as B-piece buyers, will frequently purchase all of the below-investment-grade bonds within a securitization, with the highest-risk tranche, the unrated, generally purchased at a discount.

Conversion Profit

Through early 1998, profits of 1.5% to 2% were available through the conversion of whole loans to CMBS. Profits of 5% to 6% had been available prior to fall 1997, but these were largely a function of rapid spread tightening, discussed later in this chapter. Conversion profit is due to the difference between the spread available from the underlying whole loans and the cost of debt on the ultimate securities (bonds). The cost of debt comprises the interest payable on the securities and the cost associated with completing the securitization. The interest cost in early 1998 approximated 100 basis points. Expenses at that time approximated 1.5%, which equates to approximately 20 basis points on an amortized basis.

These components, combined, resulted in an aggregate, "fully loaded" cost of debt approximating 115 to 120 basis points (the breakeven level). To the extent that the spread on the underlying mortgage loans exceeds this breakeven level, there will be a conversion profit on the issuance. While the profit on individual securitizations will vary over time, conversion profits should continue to exist, simply because the tranching allows investors to purchase the specific risk levels they desire.

Note, however, that quality differences in the underlying pool can result in greatly differing subordination levels, which can significantly impact the cost of debt. Therefore, higher spreads on the underlying mortgage loans may not result in higher profitability since the spreads may be coincidental with lower-quality loans requiring accordingly higher subordination levels. Consequently, a pool of loans with an average spread of 145 basis points over Treasuries may result in no profit, while a pool with an average spread of 120 basis points, consisting entirely of high-quality assets, may be profitable.

The size of the pool is also an important contributor to the profit margin, as fixed costs are better spread over larger pools. Therefore, CMBS issuers frequently team up to take advantage of these economies of scale. The down side to these larger pools is that the asset-level underwriting is complicated due to the higher number of assets. Further, the macro-level underwriting, which involves evaluation of both the underwriter and the underwriting as a process, is complicated due to the multiple underwriters.

Profit potential is the primary motive for involvement in the issuance of CMBS. For the investment bank issuer, CMBS issuance provides an additional product for that bank's bond department to trade. This provides fee income and may be an operational benefit, as well, since the lack of a readily salable product could hurt the bank's ability to retain its most capable bond traders.

The primary risk in the issuance of CMBS product lies in aggregation, the risk that required spreads will widen prior to the closing of the securitization, reducing the value of the loans and potentially resulting in a loss upon securitization. Theoretically, an upward movement in Treasury rates would also diminish the value of the underlying mortgage loans. But Treasury rate moves can be substantially hedged by the sale of Treasuries and, therefore, the risk can be largely mitigated. While a significant portion of the profit realized on CMBS issuance from late 1996 through mid-1997 was a result of spread-tightening, comparable losses could be encountered in the event of a corresponding spread-widening.

INSURANCE COMPANY RATINGS/KEY CONCEPTS

The insurance company rating process focuses on eight key areas:

- Industry risk.
- Management of corporate strategy.
- Business review.
- Operational analysis.
- Capitalization.
- Liquidity.
- Investments and investment performance.
- Financial flexibility.

Capitalization, liquidity, and investments and investment performance are discussed in depth in this chapter's Impact Study section.

Industry Risk

Risks that are generic to all companies within the industry are analyzed based upon:

- Potential threat of new entrants.
- Threat of substitute products/services.
- Rivalry among existing firms.
- Bargaining power of buyers/suppliers.

Management and Corporate Strategy

This analysis covers four key elements:

- Strategic positioning of the company, which addresses the planning process, whether the strategic plan is consistent with corporate capabilities, and whether the plan makes sense in the marketplace.
- Operational skills, the ability to implement corporate strategy.
- Financial risk tolerance based on balance-sheet management, specifically debt level relative to total capitalization.
- Organizational structure consistent with company strategy.

Business Review

The business review entails both qualitative and quantitative analyses of a company's fundamental characteristics and the source of competitive advantage and/or disadvantage. This review includes a specific evaluation of the way in which various aspects of the business contribute to the absolute level, growth rate, and quality of the revenue base. The following quantitative factors are reviewed:

- Compound growth rate of revenue during the past five years.
- Distribution of revenue by business unit.
- Geography, product, and distribution channel.
- Market share of the firm as a whole and by major product lines.
- Organizational structure both legally and functionally.

Qualitative analysis addresses:

- Quality of the distribution system.
- Diversity and economic viability of product lines.
- The degree of competitive advantage enjoyed due to distribution capabilities, product structure, investment capabilities, quality of service, cost structure, and market segment dominance.

Operational Analysis

To evaluate an insurance company's ability to capitalize on strategy and business strengths, the operational or earnings analysis focuses on underlying economic profitability rather than stated statutory net gain. Key determinants of a life/health insurer's operational efficiency include a review of persistency (level of policy renewal), expense structure, mortality/morbidity experience, effective tax rate, pricing policies, and actual performance versus pricing. The trend and degree of stability of a company's earnings are also important considerations. The key ratios are:

- Lapse ratio (by major product lines).
- Accident and health combined ratios.
- General expense ratio.
- Expense ratio.
- After-tax return on assets.
- Pre-tax return on revenues.
- After-tax return on capital.

CAPITALIZATION

This analysis involves a review of both the insurance company's current and prospective capitalization, focusing primarily on surplus, and capital requirements.

Capital Adequacy Model

Standard & Poor's has developed a capital adequacy model that produces a ratio based on adjusted capital and surplus, minus realistic investment losses, divided by charges for certain liabilities and risks:

$$\frac{\text{Adjusted capital \& surplus minus asset-related risk charges}}{\text{Charges for mortality, morbidity, expense, interest rate, and general risk}}$$

Asset Charges The insurer's investment portfolio quality is evaluated to establish a reasonable estimate of expected losses over a period of several years. The present value of these expected losses is treated as an appropriate investment reserve charged against surplus. Surplus is adjusted for any explicit statutory loss reserves that an insurer may already have set aside.

Liability Charges Capital is allocated to support an insurer's liabilities based on differing risk characteristics of various lines of business. These allocations reflect assumptions about the threshold level of capital necessary to absorb — in aggregate — mortality, morbidity, lapse rate, product loading, and interest rate mismatch risks for securely rated companies. The model also provides a means of allocating an appropriate capital level to support subsidiaries or other operations in a prudent manner; that is, at an investment-grade or secure rating level.

Qualitative and Quantitative Adjustments A vital part of the assessment of an insurer's capital adequacy incorporates both qualitative and quantitative adjustments. These quality-of-capital issues may include:

- Changes to bond and/or mortgage factors used in establishing prudent loss reserves.
- Asset concentrations.
- Line-of-business concentrations or unusual product features.
- Ability to generate capital internally and self-fund growth through statutory earnings.
- Capital needs of a parent, affiliate, or subsidiaries.
- Quality of asset-liability management techniques.
- Reinsurance usage.
- Other contingent liabilities that may warrant a charge against capital (such as, bond guarantees).

The analysis of capitalization for insurers also incorporates applicable ratios related to financial leverage usage and fixed charge coverage:

- Total debt to capital — long-term debt to capital.
- Short-term debt to capital.
- Fixed charge coverage.
- Preferred stock to capital.
- Fixed charge coverage of preferred dividends.

Risk-Based Capital

Another proxy for the capital strength of an insurance company is the level of risk-based capital and the risk-based capital ratio. RBC is intended to ensure capital adequacy in insurance companies, reduce the effective yield of certain higher-risk investments by increasing the capital required when making those investments (thus reducing financial leverage), and provide target levels below which additional regulatory oversight is required. This is accomplished by addressing the related surplus levels necessary to compensate for the varying levels of risk inherent in different business or investment areas. The insurer has an incentive to maintain RBC above a minimum level, due both to rating concerns and because additional regulatory oversight is affected. Also, below certain threshold levels of RBC, additional regulatory oversight is affected, as shown in Exhibit 2. Currently, most insurers have comfortable levels of RBC, so that RBC level is not a primary consideration in day-to-day investment decisions.

Exhibit 2: Regulatory Action Levels Regarding RBC

RBC Level	Regulatory Action
1	2.50+	No Action
2	2.00 - 2.50	*Trend Test.* Firms for which the ratio falls into the range warranting a trend test must calculate the greater of the decrease in the margin between the current year and the prior year and the average of the past three years, assuming that the decrease could occur again in the coming year. A company that trends below 1.9 × its base-adjusted capital triggers a plan-level regulatory action.
3	1.50 - 2.00	*Plan Level* (Company Action Level Event). At this level, regulators require that an insurer submit a comprehensive financial plan, which contains explanations, proposed solutions, a four-year projection, and identification of problems within the company. The regulators must then either approve or deny the plan.
4	1.00 - 1.50	*Action Level* (Regulatory Action Level Event). At this level, the insurer will submit a revised RBC plan, while the regulator will perform an examination of assets, liabilities, and operations of the insurer and subsequently issue a corrective order indicating the desired remedies. The expense of this level of action is borne by the insurer.
5	0.70 - 1.00	*Authorized Control Level.* At this level, the regulator shall issue a corrective order and, if deemed necessary, place the company under regulatory control.
6	0.00 - 0.70	*Mandatory Control Level.* At this level, the regulator shall place the company under regulatory control.

Categories of Risk Business areas and investments are categorized within one of four basic categories of risk:

- C 1 — asset default.
- C 2 — insurance.
- C 3 — interest rate.
- C 4 — general business hazard.

Mortgage loans comprise one component of the C 1 asset default risk category, as shown in Exhibit 3. A summary of all categories of C 1 risk-based capital factors appears in Exhibit 4.

Calculation The two pertinent RBC calculations are the aggregate RBC, which totals the risk-based capital required for all components of risk, and the mortgage loan component of C 1, or asset default risk.

Exhibit 3: Components of RBC Categories

Asset risk (C 1)	Bonds
	Mortgages
	Preferred stock
	Unaffiliated common stock
	Affiliated common stock
	Separate accounts
	Real estate
	Other invested assets
	Subtotal
Asset concentration factor	Miscellaneous assets
	Reinsurance
	Off-balance-sheet items
	Total asset risk
Insurance risk (C 2)	Health insurance — individual
	Health insurance — group
	Life insurance — individual
	Life insurance — group
	Premium stabilization reserves
	Total insurance risk
Interest rate risk (C 3)	Low risk
	Medium risk
	High risk
	Adjustment for cash-flow testing
	Total interest rate risk
Business risk (C 4)	Life and annuity
	Health
	Total business risk

Exhibit 4: Summary of C 1 Risk-Based Capital Factors

NAIC Category	Rating	RBC Factor
BONDS		
1	AAA-A	0.003
2	BBB	0.010
3	BB	0.040
4	B	0.090
5	CCC	0.200
6	In or Near Default	0.300

NAIC Category	RBC Factor Commercial	RBC Factor Residential
MORTGAGES		
In Good Standing	0.03	0.005
90 Days Overdue	0.06	0.010
In Foreclosure	0.20	0.200

NAIC Category	RBC Factor
REAL ESTATE	
Company Occupied	0.10
Investment	0.10
Foreclosed	0.15
COMMON STOCK	
Unaffiliated Companies	0.30
Affiliated Companies	Not a component of C 1
U.S. Life	% Owned × RBC
U.S. P&C	% Owned × RBC
Investment Subsidiary	% Owned × RBC
Foreign Insurers	1.00
Other	0.30
SEPARATE ACCOUNTS	
With Guarantees	
Indexed	0.003
Not Indexed	Subject to the risk of the underlying assets
Without Guarantees	0.100
OTHER LONG-TERM ASSETS	
Due to the diverse nature of these assets, RBC is calculated by applying different risk factors according to the type of assets.	
REINSURANCE	
0.005 for all reinsurance with authorized, unaffiliated companies	
MISCELLANEOUS	
Cash	0.003
Short Term Investments	0.003
Premium Notes	0.05
Collateral Loans	0.05
Write-ins	0.05

No factor for interest rate swaps or policy loans.

Aggregate RBC/RBC Ratio The aggregate RBC is calculated as follows:

The risk-based capital ratio is calculated as follows:

$$RBC = 0.5 \times [\ C\text{-}4 + \sqrt{(C\ 1 + C\ 3)^2 + (C\ 2^2)}\ ]$$

Total actual capital $\div$ Aggregate RBC = RBC ratio

Mortgage Loan Portfolio Component of C 1, Asset Default Risk The National Association of Insurance Commissioners (NAIC), has established RBC risk factors for various types and classifications of mortgage loan investments. These factors are multiplied by the outstanding balance of each mortgage type/classification to arrive at a preliminary RBC level. For residential mortgages and commercial mortgages in good standing, this preliminary RBC level is then multiplied by the experience adjustment factor (EAF) to arrive at a required RBC level for that particular mortgage type/classification. (Loans in foreclosure, loans more than 90 days past due, and due/unpaid taxes have very high RBC factors and, therefore, the preliminary RBC level is not adjusted by the EAF.) The required RBCs for each type are summed to arrive at a total RBC for the mortgage loan component of C 1. The impact study contains a comparison of the RBC ratios resulting from investment in CMBS versus investment in mortgage loans. Exhibit 5 demonstrates the impact of different EAFs on the RBC requirement,and Exhibit 6 defines the types and classifications of loan investments.

Liquidity

The liquidity analysis evaluates the interrelationship between liquid assets (sources), which are those readily convertible to cash, and liabilities (demands). The demands analysis focuses on those liabilities that are subject to a sudden shortening of term (withdrawal) which, consequently, could become calls on the company's cash position.

To help analyze the effective liquidity of an insurance company, factors are applied to investment assets to reflect the ability to turn these assets into cash. The balance of the specific asset is multiplied by the factor to determine what is, in essence, an effective liquidity balance. The balances for all individual assets are added to determine an aggregate level of liquidity. A full listing of liquidity factors appears in Exhibit 7.

Exhibit 5: Definition and Calculation of EAF

DEFINITION

The experience adjustment factor (EAF), also commonly referred to as the Mortgage Experience Adjustment (MEA) Ratio, is a ratio used to compare the historical quality/performance of an insurance company's mortgage portfolio to that of the average portfolio within the industry. The EAF is calculated by dividing the eight-quarter average of the subject company's Normalized Loss Ratio (NLR), by the eight-quarter average of the Industry Normalized Loss Ratio, which is an average of the NLRs for all insurance companies.

FORMULAS

    Quarterly Normalized Loss*
    The NLR is computed as follows:

		Multiplier
	Average level of restructured loans for the quarter	0.010
+	Average level of overdue loans for the quarter	0.020
+	Average level of in-foreclosure loans for the quarter	0.025
+	Mortgage loan foreclosures during quarter	0.120

    Quarterly Normalized Loss Ratio*

$$\frac{\text{Quarterly Normalized Loss}}{\substack{\text{Average Level of Total Mortgages for the Quarter,}\\\text{Plus 1/2 of Mortgages Foreclosed During the Quarter}}}$$

    Company Experience Adjustment Factor*

$$\frac{\text{Eight-Quarter Average of Company NLR}}{\text{Eight-Quarter Average of Industry NLR}}$$

*Quarterly averages are determined by adding the beginning balance to the ending balance and dividing by two.

The EAF is multiplied by the RBC balance for commercial mortgages in good standing, to calculate an adjusted RBC level. This RBC level is the value used in calculating total RBC.

(Note, however that the EAF used in the calculation has a lower limit of .5, and an upper limit of 3.5. Any calculated EAF values that fall above or below those limits are adjusted downward or upward to the limit, accordingly, prior to making the adjustment to RBC. Therefore the effective RBC factor, defined as the 2.25 RBC factor × the EAF, has a range of 1.125% to 7.875%)

Exhibit 6: Simplified Risk-Based Capital Calculations

Scenario One	Balance $ Million	RBC Factor %	RBC Before Factor $ Million	EAF Factor %	RBC After Factor $ million
Commercial Mortgages					
Good Standing	$900	2.25	20.250	1.00	20.25
>90 Days	15	15.00	2.250	1.00	4.500
Restructured	75	7.50	5.625	1.00	11.250
In Foreclosure	20	20.00	4.000	1.00	8.000
TOTAL					44.000
Scenario Two	Balance $ Million	RBC Factor %	RBC Before Factor $ Million	EAF Factor %	RBC After Factor $ Million
Commercial Mortgages					
Good Standing	$900	2.25	20.250	2.00	40.500
>90 Days	15	15.00	2.250	1.00	2.250
Restructured	75	7.50	5.625	1.00	5.625
In Foreclosure	20	20.00	4.000	1.00	4.000
TOTAL					52.375

Liabilities are also weighted, with weightings applied to help reflect the likelihood of withdrawal, which would create an immediate need for cash. As with investments, the individual liability balances are added to determine an aggregate liability level. Exhibit 8 contains a listing of typical insurance company liabilities, as well as the appropriate weighting factor.

The aggregate level of liquidity is divided by the aggregate liability level to calculate a liquidity ratio. Exhibit 9 summarizes the rating equivalents for the differing levels of liquidity ratios, along with the distribution of the ratios for year-end 1995, for 105 insurers rated by Standard & Poor's.

Exhibit 7: Invested Asset Liquidity Factors

	Immediate Scenario %	Ongoing Scenario %
Cash and short-term investments	100	100
U.S. government securities	100	100
Agency pass-through MBS	90	90
CMOs — VADMs, PACs and TACs	90	90
CMOs — Sequentials	80	80
CMOs — Z tranches	0	50
Other CMOs	0	0
Investment-grade public bonds	100	100
NAIC 1 144A private placements	80	90
NAIC 2 144A private placements	65	75
NAIC 1 non-144A private placements	70	80
NAIC 2 non-144A private placements	40	50
Noninvestment-grade bonds	0	0
Unaffiliated public investment-grade preferred stock	100	100
Unaffiliated public common stock	70	85
Assets in securities lending programs	0	100
Funds withheld reinsurance assets	0	0

CMOs	Collateralized mortgage obligations
MBS	Mortgage-backed securities
VADMs	Very accurately defined maturities
PACs	Planned amortization classes
TACs	Targeted amortization classes

Exhibit 8: Liability Factors

Liability	Immediate Scenario %	Ongoing Scenario %
Traditional Life	30	50
Term Life	50% of UEPR	50% of UEPR
Interest-sensitive life	50	50
Single premium deferred annuities	100	100
Tax-sheltered annuities	100	100
Flexible premium deferred annuities	100	100
Single premium immediate annuities	100	100
Other individual annuities	100	100
Supplementary contracts	30	50
Variable life and annuities	0	0
Individual accident and health	50% of UEPR	50% of UEPR
Individual disability	50% of any cash value	50% of any cash value
Structured settlements	100	100
Guaranteed investment contracts	100	100
Group annuities and other deposit funds	100	100
Group accident and health	50% of PSR and UEPR	50% of PSR and UEPR
Group Life	50% of PSR and UEPR	50% of PSR and UEPR
Group long-term disability	50% of PSR and UEPR	50% of PSR and UEPR
Health claims reserves	100	100

PSR   Premium stabilization reserve   UEPR
Unearned premium reserve

Exhibit 9: Rating Standards

Rating Category		Liquidity Ratio %	Company Distribution Number of Companies
AAA	(Superior)	260 plus	12
AA	(Excellent)	220 to 259	56
A	(Good)	180 to 219	31
BBB	(Adequate)	140 to 179	6
BB	(May be adequate)	100 to 139	0

INVESTMENTS AND INVESTMENT PERFORMANCE

This analysis entails three primary steps: review of asset allocation; evaluation of credit risk, relative yield, and diversification; and consistency with liability structure.

Review of Asset Allocation

Asset allocation is the choice of how much to invest in each broad asset class — stocks, bonds, cash, real estate, foreign securities, gold, and, possibly, others — to achieve the best portfolio given the investing objectives and constraints.

Credit Risk, Relative Yield, and Diversification

Credit risk relates to the risk of default or loss on the fixed-income portfolio. Relative yield relates to the yield on investment relative to the inherent risk of the investment. To maximize the relative yield, each investment must provide the maximum level of return for a given level of risk, or, alternatively, the minimum level of risk for a given level of return. Diversification relates to the level of exposure the company has to one asset class, industry, geographic location, or time horizon. The primary diversification items that relate to CMBS and mortgage loan investment are property type, market or geographic diversification, and time or maturity diversification.

Consistency with Liability Structure

This analysis compares the liabilities of the company, such as policy payoffs and annuity payments, with the company's asset mix. Ideally, assets and liabilities should be well matched in the sense that anticipated inflows of cash are about the same as anticipated outflows of cash. Interest rate management and duration matching are also key issues, as detailed in Exhibit 10.

Financial Flexibility This is a qualitative analysis which addresses capital requirements and capital sources. Capital requirements refer to extraordinary needs for either short-term liquidity or long-term capital. Capital sources refer to the company's level of access to the means to address these needs, other than cash from operations. Typical sources would be domestic and foreign capital markets, with demonstrated access to equity; long-term public debt; and commercial paper. The sources of capital could be the sale of assets with unrealized capital gains or the ability to obtain reinsurance.

Exhibit 10: Duration and Convexity

Duration

Duration is the sensitivity of a security's price or a portfolio's value to a change in interest rates. A portfolio with a longer duration will be more sensitive to interest rate swings than one with a shorter duration, because the longer the duration the greater the period over which the cash flow of the portfolio is being discounted. All other factors being equal, the duration of an investment increases with term to maturity, decreases with increases in yield, and decreases with the frequency of payments.

In addition to providing an easy method to evaluate a portfolio's sensitivity to interest rate swings, duration can also be used in an attempt to limit the interest rate risk within the portfolio. This is accomplished by matching the duration of the assets in the portfolio with the duration of the liabilities through a process known as immunization.

Negative Convexity

Convexity deals with changes in portfolio value that are not predicted by the use of duration. In theory, due to the inverse relationship of return requirements to the value of a fixed-income portfolio, the value of a portfolio should approach infinity if the return requirement becomes sufficiently low. Obviously there are certain limits, and these limits represent a good example of what is meant by negative convexity. Negative convexity refers to the situation in which the increase in the value of either a fixed-income instrument or a portfolio of fixedincome instruments, is less than would be indicated by the reduction in required yield. This is a major concern for real estate loans.

The primary reason for negative convexity is the lack of true call protection, or the implicit put in a nonrecourse loan. While whole loans are structured to provide theoretical call protection via yield maintenance or defeasance requirements, this protection breaks down in the event of default on a nonrecourse loan. The reason it breaks down is that a lender can look no further than to the value of the collateral to enforce any remedies and, therefore, there is no additional financial backing for the yield maintenance or defeasance requirements. In essence, the borrower on a nonrecourse loan has a right at any time to convey title to the property to the lender in full satisfaction of his obligations. This creates an implicit put that the borrower can exercise at such time as the property, subject to the underlying debt, is not financially viable.

Since the lender can ultimately look no further than the collateral for satisfaction of the loan obligation, a loan's value should never materially exceed the value of the underlying collateral, notwithstanding interest rate movements.

IMPACT STUDY

The impact of a securitization strategy has been evaluated in light of three of the eight key rating agency areas of consideration: capitalization, liquidity, and investments/investment performance.

Capitalization

To evaluate the impact of capitalization on the RBC calculation, two analyses were performed: the impact of investment in CMBS versus mortgage loans on a one-time basis and the impact of ongoing investment in the two investment types. Both analyses started with a model insurance company balance sheet, with certain assumptions as to investment mix and existing RBC and EAF ratios. The impact of these investment decisions on an actual company's RBC would be contingent upon these company-specific factors.

Existing Portfolio Analysis This analysis, as detailed in Exhibit 11, compares the RBC ratio of the company assuming investment in whole loans, investment in CMBS, and investment in investment-grade CMBS only.

Ongoing Investment Analysis

This analysis compares the long-term implications of using a securitization strategy to affect exposure to commercial real estate debt.

For the analysis, three sets of financial statements were prepared, reflecting three investment scenarios. The first assumed that the insurance company invested $200 million annually. The second assumed that the company invested in an equal level of CMBS (or, alternatively, of originating the same level of loans, but immediately securitizing the loans and holding all of the securities in-house). The third projection shows the same level of investment, but assumes that the funds used for noninvestment-grade pieces in Scenario Two were instead invested in investment-grade (NAIC 1 and NAIC 2) bonds. Exhibits 12, 13, and 14 summarize the results of the three investment scenarios.

Exhibit 15 summarizes the RBC ratings pertaining to the three scenarios.

Exhibit 11: Comparative Ratios in Portfolio Analysis

		With Whole-Loan Investment	*With CMBS Investment*	*With Investment-Grade CMBS*
Asset Base				
Bonds		6,400		
Mortgages		1,000		
Other		1,200		
		8,600		
RBC Calculation	factor			
Bonds	0.30%	19		
Mortgages	2.25%	23		
Other	30.00%	360		
Replace Mortgage Portfolio with CMBS		N/A	1,000	1,000
NAIC 1	81.5%	N/A	815	815
NAIC 2	7.0%	N/A	70	70
NAIC 3	7.0%	N/A	70	70
NAIC 4	3.5%	N/A	35	35
Unrated	1.0%	N/A	10	10
				(115)
Sell below investment grade (NAIC 3, 4 and unrated) (115)				
Reinvest in NAIC 1	80%	N/A	N/A	92
Reinvest in NAIC 2	20%	N/A	N/A	23
Bond distribution after sale and investment				
NAIC 1		N/A	N/A	907
NAIC 2		N/A	N/A	93
Effect on C1				
FASIT Adjustment				
C1-Base	factor	402	402	402
Remove from Mortgages	2.25%	N/A	(23)	(23)
Add to Bonds NAIC 1	0.30%	N/A	2	3
Add to Bonds NAIC 2	1.00%	N/A	1	1
Add to Bonds NAIC 3	4.00%	N/A	3	—
Add to Bonds NAIC 4	9.00%	N/A	3	—
Unrated	30.00%	N/A	3	—
Adjusted C1		402	391	383
C2		150	150	150
C3		50	50	50
C4		25	25	25
Adjusted Covariance		501	491	483
Total Adjusted Capital		1,320	1,320	1,320
Adjusted Ratio		263%	269%	273%

Exhibit 12: Balance Sheet — Investment in Whole Loans

Plan 1998-2000		1997	1998	1999	2000	2001	2002
New Money Investment in Mortgages		200	400	600	800	1,000	1,200
Asset Base							
Bonds Investment Grade	assumed	6,000	6,400	6,750	7,150	7,500	7,900
Bonds Noninvestment-	6%	400	400	450	450	500	500
Grade Mortgages	(rounded)	1,000	1,200	1,400	1,600	1,800	2,000
Other		1,200	1,300	1,400	1,500	1,600	1,700
		8,600	9,300	10,000	10,700	11,400	12,100
RBC Calculation	factor						
Bonds	0.30%	18	19	20	21	23	24
Mortgages	2.25%	23	27	32	36	41	45
Other	30.00%	360	390	420	450	480	510
C1		401	436	472	507	543	579
C2		150	155	165	170	180	190
C3		50	50	50	55	60	60
C4		25	30	30	30	30	30
Covariance		500	540	577	618	659	696
Total Adjusted Capital		1,320	1,430	1,530	1,640	1,750	1,850
Ratio		264%	265%	265%	266%	265%	266%

Exhibit 13: Balance Sheet with New Investment in CMBS

		1997	1998	1999	2000	2001	2002
Adjusted Asset Base							
Bonds - Investment Grade		6,000	6,577	7,104	7,681	8,208	8,785
Bonds - Non-Investment Grade		400	423	496	519	592	615
Mortgages		1,000	1,000	1,000	1,000	1,000	1,000
Other		1,200	1,300	1,400	1,500	1,600	1,700
		8,600	9,300	10,000	10,700	11,400	12,100
New Money investment to							
FASIT structure		200	400	600	800	1,000	1,200
NAIC 1	81.5%	163	326	489	652	815	978
NAIC 2	7.0%	14	28	42	56	70	84
NAIC 3	7.0%	14	28	42	56	70	84
NAIC 4	3.5%	7	14	21	28	35	42
Unrated	1.0%	2	4	6	8	10	12
		200	400	600	800	1,000	1,200
Effect on C1							
FASIT Adjustment							
C1 - Base	factor	401	436	472	507	543	579
Remove from Mortgages	2.25%	(5)	(9)	(14)	(18)	(23)	(27)
Add to Bonds NAIC 1	0.30%	0	1	1	2	2	3
Add to Bonds NAIC 2	1.00%	0	0	0	1	1	1
Add to Bonds NAIC 3	4.00%	1	1	2	2	3	3
Add to Bonds NAIC 4	9.00%	1	1	2	3	3	4
Unrated	30.00%	1	1	2	2	3	4
Adjusted C1		398	432	466	499	533	566
Adjusted Covariance		498	536	571	610	649	684
Adjusted Ratio (%)		265	267	268	269	270	270

Exhibit 14: Balance Sheet with New Investment In Investment-Grade CMBS

Adjusted Asset Base		1997	1998	1999	2000	2001	2002
Bonds - Investment Grade		6,000	6,600	7,150	7,750	8,300	8,900
Bonds - Non-Investment Grade		400	400	450	450	500	500
Mortgages		1,000	1,000	1,000	1,000	1,000	1,000
Other		1,200	1,300	1,400	1,500	1,600	1,700
		8,600	9,300	10,000	10,700	11,400	12,100
New Money Investment		200	400	600	800	1,000	1,200
NAIC 1	81.5%	163	326	489	652	815	978
NAIC 2	7.0%	14	28	42	56	70	84
NAIC 3	7.0%	14	28	42	56	70	84
NAIC 4	3.5%	7	14	21	28	35	42
Unrated	1.0%	2	4	6	8	10	12
		200	400	600	800	1,000	1,200
Sell below investment grade							
(NAIC 3, 4, and Unrated)		(23)	(46)	(69)	(92)	(115)	(138)
Reinvest in NAIC 1	80%	18	37	55	74	92	110
Reinvest in NAIC 2	20%	5	9	14	18	23	28
Bond distribution after sale and reinvestment							
NAIC 1		181	363	544	726	907	1,088
NAIC 2		19	37	56	74	93	112
		200	400	600	800	1,000	1,200
Effect on C1							
FASIT Adjustment							
C1 - Base	factor	401	436	472	507	543	579
Remove from Mortgages		(5)	(9)	(14)	(18)	(23)	(27)
	0.0225						
Add to Bonds NAIC 1	0.003	1	1	2	2	3	3
Add to Bonds NAIC 2	0.010	0	0	1	1	1	1
Adjusted C1		397	429	460	492	524	556
Adjusted Covariance		496	533	566	603	641	675
Ratio (%)		266	268	270	272	273	274

Exhibit 15: Summary of RBC Ratings

	1997	1998	1999	2000	2001	2002
Scenario 1	264	265	265	266	265	266
Scenario 2	265	267	268	269	270	270
Scenario 3	266	268	270	272	273	274

Liquidity

A quantitative comparison of the impact of CMBS investment on liquidity was completed using the S&P liquidity model. Exhibit 16 shows the liquid investment levels resulting from the same three investment scenarios detailed within the capitalization analysis. An arbitrary adjusted liability level of $3 billion was used to prepare the analysis. The resulting liquidity ratios are summarized in Exhibit 17.

Exhibit 16: Liquid Investment Levels for Scenarios 1-3

	Whole Loan			CMBS			Senior CMBS		
	Inv. Level	Weighting Factor	Weighted Level	Inv. Level	Weighting Factor	Weighted Level	Inv. Level	Weighting Factor	Weighted Level
Cash and short-term investments	150	100%	150	150	100%	150	150	100%	150
U.S. Government Securities	150	100%	150	150	100%	150	150	100%	150
NAIC 1 144A private placements	6,400	90%	5,760	6,400	90%	5,760	6,492	90%	5,843
NAIC 2 144A private placements		75%	0	75%	0		23	75%	17
Investment grade CMBS		80%	0	885	80%	708	885	80%	708
Noninvestment-grade bonds		0%	0	115	0%	0		0%	0
Unaffiliated public common stock	1,200	85%	1,020	1,200	85%	1,020	1,200	85%	1,020
Mortgage Whole Loans	1,000	0%	0	0	0%	0		0%	0
Totals	8,900		7,080	8,900		7,788	8,900		7,888

Exhibit 17: Summary of Liquidity Ratios

Strategy	Weighted Liquid Assets	Weighted Liability	Liquidity Ratio
Whole loan investment	7,080	3,000	2.36
Securitized debt investment	7,788	3,000	2.60
Investment-grade investment	7,888	3,000	2.63

Using the liquidity ratio as a proxy for actual liquidity would indicate a much higher level of liquidity resultant from CMBS investment than from whole-loan investment. However, the difference may be as much a result of the very conservative assessment of the liquidity of mortgage loans used within the liquidity model, as of any real difference in the liquidity within the portfolio. Senior CMBS is highly liquid at this time, and investment therein must be considered more liquid than comparable levels of mortgage whole loan investments. However, the appetite for whole loans by conduits has created a high level of liquidity for mortgage loans and, consequently, mortgage loans may be more liquid than nonrated securities because of the relative difficulty in securitizing nonrated securities. Therefore, investment in CMBS "across the spectrum," meaning the purchase of all tranches of bonds created through a securitization, may not be materially more liquid than investment in mortgage loans.

Analysis of Impact on Capitalization and Liquidity

In both the existing portfolio analysis and the ongoing investment analysis, investment in senior CMBS resulted in the highest RBC level, with mortgage loan investment resulting in the lowest RBC (although the differences were not material). There is a more significant differentiation in looking at the calculated liquidity ratios, with the 20+ basis point difference likely resulting in a difference of one rating level as it relates to liquidity. These results are not surprising, given that the greatest RBC difference occurred when only investment-grade CMBS were held and, therefore, virtually all of the risk inherent in the investment pool has been sold off.

There is a cost to this stronger capital position, however, and that is the significantly reduced investment yield that will be obtained from the pool. As of early 1998, an investor could reasonably expect a return of 125 basis points over Treasuries for mortgage loans, 110 basis points over Treasuries for investment in a full securitization, and 65 to 75 basis points over Treasuries for investment in investment-grade-only CMBS.

Obviously, this relationship could change at any time.

    This tradeoff has to be evaluated in light of the specific insurer's risk tolerance, return requirements, liquidity needs, and capital charges. Further, in the event that these internal considerations, other financial conditions, or environmental conditions cause RBC and liquidity concerns to become greater or lesser in the future, the relative advantage of CMBS investment would increase or decrease accordingly.

INVESTMENTS AND INVESTMENT PERFORMANCE

The impact of CMBS investment on an insurance company's investment performance will be evaluated in light of the previously identified components of investment performance. In the earlier section on investments and investment performance, the primary components in this area were identified as credit risk, relative yield, diversification, liability matching, interest rate management, duration matching, and immunization.

Credit Risk

The absolute level of credit risk is related to the tranche in which the insurance company chooses to invest. Clearly, investment that is limited solely to triple-A and double-A-rated CMBS will contain less risk than most whole-loan investments. (The exception will be whole loans containing low loan-to-value ratios and those on which the underlying collateral contains a significant number of long-term credit leases.) But investment in lower investment-grade (A or BBB) CMBS is probably comparable in risk to that in high-quality whole loans, and investment in noninvestment-grade CMBS actually has much higher risk than that in whole loans. Therefore there is no one clear credit risk advantage through investment in CMBS versus whole loans.

    One very real advantage of investment in CMBS is that credit risk can be more easily targeted with a CMBS investment strategy than with a whole-loan investment strategy due to the ability to invest in specific tranches, with reasonably well defined risk parameters.

Relative Yield

The comparison of the absolute yield provided by CMBS investment versus whole-loan investment is, like credit risk analysis, very tranche-specific. Relative yield advantages/disadvantages do occur, but must be evaluated by the investor in light of the incremental value (or cost) attributed to RBC treatment, liquidity, and certain other characteristics of the two investments.

    As an example, assume that an investor determined that a particular mortgage loan had the risk rating equivalent to that of a BBB bond, and that the mortgage loan provided a bond equivalent yield of 105 basis points over the appropriate Treasury, while the bond was providing a 90 basis point premium. If the investor requires a high level of liquidity and, consequently, applies a 25 basis point liquidity premium to a mortgage loan, the bond would be the preferred investment. Alternatively, an investor with lesser liquidity needs, or who has consciously allocated a portion of his investment dollars to assets of limited liquidity, might add only a five-basis-point premium and, therefore, would view the mortgage loan as the preferred investment.

A final consideration is that relative yields of securitized investments vis-à-vis mortgage whole loans will vary over time, and these changes will impact the calculus of determining the preferred investment. Issues that may impact the relative yield over time are:

- Subordination levels, which will impact the ultimate cost of debt for a securitization.
- Securitization costs, which also will impact the cost of securitized debt.
- Bond pricing, which impacts the cost of debt.
- Whole-loan spreads.
- Supply and demand.
- Market assessment of real estate fundamentals.

Diversification

Securitized investments, other than in single asset pools, typically provide a high level of diversification relative to property type and geography. To obtain a comparable level of diversification within a whole-loan portfolio, an investor would probably have to invest in a minimum of 50 to 100 loans. As such, for investors with smaller levels of investment (say, $500 million or less), this property type and geographic diversification is probably better attained through securitized investment. This is also true for investors that have limited sourcing capabilities which might cause them to invest disproportionately in a limited number of markets.

Another key component is time diversification, relating to the maturity schedule of the underlying whole loans. While securitized investment provides for geographic and property type diversification, it does not typically provide for adequate time diversification, since many of the underlying loans supporting conduit offerings have similar maturities. If these maturities are coincident with a period of high Treasury rates or weak real estate markets, the extension risk within the pool will be substantial. Arguably, this is the greatest risk embedded in most of the new conduit offerings. To obtain time diversification, an investor in securitized debt should invest in multiple pools and, to the extent possible, seek an investment mix that contains seasoned as well as conduit pools.

A whole-loan investor may theoretically create time diversification by laddering his maturities but, in practice, market competition as well as borrower predisposition to borrow at standard maturities (that is, five, seven, and 10 years), may preclude him from selecting maturities as specifically as would a typical fixed-income investor. Both investment types can develop time diversification via continued investment, which would ultimately provide time diversification across the investment pool.

Liability Matching

In theory, CMBS investment should allow for better liability matching than does whole-loan investing. The ability to invest in specific term securities when purchasing CMBS should allow a much better matching of assets to liabilities through investment in CMBS. In practice, however, the extension risk discussed previously may impair the use of CMBS investment for liability matching, as extensions may make the perceived match somewhat illusory.

Securitization of an Existing Portfolio

The securitization of all or part of an existing portfolio can provide a number of benefits to the insurance company. These benefits include more favorable RBC treatment and liquidity, an opportunity to take advantage of the arbitrage advantages that may be available between the private market and public market, and the reduced costs of managing a CMBS portfolio. (The reduced costs will be discussed briefly in a later section on the capacity to invest in and manage assets.) The benefits related to RBC and liquidity will not be revisited here, as the benefit of securitizing an existing portfolio will be similar to that of simply investing in this asset class at the outset.

As mentioned earlier, there was a 1.5% to 2% arbitrage advantage available as of early 1998 through the conversion of mortgage whole loans to CMBS. This meant that an existing portfolio could have been "sold" for approximately 102 cents on the dollar, net of securitization costs, resulting in an immediate gain equal to 2% of the portfolio invested.

Note, however, that due to statutory accounting requirements, the "gain" would not have been recognized immediately but, rather, would have been amortized over the life of the sold mortgages through the interest maintenance reserve (IMR), "a reserve that absorbs the realized net gains and losses ... from the sale of fixed-income securities by U.S. life and health insurance companies."[2]

Also, to the extent that the company securitized the entire portfolio and immediately repurchased all of the newly issued securities, the "gain" would be somewhat illusory, in that the company would still be holding precisely the same economic interests with the same risk and return attributes, albeit in a different vehicle, as before the securitization. Further, the cost of the securitization would not be offset by any real increase in cash flow as, again, the economic interests are the same. The insurer may have a real benefit in such a transaction however, in the event the company's RBC position was such that the investment options were limited and, thus, by converting the mortgage portfolio into a bond portfolio, the company gained the opportunity to invest in other higher-yielding asset classes. Also, to the extent that the company was at such a low RBC level as to be under the jurisdiction of the regulators, the conversion to a securitized investment might allow the company to have more flexibility in its ongoing operations without having to liquidate certain investments, potentially at a loss.

There may be an additional arbitrage advantage in the event that the company chooses to contribute the below-investment-grade bonds resulting from the securitization into a mortgage REIT. This is because assets within the mortgage REIT may receive additional valuation benefits that are attributable to an operating company.

There are certain shortcomings with this approach, however. First, any gain would also be subject to the IMR treatment. Second, to the extent that the company did in fact sell the assets into a REIT, through an "UPREIT" transaction, the company would lose management control of the contributed assets, and would run the risk of contributing into an overvalued REIT (in which case the REIT shares received in return for the securities would actually be of less value than the contributed securities). Finally, the investment value would be subject to the performance of the REIT as a whole. Another possible execution for the noninvestment-grade securities would be the securitization (re-REMIC) of the investment-grade securities into another securitization.

PORTFOLIO VALUATION/BENCHMARKING

One possible benefit of the securitization process is the potential use of a

---

[2]Elizabeth A. Mulligan and Gene Stone, *Accounting and Financial Reporting in Life and Health Insurance Companies*, Life Office Management Association Inc. (Atlanta: 1997), 684.

securitization model as an aid to portfolio valuation and performance measurement. Most fixed-income investments can be marked to market daily to provide ongoing valuations and, further, can be benchmarked against some appropriate index as a means of evaluating relative performance against a peer group. The inability to perform such daily valuations and benchmarking is a significant shortcoming inherent in commercial mortgage loan investment. This inability creates four adverse impacts:

- Commercial mortgage loans are carried on the books at values that may not be reflective of actual market value.
- Manager performance is virtually impossible to track, other than on an *a posteriori* basis after all loans in the portfolio have been repaid.
- Pricing is difficult because the impact of any single investment on the portfolio as a whole is difficult to ascertain.
- Trends in the marketplace are difficult to track on a real-time basis.

While significant strides have been made in developing methodologies for the benchmarking of commercial mortgage loans, there are three difficulties/problems which make accurate valuation and benchmarking difficult, if not impossible: the necessity for accurate loss projections, an implicit liquidity assumption, and negative convexity.

Loss Projections

The requirement to make specific loss projections on an asset-by-asset basis complicates mortgage loan benchmarking efforts. Unlike MBS performance, which can generally be projected with reasonable accuracy via econometric and actuarial methods, the performance of a commercial portfolio, which is driven by the performance of each underlying asset, must be evaluated from the bottom up. Without specifically reviewing the collateral supporting every mortgage loan in a portfolio it is impossible to value the portfolio accurately. Aggravating this is the difficulty in accurately projecting individual loan performance, even given a rigorous process of surveillance and asset management.

Implicit Liquidity

Implicit in any benchmarking process is the assumption that the underlying assets are marketable at the determined "market value." A theoretical value predicated upon a bond pricing methodology requires that the underlying asset is as marketable as a bond. Historically this has not been true with commercial mortgage loans, although the appetite for mortgages by the CMBS issuers through early 1998 greatly improves the marketability. This marketability problem renders any mortgage valuation, other than on a hold-to-maturity basis, somewhat suspect.

Negative Convexity

The negative convexity experienced by mortgage loans also makes benchmarking difficult. The cap on the value of the mortgage note makes it trade in a way that differs from other fixed-income products.

Virtual Securitization

A "virtual" securitization that would simply involve the running of a commercial loan asset pool through a securitization model could help alleviate these benchmarking concerns. The basic idea would be to simply evaluate the mortgage loan pool as if it were to be immediately securitized, and determine the value of the pool, as securitized, by determining the aggregate value of the securitized execution, net of the costs that would be involved in such an execution. This would allow a portfolio manager, on a real-time basis, to both value the portfolio and compare the performance of the portfolio against an appropriate index. The use of a CMBS model somewhat mitigates the three benchmarking difficulties, as follows.

Loss Projections Since the potential losses on CMBS are borne primarily by the first-loss tranches, which are bought at a discount with certain loss assumptions built in, precise loss projections are not as critical to the valuation of a CMBS portfolio.

Liquidity Since the bulk of the securities within a CMBS issuance are highly liquid, it can be assumed that the value of the CMBS is rapidly attainable within the market. Therefore, the ascribed value can be assumed to be truly a market value, although the liquidity of CMBS in a weak market has not yet been tested.

Negative Convexity Senior CMBS should trade similarly to other fixed-income investments and are not subject to the same level of negative convexity concerns as are commercial mortgages. The first-loss tranches are purchased at substantial discounts, and have significantly higher coupon rates, resulting in a corresponding shorter duration. They are therefore less sensitive to interest rate movements.

Results
Because of these considerations, a generally accepted virtual securitization process could greatly enhance the ability to accurately value and benchmark commercial mortgage loan portfolios.

CAPACITY TO INVEST IN AND MANAGE ASSETS
There are certain noninvestment considerations, based upon characteristics of CMBS versus whole-loan investment, that should be evaluated in making an investment decision between CMBS and whole loans. A comparison of these characteristics is shown in Exhibit 18.

Exhibit 18: Noninvestment Considerations

Characteristic	Whole Mortgage Loans	CMBS
Implementation Cost	High	Low
Recurring Overhead	High	Low
Investment/Sourcing Control	Moderate	Moderate
Flexibility	Low	High
Expertise Requirements	High	Low to Moderate
Technological Requirements	High	Low

Investment in CMBS is favored by an analysis of these noninvestment considerations. The primary operational benefit in investing in CMBS is that there are both fewer barriers to entry and lower ongoing costs. This is due to the fact that the infrastructure, both in manpower and hardware/software, required to invest in and manage CMBS is much less than that required to invest in and manage whole loans. The cost and expertise required for both sourcing and originating whole loans will make these investments less desirable than CMBS for those companies that do not have the existing staff and systems capacity, and are unwilling to make the substantial investment in staffing and systems necessary to source and manage these investments. For an institution that has the existing infrastructure, has the capacity to make sufficient investment to justify the overhead costs, and has a long-term commitment to mortgage loan investment, this advantage of CMBS investment is mitigated.

INSURER AS SECURITIZED DEBT ORIGINATOR

Another opportunity for the insurance company within the CMBS market is the use of the company's existing origination network to create product for contribution into CMBS issuances. Depending on the nature of the role that the insurer is taking, these contributions could result in the sharing of issuance profit, and/or the retention of servicing fees. There are three general roles, along a continuum, that the insurer could play within such a process. These roles are as an occasional contributor to CMBS issuance's, on a one-off basis, as a seller/servicer that would contribute a high volume of loans to a CMBS issuer, and as an aggregator/issuer.

Occasional Contributor to CMBS Issuances

This would involve, on an ad hoc basis, the contribution of mortgage loans to a CMBS issue. These would likely be loans that did not fit the insurer's specific lending parameters or those which would result in an overconcentration of loans in one market. This type of contribution could be run through either an ongoing relationship or by simply selling to the highest bidder at the time the loan becomes available. This approach would likely result in the insurer receiving no additional benefits in the form of servicing retention or profit-sharing.

Insurer as Seller/Servicer of Loans on an Ongoing Basis

This would involve some type of contractual relationship in which the insurer would align itself with an issuer and would agree to provide a certain fixed amount of loans to the issuer. The insurer in this scenario would retain servicing on the portfolio and would share in the profitability of the issuance, after attainment of a certain threshold of profit for the issuer. In this scenario, the insurer would have an option of closing the loans in its own name or, alternatively, of having the ultimate issuer close the loans in its name. A shortcoming of this type of program is that many insurers source all or most of their loans through correspondents, who are thus the primary borrower contacts during origination. To the extent that the insurer is simply acting as intermediary between the correspondent and the issuer, there is a question regarding the level of value added that is being provided by the insurer. Obviously, an insurer that largely sources loans on a direct basis does not have this concern.

Insurer as Aggregator/Issuer

The final step along the continuum would be for the insurer to originate and aggregate the loans and be a direct issuer of the CMBS. Given the economies of scale discussed earlier in this chapter, it is likely that the issuance would be in partnership with one or more other issuers. The insurer would be a welcome partner to many investment banks in this type of issuance because the partnering bank would not have to share in the bond sales profit with the insurer. The risk in this type of transaction to the insurer is that if interest spreads widen during the aggregation period, the profit on the pool will be eliminated and the issuance could go off at a loss. Since the insurer does not receive either the economic or marketing benefits of the bond sales, there is no benefit in the transaction if the insurer does not profit on the conversion. This risk can be somewhat mitigated if the insurer only generates loans for the CMBS program that it would be willing to hold in portfolio, at the appropriate spread. If the insurer does have the willingness and the capital capacity to hold the loans, then the primary aggregation risk is that the insurer's portfolio might be somewhat overweighted in mortgage loans. This problem would be somewhat exacerbated by the fact that the overweighting has occurred at a time when the market has implicitly downgraded the value of mortgage loans, as indicated by the spread widening.

One benefit to the insurer from involvement in any CMBS contribution program is that it allows the insurer's origination staff to stay in the market. This should allow the insurer to have a ready flow of mortgage loan investment opportunities at those times in which they are most favorable, and will also allow the insurer to support the overhead inherent in mortgage loan origination and servicing. Furthermore, the insurer will continually be able to stay abreast of the capital market treatment of mortgage loans, which may provide the company with insights as to when investment in CMBS or mortgage loans are more favorable or, alternatively, when a capital markets execution for portfolio balancing might be favorable.

One concern that might impact the decision to choose either option two or three, as detailed earlier, is the different mindset required for conduit origination. Many insurance company originators are underwriters first, with marketing taking a secondary role. This will not work in the conduit arena in which competition creates the need for aggressive marketing simply to see the potential loan opportunities. The conduit arena further requires loan decisions to be made in a fairly short time frame, frequently with less than optimal information. One solution is to have a segregation of duties between the conduit originators and the general-account originators. This may not be viable for those insurers with relatively small staffs, and/or an inability or unwillingness to commit to such a program long-term.

FASIT STRUCTURE

A financial asset securitization trust (FASIT) is a REMIC-like pass-through vehicle that may make it easier for an insurance company to take advantage of securitization benefits. The key characteristic that will allow the insurance company to use this vehicle is that the FASIT allows ongoing contributions to the pool, with individual bond issuances available, representing each individual mortgage loan. This may give the insurance company investor the opportunity to transform a mortgage loan immediately into a securitized instrument. This would grant the insurer the benefits appurtenant to a securitized investment at the outset while avoiding the aggregation concerns.

An ideal arrangement may be for the insurance company to align itself with a B-piece investor, who would immediately purchase the below-investment-grade investments for inclusion in an existing investment portfolio, for a potential re-REMIC or for inclusion in a proprietary mortgage REIT. The benefit of this structure is that the B-piece investor would have a steady flow of investment product, with an ability to be involved in the underwriting of the underlying mortgage loans. Also, the securitization could be completed at a lower cost due to elimination of the higher cost resulting from the sale of below-investment-grade securities.

A concern with the FASIT structure is that the continual ability to place new assets into the FASIT, along with the ability to pull assets out, will likely result in FASIT structures being rated more conservatively than comparable REMIC structures, due to the inherent unknowns within the portfolio. This shortcoming is probably a permanent structural problem with the FASIT structure, one that may result in the FASIT being primarily utilized for private transactions, in which the tranching may be less critical.

Howard Esaki is a principal in the fixed-income research department at Morgan Stanley Dean Witter, where he is responsible for CMBS research.

Previously, Esaki worked at the Federal Reserve Bank of New York, Lehman Brothers, and Moody's Investors Service.

He holds an undergraduate degree from Princeton University and a Ph.D. in economics from Yale University.

Institutional Investor selected Esaki as a member of its All-America Fixed-Income Research Team in 1996 and 1997.

Joseph Philips is a vice president in the fixed-income research department at Morgan Stanley Dean Witter, where he is responsible for mortgage and cross-sector strategy.

Before joining MSDW, Philips worked at Salomon Brothers for eight years.

He holds a master of science degree in engineering from the State University of New York at Stony Brook and a master's degree in business administration from the University of Illinois at Urbana-Champaign.

Chapter 8

Investing in Multifamily MBS

Howard Esaki
Principal
Morgan Stanley Dean Witter

Joseph Philips
Vice President
Morgan Stanley Dean Witter

Investor focus on commercial and multifamily mortgage-backed securities has been increasing as the market has grown to a total capitalization of over $100 billion. Including issuance by Fannie Mae, Freddie Mac, and Ginnie Mae, about 30% of the CMBS market consists of securities backed by multifamily mortgages. We estimate that the market capitalization of multifamily MBS exceeded $30 billion at the end of 1996. Of this total, more than two-thirds was issued by government sponsored enterprises (GSEs) or Ginnie Mae (including the FHA and the RTC), with the remainder private label.

Annual issuance of multifamily MBS, as shown in Exhibit 1, has ranged from $8 billion to $16 billion over the past four years, with about two-thirds issued by Fannie Mae or Ginnie Mae/FHA. In addition, in 1996, about $3 billion in "private label" MBS backed exclusively by multifamily loans was issued and another $3.6 billion of multifamily loans was in mixed-pool CMBS. Focusing specifically on multifamily agency MBS issuance, as shown in Exhibit 2, this sector is dominated by Fannie Mae. In fact, Fannie Mae, as shown in Exhibit 3, also issued the five largest multifamily REMICs in 1996.

Exhibit 4 shows the size of the total mortgage market at year-end 1996. Since only about 15% of the $300 billion in outstanding multifamily mortgage debt has been securitized, we believe that the size of the multifamily MBS market could grow significantly. We think that securitization of multifamily loans could reach 50% in the next 10 years, which implies net new additions of $10 billion annually in multifamily securitizations over the next decade.

The major issuers in the multifamily MBS market are Fannie

*Exhibit 1: Multifamily MBS Issuance**

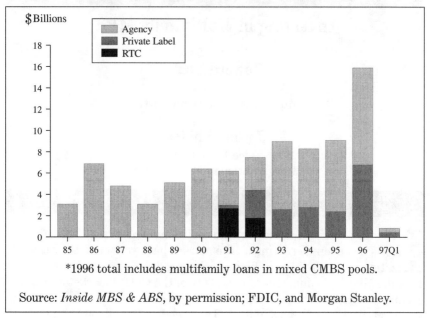

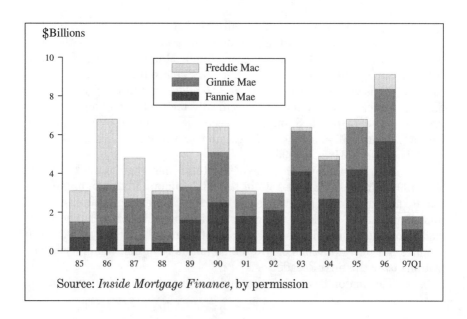

Exhibit 3: Domestic Multifamily MBS REMICs in 1996

Amount ($MM)	Issuer	Seller/Borrower	Pricing Date
319.9	Fannie Mae Multi-Family Remic Trust, 1996-M6*	Donaldson, Lufkin & Jenrette	09/26
303.0	Fannie Mae Multi-Family Remic Trust, 1996-M3 (Pt 1)	National Cooperative Bank	04/19
278.9	Fannie Mae Multi-Family Remic Trust, 1996-M7*	Donaldson, Lufkin & Jenrette	11/12
206.4	Fannie Mae Multi-Family Remic Trust, 1996-M1 (Pt 1)	Bankers Trust	03/03
194.9	Fannie Mae Multi-Family Remic Trust, 1996-M5 (Pt 1)	NationsBanc, J.P. Morgan	08/23
178.8	Condor One/HUD Bond Trust, 1996-1	HUD, Whitehall Street	06/27
169.3	Fannie Mae Multi-Family Remic Trust, 1996-M4	Donaldson, Lufkin & Jenrette	07/15
157.0	Fannie Mae Multi-Family Remic Trust, 1996-M2 (Pt 1)	Citibank FSB	03/06
152.7	Morgan Stanley Capital I Inc., 1996-BKU1	Bank United FSB	01/24
129.6	NYC Mortgage Loan Trust, 1996	New York City	06/12
127.8	Paine Webber Mortgage Acceptance Corp., 1996-M1	NHP Inc., Cardinal Realty	12/17
86.2	Fannie Mae Grantor Trust, 1996-T3	Donaldson, Lufkin & Jenrette	05/09
25.0	The Money Store Trust, 1996-C/A-15	The Money Store	09/19
21.1	Fannie Mae Multi-Family Remic Trust, 1996-M5 (Pt 2)	NationsBanc, J.P. Morgan	09/26
20.0	The Money Store Trust, 1996-B, Class A-16	The Money Store	06/21
17.9	Fannie Mae Multi-Family Remic Trust, 1996-M1 (Pt 2)	Bankers Trust	05/10
16.5	Fannie Mae Multi-Family Remic Trust, 1996-M2 (Pt 2)	Citibank FSB	03/06
10.0	The Money Store Trust, 1996-D/A-16	The Money Store	12/26
9.8	Fannie Mae Multi-Family Remic Trust, 1996-M3 (Pt 2)	National Cooperative Bank	04/02
Total 3005.0			

*Backed by Ginnie Mae project loans
Source: *Commercial Mortgage Alert*, Hoboken, N.J., 1997, by permission.

Exhibit 4: Size of the Mortgage Market ($ Billions); 1996 Q4

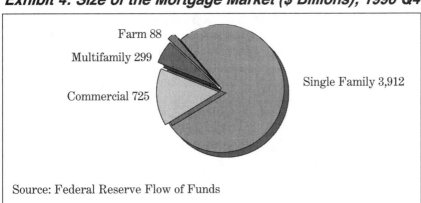

Farm 88
Multifamily 299
Commercial 725
Single Family 3,912

Source: Federal Reserve Flow of Funds

Mae, Ginnie Mae/FHA, private-label issuers, and Freddie Mac. The RTC is no longer in existence, but nearly $2 billion in RTC multifamily securities remained outstanding at the end of 1996. In the following sections we discuss the major programs of each issuer. The final sections review recent spreads for multifamily MBS and present our opinions of the relative value of the sector.

FANNIE MAE MULTIFAMILY PROGRAMS

The single largest issuer of multifamily MBS is Fannie Mae, accounting for about two-thirds of agency multifamily securitization in 1996. Fannie Mae issued a record $5.7 billion of multifamily MBS in 1996, an increase from $4.4 billion in 1995. In the first quarter of 1997, Fannie Mae issued $1.1 billion in multifamily MBS, up about 5% from the first quarter of 1996. Over 90% of Fannie Mae issuance was backed by fixed-rate mortgages in 1996, up from less than two-thirds in 1995.

The four main Fannie Mae programs are:
- Delegated Underwriting and Servicing (DUS).
- Alternative Credit Enhancement Structures (ACES) and Wisconsin Avenue Securities (WAS).
- MBS Swaps.
- The Fannie Mae Aggregation Facility.

Fannie Mae has stated that it has a $50 billion commitment to provide financing to the multifamily sector between 1994 and the year 2000.

The Fannie Mae DUS Program

Fannie Mae created the Delegated Underwriting and Servicing (DUS) program in 1988 to streamline the underwriting process and help fulfill its commitment to multifamily housing. Under the program, the specially approved lenders listed in Exhibit 5 may underwrite, close, service, and sell mortgages to Fannie Mae without prior review by Fannie Mae. DUS lenders benefit from this special relationship because they have greater autonomy in underwriting and servicing and can also be more competitive given that DUS loan rates are lower than in the prior approval program. Before this program, the process was lengthier due to the agency's need to underwrite and approve the transaction in advance of purchase.

Currently, there are 26 approved DUS lenders that have originated and sold to Fannie Mae almost $6 billion of loans through the end of 1996. Until 1994, Fannie Mae held in its own portfolio most DUS originated loans. Beginning in mid-1994, Fannie Mae began routinely to securitize DUS loans for sale in the secondary mortgage market as MBS. MBS DUS have the same guarantee of full and timely payment of principal and interest as Fannie Mae's single-family securities. Current MBS DUS production averages $200 million to $400 million each month, as shown in Exhibit 6.

Loans originated under the DUS program are generally either fixed-rate balloon mortgages with five-, seven-, 10-, or 15-year terms or

Exhibit 5: Fannie Mae DUS Lender Network

American Property Financing, Inc.	New York NY
AMI Capital, Inc.	Bethesda MD
AMRESCO Capital Corporation	Dallas TX
Arbor National Commercial Mortgage	Uniondale NY
ARCS Commercial Mortgage	Hoboken NJ
Banc One Capital Funding	Reston VA
Bankers Mutual	Newport Beach CA
Berkshire Mortgage Finance	Boston MA
Collateral Mortgage	Birmingham AL
Continental, Inc.	Seattle WA
CPC Mortgage Capital	Irvine CA
Continental Wingate Associates	Boston MA
Eichler, Fayne, and Associates	Seattle WA
First Maryland Mortgage	Baltimore MD
GMAC Commercial Mortgage Corporation	Horsham PA
Green Park Financial	Bethesda MD
Greystone Servicing Corporation	New York NY
Investment Property Mortgage	New Orleans LA
KeyCorp Real Estate Capital Markets	Cleveland OH
Mellon Mortgage	Cleveland OH
Newport Mortgage Company, L.P.	Dallas TX
The Patrician Financial Companies	Bethesda MD
PW Funding	Mineola NY
Reilly Mortgage Capital	McLean VA
Washington Capital DUS	Walnut Creek CA
Washington Mortgage Financial	Vienna VA

Source: Fannie Mae

fixed-rate fully amortizing loans with 25- or 30-year terms. Variations, such as 20-year fully-amortizing loans, are also permissible. The loans are secured by mortgages on income-producing, multifamily rental or cooperative buildings with at least five units and with occupancy rates of at least 90%. The buildings may be existing or recently completed and may require moderate rehabilitation.

Loan amounts are $1 million to $50 million. There is always a loss-sharing agreement between Fannie Mae and DUS lenders in case of default. Loans must have been originated within six months of Fannie Mae's purchase.

Prepayment Protection One of the main advantages of multifamily securities over residential MBS is the prepayment protection on multifamily

Exhibit 6: Fannie Mae MBS DUS Issuance

Month	Year	Amount ($ millions)
June	1996	309.2
July	1996	230.1
August	1996	361.5
September	1996	284.8
October	1996	279.8
November	1996	322.4
December	1996	726.1
January	1997	481.4
February	1997	311.3

Source: Fannie Mae

loans. Most DUS loans have yield-maintenance premiums in the event of an early prepayment. The premium is usually yield-maintenance calculated at the relevant Treasury rate, or "Treasuries flat." Common yield maintenance terms are:

Balloon Term (Years)	Yield Maintenance Term (Years)
5	3 or 4.5
7	5 or 6.5
10	7 or 9.5
15	10
30	10

After the yield-maintenance period ends, the borrower is still required to pay a 1% premium on prepayment which is retained by Fannie Mae. This premium is waived during the last 90 days of the loan term to facilitate refinancing. Curtailments are not allowed and, consequently, the borrower is faced with the choice of either prepaying the entire loan balance or not at all.

Prepayment fees are passed through to the investor by Fannie Mae only to the extent they are received from the borrower. Fannie Mae's obligation extends only to the outstanding principal balance of the security; that is, if an MBS DUS defaults as a premium security, the investor receives a minimum of par but may lose some or all of the premium.

Most DUS loans can be assumed by a new, and creditworthy, borrower on payment of a 1% assumption fee that is not passed through to the investor. Given that the pricing speed assumption of DUS is usually 0% CPR, the assumability option does not add any negative convexity to the security.

The yield maintenance premium is calculated as the greater of (a) 1% of the unpaid principal balance (UPB), and (b) the UPB times the present value of the stream of cash flows represented by the difference between the DUS coupon and a prespecified Treasury. The Treasury selected generally matures at the end of the yield-maintenance period and its yield is used as the discount rate. For example, the prepayment fee for a DUS pool with seven-year yield maintenance and the characteristics discussed in this chapter is calculated as seen in Exhibit 7.

The prepayment fee actually due from the borrower is calculated by substituting the note rate for the coupon in the calculation shown in Exhibit 7.

The difference between the fee received and the fee paid to the investor is shared by FNMA and the lender.

Exhibit 7: Sample Yield Maintenance Calculation

Loan Term	10 years
Closing Date of Note	September 30, 1990
Yield Maintenance Period	7 years
Prepayment Date	September 30, 1994
UPB as of Prepayment Date	$6,161,329
Time to End of Yield Maintenance	1,187 days = 3.2521 years
Net Coupon	7.675%
Treasury Yield on Prepayment Date	4.18%

The prepayment fee received by the investor is the greater of:
(a) 1% of UPB = 0.01 × $6,161,329 = $61,613.29; and
where N = the time to balloon as of the prepayment date.

(b) $\text{UPB} \times (\text{coupon} - \text{Treasury yield}) \times \dfrac{(1 - (1 + \text{Treasury yield})^{-N})}{\text{Treasury yield}}$

where N = the time to balloon as of the prepayment date.

$= \$6{,}161{,}329 \times \dfrac{(0.07675 - 0.0418 \times ((1 - (1 + 0.0418)}{0.0418} - 3.2521 = \$642{,}340.91$

Since (b) is greater than (a), the prepayment fee = $642,340.91.

Source: Fannie Mae

Underwriting DUS lenders have strong incentives to underwrite high-quality loans. First and foremost, Fannie Mae monitors the performance of its DUS lenders. In addition, when a DUS loan defaults, losses up to the first 5% of the UPB are borne solely by the lender and losses in excess of 5% are shared by Fannie Mae and the lender according to a formula. The lender's share of the loss is limited to 20% — 40% of the UPB. Not a single default has occurred in the MBS DUS program since its inception in August 1994. In addition, as of the third quarter of 1996, there were no delinquencies in the MBS DUS program.

For pricing and underwriting purposes, Fannie Mae categorizes DUS loans into one of four credit "tiers" based on debt-service coverage and loan-to-value ratios. Tier 4 loans, as shown in Exhibit 8, have the highest credit quality, while Tier 1 loans have the lowest. Most DUS loans tend to fall into the middle two tiers. Tier 1 loans are extremely rare. Fannie Mae may also designate loans with a "+" in each category, based on subjective criteria such as property location and management. A "+" reduces the guarantee fee by about 10 basis points.

Exhibit 8: DUS Underwriting Tiers

	Minimum Debt Service Coverage Ratio	*Maximum Loan-to-Value Ratio*
Tier 1	1.15	80%
Tier 2	1.25	80%
Tier 3	1.35	65%
Tier 4	1.55	55%

Source: Fannie Mae

The MEGA Program In August 1996, Fannie Mae introduced a MEGA program that allows for the combination of multiple DUS pools. MEGA pooling creates a security backed by multiple borrowers from many geographic areas. Instead of accumulating many pools backed by individual loans to mitigate default and prepayment risk, an investor can now buy a single MEGA pool and achieve the same effect. Liquidity of this sector should also be enhanced by the program.

To be eligible for a MEGA pool, loans must have coupons within a 100 bp range and must have a similar balloon or amortization term. In actual practice, Fannie Mae allows pools with the same "subtype" and coupons within a 100 basis point range to be combined into a MEGA. MEGAs of MEGAs are allowed. The fee schedule for the program is shown in Exhibit 9.

Exhibit 9: MEGA Fee Schedule

Mega Current Face ($ millions)	Fee
>100	2+/32
75 - 99.99	3/32
50 - 74.99	3+/32
25 - 49.99	4/32
10 - 24.99	5/32
5 - 9.99	5+/32
3 - 4.99	6+/32
0 - 2.99	$7,000

Source: Fannie Mae

The ACES and Wisconsin Avenue Securities Programs

The ACES (Alternative Credit Enhancement Structure) program allows non-DUS lenders to swap multifamily loans for Fannie Mae securities. The collateral in ACES deals may be from seasoned portfolios or from new conduit originations and may have various loan terms and prepayment protection. Through the end of 1996, Fannie Mae had issued about $5 billion in ACES transactions. There are two basic ACES structures:

- The REMIC structure, which includes:
  The Wisconsin Avenue Securities (WAS) REMIC
  The MBS REMIC
- The A/B grantor trust.

The WAS REMIC structure allows the lender to swap multifamily loans for senior and subordinated REMIC certificates. The senior security is guaranteed by Fannie Mae. The subordinate security is not guaranteed by Fannie Mae and is appropriately sized to provide the necessary credit enhancement to the senior. The subordinate is offered via a private placement memorandum.

In contrast, in the MBS REMIC structure, the lender first swaps multifamily loans for Fannie Mae MBS which are then placed in a REMIC. A portion of the MBS certificates is set aside in a custodial account to provide first loss protection to the senior securities. The WAS REMIC is more efficient than the MBS REMIC given that the loans do not need to be first securitized before being put into the REMIC.

The A/B structure is similar to the MBS REMIC to the extent that the lender swaps loans for MBS. However, a portion of the MBS, essentially the B piece, is set aside in a custodial account to cover losses. Unlike the A piece, which is sold in its entirety to investors, only the interest cash flows of the B piece are sold, with its principal flows being retained by Fannie Mae for a designated period of time. Given its efficiency, the WAS REMIC program is currently the most popular ACES structure.

MBS Swaps

Under this program, the lender swaps multifamily mortgages for Fannie Mae MBS with full, partial, or no recourse to the lender. Recourse obligations must be collateralized with Fannie Mae-approved collateral or backed by a corporate guarantee. The corporate guarantee (uncollateralized) option is available only to institutions rated single-A or better. If the rating falls below single-A, the corporate guarantee must be collateralized by short-term triple-A quality collateral. Non-recourse MBS swaps are also permissible and typically involve high quality, cross-collateralized, cross-defaulted multifamily mortgages to a single-purpose entity.

The Aggregation Facility

In December 1996, Fannie Mae announced a new multifamily conduit-like lending program, the Fannie Mae Aggregation Facility, which "permits lenders to sell individual loans to Fannie Mae for cash on an 'as originated' basis." Initially, Fannie Mae will open the program only to approved DUS lenders, but plans to expand the program in the future to other lenders. Unlike the DUS program described in a previous section, lenders do not share in any losses from loan defaults. Exhibit 10 compares Fannie Mae multifamily programs, and Exhibit 11 provides details of Fannie Mae delinquency rates.

According to Fannie Mae, "lenders participating in the Aggregation Facility will originate loans under standardized underwriting and origination requirements utilizing Fannie Mae Loan documents."

Exhibit 10: A Comparison of Fannie Mae Multifamily Programs

	DUS	ACES	Aggregation
Lenders	DUS only	All	DUS only*
Prior Approval Required	No	Yes	Yes
Lender shares in loss	Yes	No	No
Prepayment Protection	Yes	Yes	Yes
Loan Age Restrictions	Max. 6 months	None	None
FNMA Guarantee	Yes	Senior only	Senior only
MEGA Program	Yes	No	No

*Program may be expanded later to include non-DUS lenders.

Exhibit 11: Multifamily Delinquency Rates

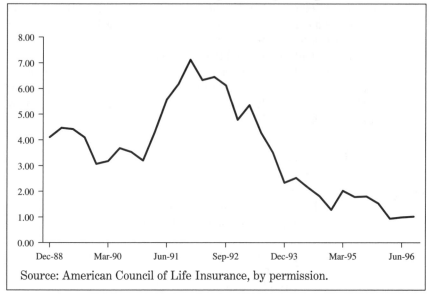

Source: American Council of Life Insurance, by permission.

After accumulating loans under the new aggregation facility, Fannie Mae will issue a WAS REMIC. The liquidity of WAS REMICs should be enhanced by increased issuance under the Aggregation Facility.

CREDIT PERFORMANCE OF MULTIFAMILY LOANS

Although Fannie Mae does not publish delinquency statistics on loans in individual securitization programs, the overall delinquency rate on Fannie Mae multifamily loans is low. As of December 31, 1996, the number of "seriously delinquent" loans in Fannie Mae's portfolio and MBS outstanding[1] was 0.68% of the current balance of the loans. Fannie Mae defines "seriously delinquent" as being 60 or more days delinquent or in foreclosure.

The percentage of "seriously delinquent" loans has declined from a peak of over 3% in the last quarter of 1991. We attribute the decline to three factors: improvements in underwriting, the recovery of the commercial real estate markets, and an increase in the number of loans serviced. At the end of 1996, Fannie Mae had 5,472 loans with an unpaid balance of $18.7 billion, up from 2,637 loans with an unpaid balance of $9 billion at the end of 1991. Many of the properties backing Fannie Mae loans

---

[1]This includes just loans that fall into the "shared risk" and "at risk" categories (excluding ACES).

thus operate at recently underwritten cash flows.

By way of comparison, the delinquency rate on apartment loans reported by the American Council of Life Insurance was 0.48% at the end of 1996, the lowest of any property type measured by the ACLI. The delinquency rate on all commercial loans tracked by the ACLI was 1.79% at the end of 1996. At the end of 1996, Fannie Mae had just 27 properties in REO, with an unpaid balance of $49 million, or 0.26% of outstanding balances. The number of REO properties has declined from 60 at the end of first-quarter 1995.

GINNIE MAE/FHA

Within the agency multifamily market, the second largest issuer in the agency market is the Government National Mortgage Association (GNMA). Project loans may be made under a number of Housing and Urban Development Department programs, including:

221(d)4:	Construction or permanent financing
223(f):	Refinancing
223(a)7:	Accelerated refinancing
232:	Nursing home/assisted living
241(f):	Equity take-out second mortgage.

All Ginnie Mae securities are backed by loans originated by the Federal Housing Administration (FHA) and are either permanent loan certificates (PLCs) or construction loan certificates (CLCs).

PLCs are usually 35-year fully amortizing fixed-rate mortgages. Prepayment protection is either (1) a five-year lockout followed by declining penalty points (5, 4, 3, 2, 1) over the next five years or (2) a 10-year lockout. Many PLCs begin as CLCs and are converted to PLCs upon completion of the construction project. CLCs trade at wider spreads than PLCs because of liquidity and uncertainty associated with funding a construction loan. Exhibit 12 shows some of the major differences between Ginnie Mae and FHA project loans, followed by a profile in Exhibit 13.

Ginnie Mae issued $2.7 billion of multifamily MBS in 1996, up from $2.2 billion in 1995. In the first quarter of 1997, issuance was $670 million. Monthly issuance usually falls in the range of $150 million to $350 million. As of March 1, 1997, only 0.87% of GNMA multifamily loans were delinquent for 60 days or more. Effective April 1, 1997, Ginnie Mae reduced pool processing time to five days from 10 days and added other features to streamline its multifamily MBS program.[2]

---

[2]See *Inside MBS & ABS* (May 1, 1997): 3.

Exhibit 12: Characteristics of Ginnie Mae and FHA Project Loans

	Ginnie Mae	FHA
Government guarantee	explicit	implicit
Principal payment in case of default	100%	99%
Delay days	44	54
Delivery	PTC	physical
Data on Bloomberg	yes	no

Exhibit 13: A Profile of Ginnie Mae Multifamily MBS

Issuer:	Ginnie Mae approved mortgage lender
Issue Type:	GNMA I
Underlying Mortgages:	FHA Insured multifamily mortgages
Pool Types:	Construction Loan Securities
	(CL) Security rate remains constant with conversion to permanent loan
	(CS) Security rate changes with conversion to permanent loan
	Project Loan Securities
	(PL) Level payment permanent securities
	(PN) Non-level payment permanent securities
	(LM) Securities for Mature Loans. Loans pooled after more than 24 months of amortization
	(LS) Securities for Small Loans. Loans of no more than $1M
Securities Interest Rate:	Fixed; at .25% to .50% below the interest rate of the underlying mortgage(s)
Guaranty:	Full and timely payment of principal and interest
Guarantor:	Ginnie Mae (full faith and credit of the United States)
Principal and Interest:	Paid monthly to securities holders
Maturity:	Varies, typically 40 years
Minimum Certificate Size:	$25,000 (may be less for aged securities)
Transfer Agent:	Chase (formerly Chemical Bank)

Source: Reprinted from Ginnie Mae website, www.ginniemae.gov, 1997.

FREDDIE MAC

Freddie Mac, a large issuer in the 1980s, has reduced its role in the multifamily securitization market in the 1990s. The agency has recently begun to increase its multifamily loan production. Freddie Mac issued $770 million of multifamily MBS in 1996, up from $355 million in 1995.

Almost all of the issuance was in November and December. In 1986, Freddie Mac issued over $3 billion of multifamily MBS, but has issued less than $1 billion per year since 1990. In the first quarter of 1997, Freddie Mac did not issue any multifamily MBS.

In 1996, Freddie Mac purchased about $1.5 billion of multifamily loans for its portfolio. As of November 1996, the delinquency rate on Freddie Mac's multifamily portfolio was 2.30%, down from 3.36% a year earlier.

Program Plus

Freddie Mac's Program Plus is similar to Fannie Mae's DUS program. Under the program, Freddie Mac pre-approves multifamily lenders with "local market expertise." Since 1993, Freddie Mac has financed $5.3 billion (1,400 properties) under Program Plus.

To be eligible for Program Plus, loans must be between $5 million and $50 million and have the following characteristics:
- Terms of 7, 10, 15, 20, or 25 years.
- Amortization period of 20, 25, or 30 years.
- Maximum LTV of 75%.
- Minimum DSCR of 1.3.

The yield-maintenance terms of the loans are:

Term (Years)	Yield Maintenance (Years)
7	6.5
10	9.5
15	14.0
20	15.0

A list of the Freddie Mac-approved Program Plus seller/servicers is shown in Exhibit 14.

RESOLUTION TRUST CORPORATION

In 1991 and 1992, the RTC issued 11 multifamily MBS with a total balance of $4.5 billion. The transactions, known as M-Series, were backed by pools of multifamily loans from thrift institutions taken over by the RTC. As of February 1997, the remaining balance of M-Series transactions was $1.8 billion.

Although many M-Series deals have high rates of delinquency, most remain well protected from credit losses by high cash reserves. The one notable exception is 1991-M2, which has exhausted its cash reserves through losses on liquidated loans. Moody's and Standard & Poor's have downgraded the transaction several times.

Exhibit 14: Approved Freddie Mac Program Plus Seller/Servicers

Seller/Servicer	Location
AMRESCO Capital	Miami FL
Apple Bank	New York NY
Bank United	Dallas TX
Collateral Mortgage	Birmingham AL
ARCS Commercial Mortgage	Calabasas CA
Bankers Mutual	Newport Beach CA
Berkshire Mortgage	Boston MA
Columbia National	Columbia MD
Community Preservation Corp.	New York NY
Continental Savings	Seattle WA
Dorman and Wilson	White Plains NY
East New York Savings	New York NY
Financial Federal	Memphis TN
First National Bank of Omaha	Omaha NE
First Security Bank	Salt Lake City UT
Glaser Financial	Saint Paul MN
GMAC	Horsham PA
Great Lakes Financial	Beechwood OH
Hartger and Willard	Grand Rapids MI
Inland Mortgage	Indianapolis IN
John Hancock	Boston MA
L.J. Melody	Houston TX
Larson Financial	Somerset NJ
Laureate Realty	Charlotte NC
Legg Mason	Jacksonville FL
Liberty Federal	Eugene OR
Mason McDuffie	Oakland CA
Mellon Mortgage	Overland Park KS
Mitchell Mortgage	The Woodlands, TX
National Bank of Alaska	Anchorage AK
National Cooperative Bank	New York NY
Newport Mortgage	Dallas TX
Northland Financial	Bloomington MN
P/R Mortgage	Indianapolis IN
Primary Capital	Atlanta GA
PNS Realty	Pittsburgh PA
Reilly Mortgage	McLean VA
Republic National Bank	New York NY
Richter-Schroeder	Milwaukee WI
TRI Capital	San Francisco CA
Towle Real Estate	Minneapolis MN
W. Lyman Case Holding	Columbus OH
Washington Mortgage	Vienna VA
Western Mortgage	Salt Lake City UT

Source: Freddie Mac

As of March 25, 1997 remittance reports, the delinquency rate on RTC M-Series transactions, was 11.98%. This delinquency rate has declined from over 16% in March 1996. As of the latest reports, the delinquency rate on M-Series transactions is still above the delinquency rate on C-Series transactions (11.07%), but the difference has narrowed over the past year, as indicated in Exhibit 15.

Exhibit 15: RTC Multifamily Delinquency Data
(as of March 1997 remittance reports)

Deal Balance	Original Balance $ Million	Current Balance $ Million	Factor	30, 60 & 90+ Days %	Fore-closures %	REO %	Total Del. %	Reserve Fund %
1991-M1	373.3	178.3	0.478	6.47	3.15	9.86	19.48	46.38
1991-M2	452.6	166.4	0.368	13.73	0.70	5.11	19.54	0.00
1991-M3	183.3	61.3	0.334	7.19	0.00	4.47	11.66	30.63
1991-M4	413.2	182.3	0.441	2.33	3.06	2.17	7.56	19.53
1991-M5	386.3	157.1	0.407	2.40	0.05	0.71	3.16	36.30
1991-M6	651.5	365.5	0.561	5.67	3.57	2.88	12.12	31.01
1991-M7	240.5	69.6	0.289	19.86	2.82	1.19	23.87	64.51
1992-M1	290.6	136.1	0.468	6.16	2.13	0.00	8.29	45.78
1992-M2	520.1	140.8	0.271	14.29	0.97	3.95	19.21	80.94
1992-M3	526.7	164.0	0.311	6.06	0.09	0.56	6.71	69.55
1992-M4	447.7	159.7	0.357	5.84	0.36	0.05	6.25	60.25
Totals								
March M-Series	4,485.8	1,780.9	0.397	7.25	1.82	2.91	11.98	41.48
February M-Series	4,485.8	1,818.3	0.405	8.09	2.25	2.75	12.73	40.57

Source: FDIC

The FDIC reports on prepayments on M-Series transactions every month, one of the few regular sources of prepayment data on multifamily loans. Prepayments on RTC multifamily deals averaged over 20% CPR in 1996. For the latest three-month, six-month, and 12-month periods, the CPR on M-Series deals has averaged 23%, 22%, and 21%, respectively. Details of RTC prepayments are shown in Exhibit 16.

Although RTC loans are not representative of the multifamily loan universe, data on them can sometimes reflect trends in commercial real estate lending. We believe that the rapid prepayment rates on RTC M-Series deals indicate the current competitive market for commercial loans and the large amount of capital flowing to the sector. As of March 1997, only $1.8 billion of RTC M-Series remained, less than 40% of the original balanceas shown in Exhibit 17.

Exhibit 17: RTC Prepayments
(% CPR; months represent remittance report date)

	Org. bal.	Rem. bal.		1996								1997			Latest		
	($MM)	($MM)	Factor	May	Jun	Jul	Aug	Sep	Oct	Nov	Dec	Jan	Feb	Mar	3mo	6mo	12mo
1991-M1	373.3	178.3	0.478	15	0	5	6	5	4	24	21	0	4	58	26	22	17
1991-M2	452.6	166.4	0.368	45	19	24	42	22	11	9	45	43	4	11	22	23	26
1991-M3	183.3	61.3	0.334	14	52	0	4	29	66	7	5	73	25	2	42	37	32
1991-M4	413.2	182.3	0.441	13	5	12	13	18	15	26	22	43	24	25	31	26	19
1991-M5	386.3	157.1	0.407	3	2	6	1	1	7	14	0	7	0	0	2	5	4
1991-M6*	651.5	365.5	0.561	40	0	4	41	6	6	30	0	28	0	29	20	16	19
1991-M7	240.5	69.6	0.289	8	8	15	64	23	40	40	37	8	15	34	20	30	27
1992-M1	290.6	136.1	0.468	44	14	22	5	3	7	36	6	45	42	21	37	28	23
1992-M2	520.1	140.8	0.271	46	14	11	82	46	22	43	19	40	15	8	22	26	38
1992-M3	526.7	164.0	0.311	12	32	34	4	15	24	7	31	24	10	8	14	18	20
1992-M4	447.7	159.7	0.357	26	28	12	6	15	13	51	10	5	10	4	28	28	22
Total	4,485.8	1,780.9	0.397	Avg.24	16	13	24	17	14	27	16	27	11	20	23	22	21

*Group 1 loans only.

Source: Morgan Stanley and FDIC.

PRIVATE-LABEL MULTIFAMILY MBS

Private-label CMBS backed by 100% multifamily loans totaled $3.2 billion in 1996, about 10% of CMBS issuance. Issuance of 100% multifamily MBS peaked at $4.3 billion in 1993 and 1994. Since 1994, however, many CMBS backed by mortgage conduit loans contain a high percentage of multifamily loans. In 1996, $6.8 billion of multifamily loans was securitized in private-label CMBS, about 20% of total CMBS issuance, as detailed in exhibits 18 and 19.

Issuers tranche multifamily MBS into credit classes ranging from triple-A to single-B and unrated. In the next section, we discuss the relative value of the various classes of private-label CMBS.

RELATIVE VALUE OF MULTIFAMILY MBS

We believe that multifamily MBS should play an important role in a diversified mortgage and CMBS portfolio. As of May 1997, our fixed-income strategy group is recommending a 4.5% allocation to CMBS in fixed-income portfolios, far above its share of fixed-income securities. Our recommendation is that CMBS investors remain fully invested in multifamily MBS, maintaining an investment close to the market share of multifamily CMBS in the total CMBS market. Relative to non-CMBS fixed income investments, investors should have an overweight position in multifamily MBS.

DUS pools represent a cheap substitute for corporates and agency debentures. In general, investors seeking positive convexity have

Exhibit 18: CMBS by Type of Property

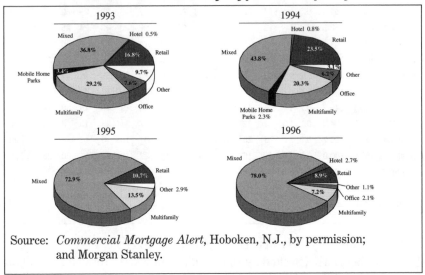

Source: *Commercial Mortgage Alert*, Hoboken, N.J., by permission; and Morgan Stanley.

Exhibit 19: Percentage of Multifamily Loans in the Largest CMBS Conduit/Seasoned Loan Transactions,

Multifamily Amt. Pricing %	($MM)	Issuer	Seller/Borrower	Date
23.5	1,926.5	Structured Asset Securities Corp.,1996-CFL	Confederation Life Insurance Co. (U.S.)	02/09
44.2	1,138.3	Merrill Lynch Mortgage Investors Inc., 1996-C2	First Union, Merrill Lynch	11/15
26.3	879.5	Asset Securitization Corp., 1996-D2	Nomura Asset Capital	02/27
28.9	782.6	Asset Securitization Corp., 1996-D3	Nomura Asset Capital	10/15
15.7	716.5	FDIC Remic Trust, 1996-C1	Federal Deposit Insurance Corp.	12/19
4.4	709.8	Structured Asset Securities Corp., 1996-C1	Lehman Brothers	09/27

Source: *Commercial Mortgage Alert*, Hoboken, N.J., 1997, by permission.

had to either go down in credit quality or accept relatively narrow spreads. DUS product offers investors a high-yielding corporate alternative with positive convexity and agency credit.

For example, spreads to Treasuries on 10-year Fannie Mae DUS with 9.5 years of prepayment lockout have trended down from 65 basis points in June 1995 to about 45 bp as of May 1997. At this level, the Fannie Mae 10/9.5s are still 15 bp wider than AAA-rated 10-year corporate bonds. However, we should point out that although DUS issues with prepayment lockouts that extend to within six months of maturity are nominally positively convex, in actual practice default risk may introduce some "trading negative convexity" in big rallies. Representative spreads are shown in Exhibit 20, followed by historic spreads in Exhibit 20 andPLC spreads in Exhibit 22.

Exhibit 20: Representative DUS Spreads (in bp)

Type	May 29, 1997	July 5, 1996
10/9.5	46 / 10-Year	55 / 10-Year
10/7	57 / 10-Year	73 / 10-Year
7/6.5	40 / 7-Year	45 / 7-Year
7/5	51 / 7-Year	60 / 7-Year

Exhibit 21: Historical Fannie Mae DUS 10/9.5 Spreads (in bp) July 1996 – May 29, 1997

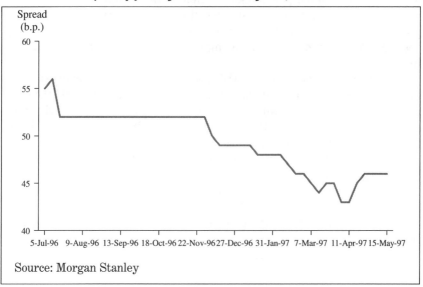

Source: Morgan Stanley

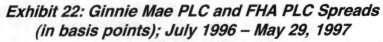

*Exhibit 22: Ginnie Mae PLC and FHA PLC Spreads
(in basis points); July 1996 – May 29, 1997*

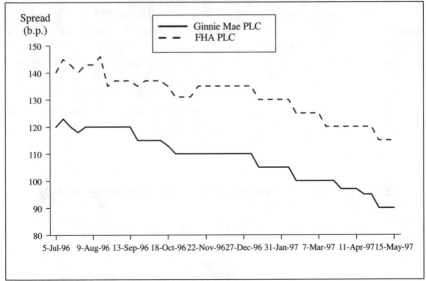

DUS that are not locked out from prepayments for the entire term, such as a 10/7 DUS can be negatively convex albeit to a lesser extent than a 30-year single-family mortgage pass-through. Even after adjusting for minimal prepayment option costs and a liquidity premium, we believe that the DUS product remains attractive relative to the corporate and agency debenture market. Liquidity has been enhanced by the MEGA program and the growing number of dealers making markets in this product.

In the private-label CMBS sector, spreads to Treasuries tightened significantly during 1996 and the first six months of 1997. Despite this tightening, CMBS maintain a spread advantage over similarly rated corporate bonds of about 40 bp to 60 bp at the investment grade level. Some selective CMBS spreads are shown in Exhibit 23.

For noninvestment-grade bonds, BB CMBS have spreads similar to corporate BBs, while single-B CMBS maintain a large advantage over corporate single-Bs. Since we believe that the credit risk of CMBS is lower than for corporates of the same rating at most rating levels, we think that CMBS still offer good relative value for the fixed-income investor.

Exhibit 23: Selected CMBS Spreads
(In basis points, as of May 29, 1997)

	3-Year	5-Year	7-Year	10-Year
U.S. Treasury	6.43	6.61	6.69	6.75

	Fixed				Uncapped Floating	
	3-Year	5-Year	7-Year	10-Year	3-Year	5-Year
Conduit*						
AAA	—	50	57	65	25	25
AA (Senior)	—	70	70	70	35	35
AA (Mezz.)	—	70	70	70	40	40
A	—	80	80	80	60	60
BBB	—	95	95	95	85	90
BBB	—	125	125	125	—	—
BB	—	215	215	215	—	—
B	—	500	500	500	—	—
Seasoned Pool**						
AAA	42	50	57	—	25	25
AA (Mezz.)	60	70	70	—	35	35
A	80	80	80	—	60	60
BBB	90	100	95	—	85	85
BB	215	215	215	—	—	—
B	500	500	500	—	—	—
Agency Multifamily						
Fannie Mae DUS 10/9.5	—	—	—	46	—	—
Fannie Mae DUS 10/7	—	—	—	57	—	—
Fannie Mae DUS 7/6.5	—	—	40	—	—	—
Fannie Mae DUS 7/5	—	—	51	—	—	—
Ginnie Mae PLC***	—	—	—	90	—	—
FHA PLC3	—	—	—	115	—	—
FHA CLC3	—	—	—	130	—	—

*For newly originated, call-protected, balloon mortgages. Assumes class B and C with multiple borrowers and zero delinquencies.

**For late 1980s originations. Assumes multiple borrowers and markets, mixed call protection, and diversified assets.

***Assumes a 10-year lockout and CLC spread to 30-Year U.S. Treasury bond.

Source: Morgan Stanley

CONCLUSION

Securities backed by multifamily mortgages are a growing sector of the MBS market. With an estimated market capitalization of $40 billion, multifamily MBS make up nearly one-third of the commercial and multifamily MBS market. We believe that multifamily MBS offer good value relative to corporate bonds. We think that fixed-income investors should be overweight in the commercial and multifamily MBS sector and, within the CMBS sector, be fully invested in multifamily MBS.

Phoebe J. Moreo is national director of real estate securitization services for the E&Y Kenneth Leventhal Real Estate Group of Ernst & Young LLP. Her group provides securitization services to issuers and investors, including transaction modeling, analytics, collateral analysis, due diligence, portfolio strategic consulting, valuation, tax reporting, investor tax strategies, and regulatory and financial statement reporting. For CMBS and whole-loan mortgage-backed securities, Moreo specializes in structuring, economic analysis, and tax strategies.

Moreo has assisted financial institutions in Latin America in adapting U.S. real estate securitization processes for their countries. She has been a frequent speaker at conduit and securitization conferences, has addressed issuer, lender, and investor groups in the United States, Argentina, Mexico, and Hong Kong.

Richard M. Levine is a senior analyst with E&Y Kenneth Leventhal's Real Estate Securitization Group, with extensive experience structuring, analyzing, and modeling CMBS and residential mortgage-backed securities. Prior to joining EYKL, Levine structured and marketed residential CMOs and other mortgage derivatives at PaineWebber and Donaldson, Lufkin & Jenrette, and developed mortgage-backed and asset-backed securities models at KPMG Peat Marwick.

Levine holds a bachelor of science degree in systems engineering from the University of Virginia and a master's degree in business administration from New York University's Stern School of Business. He is an adjunct professor of finance at the Stern School, where he teaches investment principles and corporate finance.

Chapter 9
An Investor's Guide to B-Pieces

Phoebe J. Moreo
Partner
E&Y Kenneth Leventhal
Real Estate Group

Richard M. Levine
Senior Analyst
E&Y Kenneth Leventhal
Real Estate Group

Over the past few years, traditional real estate equity investors have begun to examine CMBS B-pieces as an alternative vehicle for enhancing portfolio returns. The increasing demand for B-pieces has resulted in a dramatic tightening in spreads in BB-rated classes and increased complexity in credit tranching and bond structures. The growing market sentiment that real estate cash flows can be fine-tuned into more predictable patterns has led to the introduction of a new array of structured products that provide real estate investors with improved liquidity, greater diversification, and a means to enhance portfolio yield.

At current tightening market spreads, investors seeking consistently above-average B-piece returns must now incorporate a valuation methodology that effectively analyzes the two main components of B-piece performance: the volatility component inherent in real estate investments and the newly added issues of return fluctuations due to capital market movements. Exhibit 1 outlines the factors that play a role in B-piece valuation.

ROLE OF B-PIECES IN CMBS STRUCTURES
Subordinate CMBS tranches, or B-pieces, are below-investment-grade (BB+ or lower) securities that receive distributions of principal and interest from a pool of commercial mortgage loans after scheduled payments are committed to the investment-grade or senior certificate holders. Realized losses incurred in servicing the loans are absorbed by the B-

Exhibit 1: Valuation of B-Pieces

n Investor in a B-Piece security can be viewed as owning a T-Bond plus a short position in a put option to the borrower.

n The borrower can put (sell) the underlying real estate to the B-Piece investor at a strike price equal to the unpaid balance of the loan.

n In a true economic model, the borrower would always default on the loan if the property value is less than the loan balance.

n The B-Piece investor's required yield would be defined as the Treasury risk free rate plus the price of the option.

T-Bond Rate + Option Yield = B-Piece Investor Yield

Source: E&Y Kenneth Leventhal Real Estate Group, Ernst & Young LLP

pieces, reducing their principal balance and, consequently, lowering optimal scheduled disbursements. Realized losses are incurred when the proceeds received on liquidation are less than the sum of liquidation costs, principal and interest outstanding and servicer advances, and the interest thereon. Buyers of the first-loss class face the highest degree of cash-flow uncertainty as they are the first to receive writedowns from realized losses.

Before evaluating individual B-piece securities, investors must have a clear understanding of the role of subordination in CMBS structures. B-pieces provide credit enhancement to the investment-grade classes of CMBS. As such, an optimal B-piece investment should provide the high yield necessary to compensate the bondholder for the credit risk inherent in the structure. Determining suitable B-piece investments involves assessing underwriting of the underlying property cash flows, underwriting of the underlying mortgages, and evaluation of the CMBS structure to determine if it provides the tools necessary to manage the credit risk of the pool.

FIVE-STEP APPROACH TO ANALYSIS

An analysis of B-pieces involves qualitative and quantitative assessments of the underlying properties and their cash flows, the loans secured by these properties, and the cash flows ultimately passed through to the bondholders. A five-step approach to analyzing subordinate-class investment is recommended, in which the investor considers the following topics:

- Assessment of the underlying properties.
- Analysis of the underlying mortgage loans.
- Dynamics of the mortgage pool.
- Impact of third party providers for the CMBS.
- Thorough understanding of the CMBS structure, including principal and interest distribution rules as well as loss allocations.

UNDERLYING PROPERTY ASSESSMENT

B-piece investors must first evaluate loss potential. The credit quality of a CMBS issuance is based on the long-term performance of the commercial properties underlying a CMBS pool of mortgages. The property cash flow is not static over time but can change dramatically due to changes in physical condition, tenant mix, and economic conditions — both geographically and in the tenants' respective markets. Net operating income of the properties must be sufficient to sustain future capital expenditures and tenant improvements. Investors should obtain a thorough understanding of the quality and volatility of the operating cash flows of the underlying properties, as well as the amount of operating leverage in the properties and the strength of their revenue streams.

After examining these factors, the B-piece investor can compare cash inflows from the properties with operating expenses to determine how susceptible their earnings are to inflation and other changing macroeconomic conditions. CMBS investors should also feel comfortable that revenue streams from the properties are adequately supported by demand for space and tenant rollover provisions.

As the provider of credit enhancement, the B-piece investor needs a thorough understanding of the properties underlying a CMBS. The investor is assisted in this process by the underwriting performed by other parties, including the loan originator, the rating agencies, and the securities underwriter.

Operational and Refinance Risk

CMBS investors face two credit issues with respect to the CMBS mortgage pool: operational defaults — the risk that the property will not generate sufficient cash flow to make the monthly payments on the mortgage loan — and refinance risk — the risk that, at maturity, the property will lack sufficient value to be sold or refinanced in an amount sufficient to make the balloon payment. Operational risk is common to both fully amortizing and balloon loans, while refinance risk is common only to balloon loans. Operational risk and refinance risk can be managed only through careful underwriting at origination and strong property management throughout the life of the mortgage. These risks can be quantified using several financial ratios: debt service coverage, loan to value at origination, and loan to value at maturity.

DSCR The debt-service-coverage ratio (DSCR) is commonly expressed as the ratio of a property's net operating income (or the property's underwritten operating cash flow) to its debt-service payments.

In a study by Fitch Investors Service, DSCR was found to be a good indicator of a property's operational default risk. Loans with higher DSCRs defaulted much less frequently than loans with lower DSCRs although loans with a DSCR of 1.00 did not immediately go into default. Loss severity was also found to be correlated to DSCR; loans with a DSCR ranging from 1.00 to 1.19 experienced an average loss of 47.5% compared with an average loss of 30.7% for loans with a DSCR of 1.40 to 1.74.

Loans having similar DSCRs at origination may exhibit different propensities for operational default risk due to the volatility of their DSCRs. A property with operating expenses relatively high in relation to its revenues will have a more volatile DSCR in changing economic conditions than one having relatively small operating expenses.

LTV A relatively low loan-to-value ratio at origination (the ratio of the original loan amount to the property's value at origination) is important, as lenders have established that a borrower with equity in the property has greater incentive to continue debt-service payments in times of decreased property cash flow. The loan-to-value at maturity (the ratio of the balance of the loan due at maturity to the property's value at origination) gives an indication of the property's refinance risk.

A 10-year loan with payments based on a 15-year amortization schedule will have a more conservative loan-to-value at maturity than a similar loan on a property of equal value that calls for monthly payments based on a 25-year amortization schedule. The investor should also be certain that the property's value is realizable upon default. Attention should be focused on the loan's allowance for second mortgages and whether escrows are set up to cover taxes and insurance and what provisions, if any, are in place for ongoing replacement reserves and tenant improvements.

Timely Information DSCR and LTV analyses are meaningful only if investors are provided with timely and accurate information on loan performance. B-piece investors must investigate the originator's loan-underwriting guidelines to determine that the loan was underwritten based on current and substantial operating data and that the loan's terms provide that the investor will be able to secure updated operating information in a timely manner throughout the life of the loan.

Special Concerns B-piece investors should also be cognizant of special concerns such as environmental issues. Subordination levels of the CMBS are determined in part by environmental concerns. Properties with asbestos-containing material, soil contamination, or underground storage tanks should be carefully evaluated. Many CMBS issuances preclude foreclosure on properties where the cost to cure environmental hazards exceeds the property's value.

UNDERLYING LOAN ANALYSIS

The credit quality of a CMBS is derived from the long-term performance of the underlying loans. Having analyzed the properties, B-piece investors must evaluate issues concerning the timing of payments of the underlying mortgages that are passed through to the bondholders. There are two major credit considerations: how well the loan secures the investor's rights to underlying property cash flows, and what tools the loan provides to help manage credit risk. The latter encompasses bondholders' rights to receive timely operating information and the means to ensure that real estate taxes and insurance are always in place to protect the investor's lien interest in the underlying property cash flows.

Historical performance of the loans underlying a CMBS should be considered for new-issue B-pieces. CMBS collateralized by pools that were previously nonperforming or delinquent should be closely scrutinized to determine if these events could recur and/or if additional credit enhancement is needed to resolve these issues. Structures containing balloon loans contain more optionality than bonds secured by fully amortizing loans, since the borrower's ability to make the balloon payment depends to a large extent on its ability to refinance.

Special consideration should be accorded to CMBS collateralized by loans featuring nonstandard debt-service-payment terms and/or covenants for extension or early extinguishment of loan balance. Cash flows passed through to the CMBS investor may also be affected by loans for which the amortization schedule is tied to an index or subject to "teaser" rates where debt service increases substantially after the initial "teaser" period.

The credit quality of the mortgagees (especially large single-concentration borrowers) should also be disseminated to forecast potential delinquencies and/or defaults. A comprehensive financial statement evaluation is usually undertaken by the rating agencies, as well as a qualitative assessment of the management team. B-piece investors should be wary of CMBS structures requiring unduly large amounts of subordination due to borrower deficiencies.

Prepayment Provisions Most new commercial loans backing CMBS are structured with prepayment provisions such as lockouts (which prohibit the borrower from prepaying during a portion of the loan's life) and prepayment penalties. Lockout and prepayment penalty provisions compensate the lender for the yield lost when a borrower prepays principal. They are predicated on the assumption that a borrower will prepay if interest rates drop. Prepayment penalties are of two types: yield maintenance and fixed percentages. Yield-maintenance penalties require the borrower to make an additional payment with a prepayment of principal equal to the difference between (a) the return that the prepaid principal would earn accruing interest at the loan's coupon and (b) the return of an equivalent-maturity Treasury bond. Fixed percentage prepayment penalties have the borrower pay an additional payment equal to a fixed percent of the amount of principal being prepaid.

In most CMBS, prepayment penalties are passed through only to senior bond holders — typically the interest-only (IO) classes and any senior bond currently receiving principal. In these cases, prepayments adversely affect senior-class returns.

The B-piece buyer, however, should take a different view of prepayments. Whereas a senior bondholder's yield may be hurt by prepayments, they help a B-piece buyer by increasing his percent of the pool, providing an opportunity to obtain a rating upgrade for some or all of his investment. The key to prepayments for a B-piece investor is ensuring that prepayment provisions reduce prepayment interest shortfalls by allowing borrowers to prepay only on loan due dates.

MORTGAGE POOL DYNAMICS

After evaluating the loans on an individual basis, the B-piece investor needs to analyze the dynamics of the mortgage pool. Loan concentrations by property type, geography, and borrower must be analyzed at issuance. Additionally, CMBS investors need to focus on the mortgage pool's future composition — the concentrations of the mortgages that will be outstanding when the subordinate classes begin their scheduled principal paydown. However, diversification is useful only if the principal value of the class the investor is pursuing is not eliminated by defaults on one or two loans. Investors in first-loss classes must look at the underlying pool under the weakest-link-in-the-chain theorem, as it is the weakest loans that are most likely to be the cause of losses for such investor.

Property Type CMBS can be backed by pools containing loans of one or more property types (such as hotels, multifamily, or office). A diverse property-type mix adds to the credit quality of the pool by minimizing exposure to economic fluctuations in one sector of the real estate market. Hotel properties often have more operating leverage and can exhibit greater DSCR variances throughout their term. Unanchored and weakly anchored retail centers may suffer most from economic downturns. Pools backed by poor-quality properties carry more risk of insufficient debt coverage due to decreases in value associated with obsolescence and greater maintenance requirements. B-piece investors should weigh all these factors when considering whether the loss severity and delinquency assumptions are adequate.

Geographic Concentrations Properties in California are more susceptible than those in other states to natural disasters such as earthquakes. Many California loans are fully protected by earthquake insurance, while others may have insurance up to the probable maximum loss (PML) amount. Coastal Florida properties have risks associated with wind damage stemming from hurricanes, though some have insurance provisions. Properties in Texas generally have values more affected by economic volatility. Investors should carefully analyze state concentrations representing more than 5% of a pool.

Borrower Concentrations B-piece investors in CMBS exhibiting heavy borrower concentrations need to analyze such borrowers' abilities to manage the underlying properties and maintain their value. Investors also need to focus on such borrowers' prior credit records and how they have behaved in other workout situations.

THE IMPACT OF THIRD-PARTY PROVIDERS (SERVICERS AND TRUSTEES)

The quality of servicing plays a key role in forecasting potential losses. In many cases, the first-loss piece is held by the special servicer. This is an important consideration for other B-piece investors in the same issuance, since the special servicer's workout capabilities will be crucial in limiting losses on defaulting loans.

Servicers

The master servicer of a CMBS is responsible for the day-to-day administration of the transaction. In most cases, the master servicer acts as the primary servicer, collecting payments from borrowers and responding to inquiries from current and potential investors. In other cases, the master servicer oversees sub-servicers, but still remains responsible for providing liquidity to the CMBS issuance. The master servicer advances monthly payments due from borrowers but not received within the collection period. The master servicer receives a fee for these services and is further compensated by collecting interest on advances and float income on collections.

Operational Information The master servicer is also responsible for collecting updated borrower information and distributing it to investors, the trustee, and the special servicer. This information is crucial to B-piece investors to track their investment and determine when they should be vocal in assuring potential problems are addressed early.

The special servicer is responsible for managing and resolving all nonperforming mortgage loans. The special servicer also oversees the disposition of any REO properties. Most important to B-piece investors, though, is the provision in many CMBS pooling and servicing agreements that calls for the special servicer to alter loan payment terms, which could include the forgiveness or deferral of principal and interest payments. Often, the consent of 100% of holders of the most subordinate class of securities outstanding — among other conditions — is required for scheduled payments to be reduced or deferred. Since any resultant interest shortfall or principal forgiveness is written off immediately as a realized loss, B-piece investors must measure the special servicer's ability to restructure or refinance troubled loans.

Increasingly, the special servicer will retain the first-loss tranche for investment. This is generally viewed favorably by other B-piece holders — the special servicer will be highly motivated to protect investors' interests when its own capital is at risk. CMBS serviced by full-service entities (which act as both master and special servicer) are also viewed as more favorable to investors since transfers of troubled loans can be completed more smoothly.

Trustees

Trustees are responsible for distributing monthly cash flows to bondholders. They also may ensure that the master and special servicers are meeting their contractual obligations. Some trustees may also have backup advancing responsibilities. Trustees with deep pockets (such as money center banks or those with large corporate parents) are more likely to make timely advances and should be factored into expectations of cash-flow certainty for the B-pieces.

Operating Advisers

The operating adviser (OA) is an entity or individual elected to advise, approve, and direct the special servicing of loans, particularly relating to workouts, modifications, discounted payoffs, and other deviations due to defaulted or delinquent loans. Prior to the introduction of the OA in CMBS transactions, all decisions regarding management and liquidation of the loan portfolio were determined by the master servicer or special servicer.

OAs are elected by the first-loss subordinate class until its outstanding principal balance has eroded to approximately 25%-50% of its initial face amount; whereupon the next loss class assumes this responsibility. B-piece buyers should be aware of the terms and conditions of selection of an OA (which can vary from deal to deal) to become comfortable that estimated losses will be determined in a manner beneficial to their interests.

ANALYZING THE CMBS BOND STRUCTURE

A critical aspect in evaluating CMBS B-pieces is analysis of the CMBS bond structure. Each issuance is uniquely structured to reflect investor, issuer, and servicer preferences, varying loan attributes, and rating agency concerns.

Initial Subordination Levels

The original subordination levels of a CMBS issuance must sufficiently reflect the credit quality of the underlying mortgage pool.

Senior/subordinate percentages should seem reasonable given the credit quality of the underlying properties and loan. Investors may also evaluate the LTVs and DCSRs by bond class to confirm whether subordination effectively reflects credit stratification.

Cash Flow Allocation

The allocation of cash flows to the senior and subordinate classes is known as the "waterfall," as available cash payments cascade from bonds with the highest priority to those of the lowest payment priority. Most CMBS utilize one of two waterfall payment schemes: an interest-principal/interest-principal (IPIP) structure, or an interest-interest/principal-

principal (IIPP) allocation. Most conduit issuances have an IPIP water-fall; many single-borrower issuances and nonperforming loan issuances have an IIPP waterfall.

IPIP In the IPIP structure, the subordinate classes receive cash flows only after the senior classes are paid both interest and principal. Available cash each period is distributed first as interest to the senior bonds, then as principal to the senior bonds (with the highest rated class-es usually receiving priority). Next, cash flows are allocated to the sub-ordinate bonds. Interest accrued at the coupon rate of each bond is paid to the junior classes in order of credit quality, with any remaining cash used to make scheduled principal payments (as discussed later in this chapter) to each of the B-pieces, generally in sequential order of credit quality.

IIPP The IIPP structure is more advantageous to subordinate bondhold-ers because they receive interest payments after the senior classes are paid interest and before the senior classes are allocated principal. Thus, in periods where available cash falls short of scheduled payments, B-piece owners are given a greater likelihood to receive at least some portion of the proceeds.

Determination of Principal Distribution Amount

The principal distribution amount is defined as the amount due each peri-od to reduce the principal balance of each class in the CMBS. Most struc-tures pay principal sequentially — the highest-rated classes are paid in full before subordinate classes receive any principal. Two variations of principal determination impact the B-pieces: the interest-paid structure and the interest-impacted structure.

Interest Paid In the interest-paid structure, the principal distribution amount is defined as the sum of all scheduled principal payments received from borrowers or advanced by servicers, all balloon payments and pre-payments received from borrowers, and the principal portion of liquida-tion and REO (real estate owned) proceeds.

Principal cash flows received are passed through to bondholders, while realized losses are allocated to write down the principal balance of the most subordinate class. Interest cash flows received are kept sepa-rate from principal so that — absent interest shortfalls, appraisal reduc-tions, and payments to servicers for advances — all classes may be able to receive interest due, as shown in Exhibit 2.

Exhibit 2: Interest Paid Structure

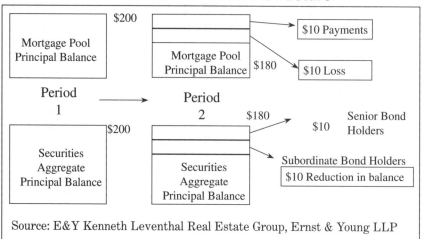

Source: E&Y Kenneth Leventhal Real Estate Group, Ernst & Young LLP

Interest Impacted The interest-impacted structure may lead to greater volatility in distributions to the subordinate classes. In this structure, the principal distribution amount is equal to all principal advanced or received, plus the principal portion of any realized losses.

Interest flows to the most subordinate class are "borrowed" and used to pay the principal distribution amount. Thus, the first-loss piece is subject to lower yields as it loses interest payments when losses are realized. In addition, the first-loss class loses distributions of scheduled principal in later periods as the amount of available cash is applied first to prior unpaid interest accruals, then to principal, as shown in Exhibit 3.

Conversely, the most senior subordinate piece may benefit from the interest impacted structure because interest foregone in early periods may eventually be returned (sometimes with accrued interest) and losses are, in essence, deferred.

Appraisal Reductions

Appraisal reductions, also known as appraisal subordination entitlement reductions (ASER) or collateral valuation adjustments (CVA), are recent CMBS structuring innovations designed to improve overall transaction credit quality. Appraisal reductions were created in response to rating agency concerns that, without such an adjustment, cash flow from mortgages likely to default would be paid to the first-loss class. The rationale behind appraisal reductions is to support proactively the credit rating of senior CMBS tranches by reducing cash-flow payments to the subordinate

Exhibit 3: Interest Impacted Structure

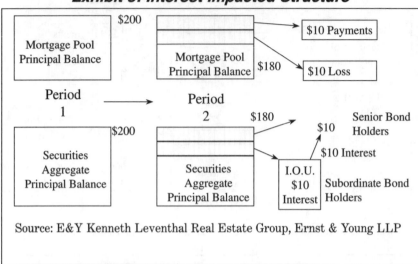

Source: E&Y Kenneth Leventhal Real Estate Group, Ernst & Young LLP

class prior to the time the realized loss associated with a bad loan is fully determined. B-piece holders (particularly owners of the first-loss class) are most adversely affected by appraisal reductions, since a large portion of their yield is derived from future interest cash flows.

Appraisal reductions are calculated on a loan-by-loan basis. Once a loan has been labeled as seriously delinquent, the special servicer will request an updated appraisal. The collateral value adjustment amount is typically equal to the excess of the principal balance of the loan plus the sum of:

- Accrued and unpaid interest not previously advanced.
- Unreimbursed advances plus interest at the advance rate.
- Any unpaid servicing and trustee fees.
- Unadvanced taxes and assessments, insurance premiums, ground rents.
- Anticipated expenses to foreclose or liquidate over 90% of the updated appraised value.

There are several methodologies for allocating the collateral value adjustment amount. In some CMBS methodologies, interest paid to the subordinate classes is reduced and the excess cash flow is used to pay down principal on the most senior class. In other types of appraisal reductions, however, the amount the servicer is required to advance on the loan is reduced. It is not always clear which classes will be impacted by such a reduction in the servicer advance. For example, if the amount of the reduction is taken from the interest portion of the advance, the most senior classes would receive their expected principal payment and only the interest cash flows of the first-loss class would be impacted. But if the reduction in the advance is applied to both its principal and interest components, the principal due to the most senior class would be reduced while the hit to the interest payment for the first-loss class would not be as severe.

B-piece investors need to pay attention to what events trigger an appraisal reduction and recognize that such adjustments come with a negative tax impact: The B-piece investor must still recognize interest income that has accrued, not just interest received.

CONCLUSION

CMBS subordinate securities offer investors a yield-rich, liquid investment that allows them to take part in the improved real estate market in a most flexible manner. However, they are investments that demand intensive monitoring and surveillance capabilities, real estate and capital markets savvy, and vigorous underwriting if an investor is to create a portfolio with real and lasting value.

Haejin Baek is a senior vice president at Lehman Brothers on the commercial mortgage trading desk. Baek was with Lehman from 1990 through 1994 and returned in 1996.

She was with Bear Stearns as a managing director in commercial mortgage trading from 1994 to 1996. Prior to trading CMBS, Baek traded adjustable-rate mortgage securities from 1990 to 1993.

She is a member of the 1997 *Institutional Investor*-ranked Third Team for commercial mortgage-backed research, along with teammate Tricia Hall.

Baek holds bachelor of science degrees in computer science and management from the Massachusetts Institute of Technology and a master's degree in business administration from the Anderson Graduate School of Management, University of California at Los Angeles.

Baek thanks Scott M. Weiner and Mary Kunka of Lehman Brothers for their invaluable assistance in writing this chapter.

Chapter 10

Relative-Value Tools for CMBS IO Analysis

Haejin Baek
Senior Vice President
Lehman Brothers

C ommercial mortgage-backed securities, once considered a small and temporary niche of the mortgage-backed securities market, continue to be issued at a record pace, with 1997 issuance expected to break 1996's record volume level of $30 billion. This explosive growth in the issuance of CMBS has resulted in a corresponding growth in the issuance of interest-only, or IO, securities stripped off these deals. These CMBS IO securities, while similar to the IO securities stripped off single-family residential loans, have many unique characteristics due to the differences between the residential and commercial mortgages that make up the collateral for the security.

Loans on commercial real estate, unlike single-family residential loans, generally offer explicit call protection that prohibits or, at the very least, provides significant disincentives to borrower refinancing. This call protection is generally in the form of a lockout provision, yield maintenance, or declining prepayment percentages — and a recent innovation, Treasury defeasance. It is customary for loans to have a combination of these forms of call protections, the most common being three to five years of lockout, then yield maintenance until six months prior to maturity of the loan. The expense, time, and resources needed to refinance commercial loans also make them much less likely to refinance than single-family loans because of interest rate movements alone.

The lack of a direct link between interest rate movements and prepayments in the commercial market makes predicting these prepayments difficult. This notwithstanding, the combination of these features and characteristics causes IO securities backed by commercial real estate loans to be much more stable than their single-family counterparts, causing them to trade at lower yields. The yield on the IO securities, though, is still much higher than that found on the comparably rated principal-paying securities from the same deals.

Despite the wide spreads and stability of CMBS IO securities when compared with single-family IO securities, the investor base has remained relatively narrow. This fact was in large part due to the limited analytical tools available to evaluate CMBS IO securities. Today, however, most Wall Street firms as well as third-party vendors can provide sophisticated tools for CMBS IO analysis, which will aid in the expansion of the investor base and the CMBS IO market overall. This chapter does not attempt to address the motivations of the commercial borrower but, instead, looks at the relative value of one CMBS IO security to another CMBS IO security from a bond perspective, using some of these tools.

ELEMENTS OF INTEREST-ONLY SECURITIES VALUATION

There are many factors which affect the valuation of IO securities, including:

- Quality of the underlying collateral.
- Call protection of the underlying loans.
- Cash-flow structure of the deal.
- Allocation of prepayment penalties.

While any one of these factors can determine the value of the IO security, it is the interaction of all these factors that determines the relative value of one IO security to another. For example, while onerous prepayment penalties on the underlying loans add value to the IO security, a disproportionate allocation of these penalties to the principal-paying bond classes may detract from the value of the IO security. Additionally, while solid call protection and fair allocation is a plus for the IO security, if the underlying loans are of poor quality and more likely to default than to prepay, what the call protection is and how the penalties are allocated become secondary issues.

Quality of Underlying Collateral and Property Types

The most important determinant of value for any commercial mortgage-backed security is the quality of the underlying loans. No amount of financial engineering can replace good, sound underwriting of the loans that are collateral for the security. Loans that are poor in quality, as measured by low debt-service coverage ratio, or DSCR, and high loan-to-value, or LTV, are more likely to default, causing an unexpected retirement of principal. High-quality loans, as measured by high DSCR and low LTV, are likely candidates for prepayment.

Call Protection of Underlying Loans

The most common forms of call protection are discussed below.

Lockout A loan that is locked out for a period of time prohibiting any prepayment during that time period is the ultimate form of call protection. The only concern is default risk.

Yield Maintenance Although there are many forms of calculation, yield maintenance generally provides for penalties based on the present value of "lost cash flows" due to prepayment. The present value, or PV, is usually calculated using the rate on the Treasury bond with a maturity closest to the maturity of the loan. Yield maintenance can also be quoted with a spread, for example, YM+50 implying that 50 basis points will be added to the Treasury yield to determine the reinvestment yield used to discount the cash flows.

Generally, yield maintenance can be calculated in two ways:

- The interest-differential method calculates the present value of the difference between the coupon on the loan and the reinvestment yield (adjusted for monthly compounding) on the principal balance being prepaid at the date of prepayment. This method does not take into account the expected amortization of the loan; instead the PV is calculated assuming the loan is a bullet.
- The notional present value, or NPV, method calculates the dif ference in present values of the loan's cash flows discounted at the mortgage rate, and discounted at the reinvestment yield (adjusted for monthly compounding). This method takes into account the expected amortization of the loan. In longer-term loans where the stated maturity and amortization terms are similar, this method will produce a lower penalty than the interest-differential method, all else being equal.

Declining Percentage Penalty Declining percentage penalty provides for a fixed percentage of the prepaid principal balance to be paid as penalty. For example, a five-year balloon loan with a declining prepayment percentage of 5-4-3-2-1 means that during the first year, 5% of the prepaid balance must be paid as penalty; 4% during the second year, etc. There may be loans that provide for one flat percentage penalty for a period of time, such as 3% for five years. This method provides for certain prepayment penalties regardless of the interest rate environment.

Treasury Defeasance An innovation in CMBS call protection is Treasury defeasance. This concept is similar to Treasury yield maintenance in that, instead of prepaying the loan, the borrower substitutes Treasury securities to replicate the cash flows of the mortgage. When the reinvestment yield is lower than the coupon on the mortgage the borrower must provide for enough funds to defease the mortgage with Treasuries. When the reinvestment yield is higher than the coupon on his mortgage, the borrower must still provide for enough funds to defease the mortgage, but that amount can be less than the balance of the loan. This feature provides the borrower with additional benefits if Treasury rates rise above his mortgage rate. This feature virtually eliminates prepayment sensitivity for the IO securities because despite any prepayments, the cash flows will be uninterrupted.

Treasury defeasance is most beneficial to the IO investor since part of the IO's cash flows are now backed by Treasury securities. Even though the IO investor will not benefit as greatly in a low interest rate environment (since they won't receive the yield-maintenance payments), the IO investor will not lose out in a high interest rate environment. This method provides for increased stability of cash flows benefiting the bond holder and creating securities that are almost completely insensitive to prepayments.

Cash Flow Structure

The Notional Balance IO securities can be stripped off various parts of the deal structure. The simplest form of IO security is a collateral IO, which is stripped off the entire mortgage pool. As a result, it is affected by prepayments and losses in the same manner as the underlying loans. Since the notional balance on the IO steps down in line with the collateral, the recovery percentage for defaulted loans does not affect the performance of the IO.

The other form of IO security is a bond IO. Unlike a collateral IO, which is insensitive to recovery/loss amounts, a bond IO can be protected from writeoffs due to losses if it is not stripped off the subordinate bond classes. However, because such a bond IO is stripped off the first classes in a deal, it can be more sensitive to faster prepayments than a collateral strip IO. In most recent transactions, the IO class has been stripped off all the bond classes, but unlike a collateral IO which strips one amount off the whole collateral, these bond IOs are created by stripping different amounts off each bond class. Depending on how the IO is stripped, it can be more or less sensitive to prepayment and recovery/loss amounts.

This chapter will use three IO securities with differing structures and call protection profiles for relative-value analysis. The first security, IO-A, has a weighted-average coupon, or WAC. The second security, IO-B, has fixed coupons stripped off all investment-grade classes as shown in Exhibit 2.

Exhibit 1: IO-A Structure

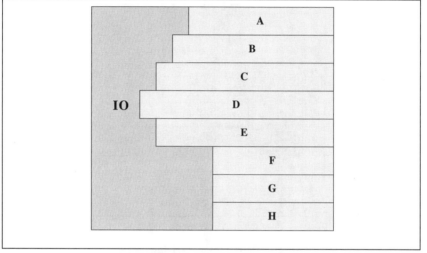

Exhibit 2: IO-B Structure

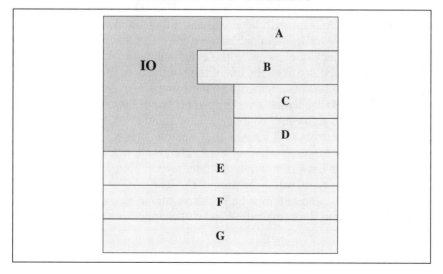

The third security, IO-C, has a WAC coupon stripped off the collateral as shown in Exhibit 3.

Exhibit 3: IO-C Structure

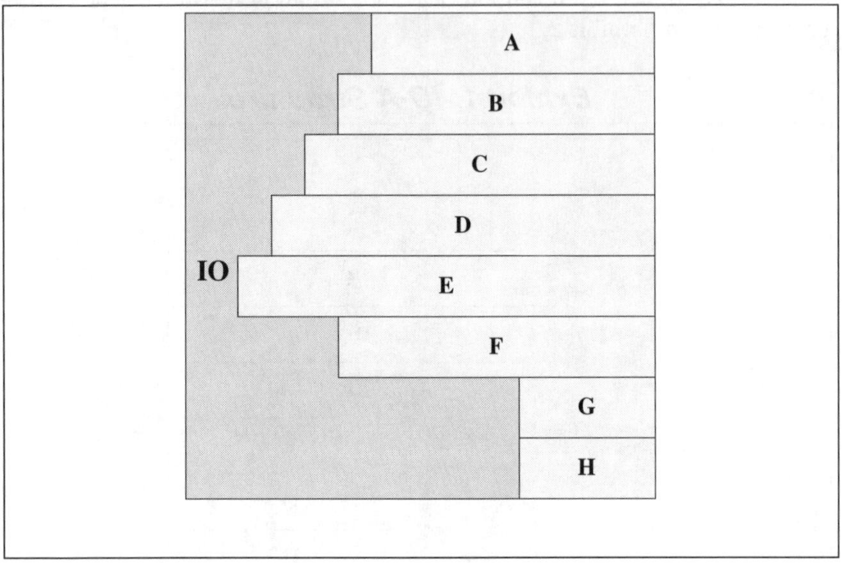

The Coupon: Fixed versus WAC IO securities can provide for fixed rates of interest over the life of the bond, or weighted average rates of interest based upon the WAC of the collateral pool. The IO security is defined by its coupon or WAC. As with bond classes, a fixed coupon IO will receive the fixed coupon on its notional balance over the life of the security. A WAC IO is subject to changes in the collateral pool with the result that coupons may fluctuate over the life of the bond due to scheduled principal paydowns as well as prepayments and/or losses/recoveries.

When IO securities are stripped off bond classes, each bond class can contribute a different "coupon," either fixed or WAC, to the IO. By stripping IO securities off classes that are not immediately affected by prepayments or losses, such as classes rated double-A through triple-B, the IO securities have protection provided by the structure of the deal as well as the underlying call protection of the loans. IO securities that have different fixed coupons stripped off different bond classes are considered WAC IOs because the aggregate WAC will change over time as the bonds pay down.

Structural Enhancements Appraisal reduction, which was introduced by the rating agencies as a means of protecting senior bond holders when loans go into default, can also have an impact on the IO security. Appraisal reduction becomes an issue when a loan goes into default and an appraisal is ordered. The difference between the loan balance and the appraisal amount plus advances to date plus expenses is termed the appraisal-reduction amount. Some methods use the appraisal-reduction amount to "fast pay" the senior classes; thereby using interest to pay down principal. When principal is paid down faster than expected, this results in a negative for the IO Class. Other methods stop the advancing on the appraisal-reduction amount, causing the subordinate class to be denied interest in the corresponding amount, although principal is not paid down any faster. Most methods, though, do not deny interest to the IO security as a result of appraisal reductions because the IO security is generally in the triple-A waterfall of the cashflow structure.

Modifications of interest rates on underlying loans may or may not affect the WAC of the IO class, depending on how the WAC of the bond classes is defined. In more recent transactions, the definition of the net WAC of the pool is defined as the net WAC at cutoff date, which means that even if a loan's coupon is modified, for purposes of the calculation of the net WAC the original rate is used, not the new modified rate. The senior bond classes, including the IO security, will not suffer a reduction in WAC, but the most subordinate bonds will.

Allocation of Prepayment Penalties

Allocation of prepayment penalties can be as important in determining relative value as the underlying call protection and cash flow structure of the different IO securities. Allocation of prepayment penalties can help overcome weak call protection of underlying loans or work to offset strong call protection by allocating more or less to the IO securities. The fairest allocation method tries to take into account the value of lost cash flow due to the prepayment and to allocate proportionately. The most typical forms of prepayment penalty allocation are outlined as follows.

Straight Allocation Straight allocation involves the payments of certain percentages to the bond classes and IO securities. Often, when most of the underlying loans provide for declining percentage penalties instead of yield maintenance penalties, the simplest method of allocation is to allocate a fixed percentage to the bond classes and a fixed percentage to the IO securities, for example, 75% to the IO security, 25% to the bond class. While this method may not always compensate the investor for lost cash flows, this allows the investor to always realize a certain amount of penalties regardless of interest rates.

Present Value of Yield Loss A prepayment of a loan may be accompanied by a significant prepayment penalty. The prepayment charges that are paid and the charges that bond holders, especially IO holders, receive should be proportionate. The method of premium allocation, referred to as PV of yield loss, attempts to compensate investors for the loss in cash flows due to the prepayment. This method is very similar to that of the yield-maintenance calculation itself, where the lost cash flows due to prepayment are discounted using a reinvestment yield. The Treasury security selected to determine the reinvestment yield is often the Treasury that corresponds to the expected maturity of the bond class that is affected.

The PV yield loss method calculates the NPV of the yield loss due to the prepayment of the loan for each of the bond classes and the IO security. The penalties are then allocated pro rata between the bond class and IO security according to their respective PV yield-loss amounts. This method tries to allocate equitably between the two classes, compensating each for the loss suffered.

Coupon Percentage Method A popular allocation method, due to its simplicity, is allocating the penalties for each class, approximating the loss in interest. This approximation is calculated as described below:

$$\% \text{ penalty due IO security} = \frac{(\text{WAC on loan} - \text{WAC on bond class})}{(\text{WAC on loan} - \text{reinvestment yield})}$$

$$\% \text{ penalty due bond class} = \frac{(\text{WAC on bond class} - \text{reinvestment yield})}{(\text{WAC on loan} - \text{reinvestment yield})}$$

This method can closely approximate the yield loss on both classes if all the loans are homogenous with similar maturity dates. By only taking into account the coupon differentials, the maturity of the loan is not factored in to the yield-loss calculations.

Bonds versus IO Securities There is a constant battle between the bond investors and IO investors regarding the allocation of prepayment penalties between bond classes and IO securities. The easiest method of dividing up prepayment charges has been to compensate the holder of the bond class affected and the IO security affected. With the growing number of conduit transactions, where the dispersion of maturities of the underlying loans can vary by as many as 10 years, it is becoming common to see bond classes that are further down the sequential pay structure being affected by prepayments with a resultant shortening of their average life. Although there is no perfect solution to this problem, the market is aware of it and continues to perfect allocations.

TOOLS OF IO ANALYSIS

Quality of Underlying Collateral

The ability of an underlying loan to prepay is just as important as the probability of the underlying loan to default. From an IO investor's perspective, both can have the same impact. Many investors will state that the perfect IO security will be backed by loans whose quality is high enough to be eligible for refinancing at a later date, but whose quality is not so poor that it may go into default anytime soon.

Call Protection of Underlying Loans

The quality of call protection of the underlying loans is also an important factor in determining relative value. Consider two different deals in which one appears to have shorter call protection; that is, the loans in one deal are not call-protected beginning three years prior to maturity versus loans in the other that are call-protected until six months prior to maturity. If the IO security is stripped off the shorter classes in the former, the shorter call protection may make no difference to the value of the IO security.

At first glance, many deals appear to have loans with very similar call-protection profiles. Further analysis may shed some light on how different some IOs can perform due to the call protection of underlying loans, bond/cash flow structure, and allocation of prepayment penalties.

The following analysis will try to isolate the impacts of the varying attributes of IO securities by presenting yield sensitivities under varying conditions. However, it is impossible to isolate completely the impact of any one element, and all data and analysis should be considered together when evaluating commercial mortgage-backed IO securities.

Yield tables applying varying prepayment speeds at varying points in the life of a loan can help to differentiate the strength of the call protection of a pool of loans. The following scenarios represent simple analysis of three different deals, all with loans with similar characteristics, except that the call protection and structure on the underlying loans are different.

    In comparison, the collateral for Deal C appears to have the strongest call protection with almost 95% of the loans having lockout for a weighted average 36 months. Deal A has fewer loans that are locked out, but the loans with lockout are locked out for a longer period on average, approximately 63 months. Deal A appears to have stronger call protection than the collateral for Deal B, with almost 64% of the pool being locked out.

    The allocation of prepayment penalties for IO-A and IO-B appears to be most equitable, while IO-C just provides for a straight allo-

Exhibit 4: Call Protection and Structure Scenarios

	Deal A	Deal B	Deal C
Coupon/WAC (bps)	127	237	133
Average Life (years)*	9.41	5.29	8.80
WA time to end of LO (months)**	63	18	36
WA time to end of CP (months)***	119	97	107
WAM	130	118	11
WAC/Fixed strips	WAC	Fixed	WAC

*Average life based on 0% CPR at maturity.
**Weighted average lockout date based only on loans with lockout.
***Weighted average call protection date based solely on loans with call protection only.

Type of Call Protection	Deal A	Deal B	Deal C
LO ➤ YM	63.7%	31.5%	94.5%
Allocation to IO	PV yield loss amount (pro-rata with bond PV yield loss amount) plus any excess	PV yield loss amount (pro-rata with Class A PV yield loss amount and prior to remaining bonds PV yield loss amount)	80%
Allocation to bonds	PV yield loss amount (pro-rata with IO)	PV yield loss amount (pro-rata with IO for Class A and sequential after IO for remaining bonds)	20%

cation of 80% to the IO and 20% to the bond classes.

The two basic yield tables are applying prepayments at the end of lockout and at the end of call protection. This allows comparison of different IO securities under simplified scenarios.

In comparing the IOs with these initial-yield tables, IO-A and IO-C have similar profiles because they are stripped in a similar manner. IO-B is affected by prepayments more because it is stripped off only the investment-grade classes, making it more sensitive to prepayments than the other two IOs. If most of the loans pay off after their call-protection periods, IO-B will be the most negatively affected.

In looking at the end-of-lockout yield tables, IO-B performs the best, because the prepayments are occurring with prepayment penalties and the allocation of prepayment penalties is most beneficial to IO-B during this period.

Exhibit 5: Allocation of Prepayment Penalties

	0% CPR	5% CPR	10% CPR	20% CPR	50% CPR
Prepayments Applied at End of Call Protection					
Corporate Bond Equivalent Yield Table					
IO-A	8.429%	8.382%	8.340%	8.271%	8.120%
Avg. Life (years)	9.41	9.37	9.33	9.28	9.18
IO-B	8.356%	8.194%	8.050%	7.807%	7.279%
Avg. Life (years)	5.29	5.26	5.24	5.20	5.13
IO-C	8.405%	8.395%	8.384%	8.361%	8.280%
Avg. Life (years)	8.80	8.80	8.79	8.78	8.74
Prepayments applied at end of Lockout					
Corporate Bond Equivalent Yield Table					
IO-A	8.429%	9.026%	9.328%	9.775%	10.481%
Avg. Life (years)	9.41	8.54	7.88	6.95	5.60
IO-B	8.356%	10.649%	13.550%	19.784%	44.302%
Avg. Life (years)	5.29	4.36	3.61	2.54	1.08
IO-C	8.405%	9.924%	11.351%	13.845%	19.010%
Avg. Life (years)	8.80	7.88	7.11	5.93	4.08

Evaluating Cash Flow Structure

To differentiate cash-flow structure between deals, the key elements to focus on are:

- What classes or collateral is the IO stripped off? This determines how prepayments and defaults affect the IO security.
- Is the coupon on the IO security a WAC or fixed rate and if it is WAC, how can the WAC change over time?

The cash-flow structure of the IO security determines its sensitivity to prepayments and defaults. A solid structure can add stability to the IO's performance. IOs stripped off investment grade classes only are more sensitive to prepayments than IOs stripped off the whole pool; they are also more sensitive to losses if recovery rates are very high. IOs that have more basis points stripped off the most subordinate and most senior classes may be more sensitive to prepayments and losses than IOs that have a fixed amount stripped off each class.

Basic default sensitivities can isolate the impact of defaults, losses and recoveries on a specific IO security. How the IO is structured and stripped will play an important role in how the bond performs under the scenarios shown in Exhibit 6.

Exhibit 6: Security Default Sensitivity

Corporate Bond Equivalent Yield Table									
0% CDR	2% CDR			4% CDR			6% CDR		
	50	70	80	50	70	80	50	70	80
IO-A 8.429%	6.404%	6.581%	6.660%	4.331%	4.708%	4.915%	2.715%	2.666%	3.178%
IO-B 8.356%	7.961%	7.388%	7.102%	7.823%	6.454%	5.866%	8.076%	5.551%	4.646%
IO-C 8.405%	6.048%	6.327%	6.496%	4.279%	4.353%	4.576%	2.776%	2.642%	2.760%

As expected, defaults affect all the IO securities but to differing degrees. IO-C performs the worst because more coupon is stripped from the lowest rated classes, therefore lower recovery rates affect IO-C more. But for IO-B, higher recovery rates hurt IO-B more since it is stripped off only the investment-grade classes. Higher recovery rates imply more principal paydowns on the senior classes, which is worse for IO-B. IO-B stands up the best under varying default scenarios because of its cash-flow structure.

Allocation of Prepayment Penalties

Once the various components of the IO security have been evaluated, it is still necessary to determine the effect of prepayment penalty allocation.

A simple analysis to compare the allocation of prepayment penalties is to run varying scenarios with prepayment penalties applied in varying interest rate scenarios, as well as scenarios which prepay certain loans, for example, longer-maturity loans versus short-maturity loans.

In comparing the three IO securities under interest rate scenarios of +/–100, +/–200 and +300, we can isolate the impact of the allocation of prepayment penalties as well as the strength of the underlying loan's call protection.

IO-B performs the best under +100 and +200 scenarios because it has a more beneficial allocation of prepayment penalties. However, in a +300 interest rate scenario the effects of prepayments surpass the benefits of prepayment penalties and IO-B can suffer negative returns. In large up interest rate scenarios, IO-C may underperform IO-A because it provides for a fixed 20% of the prepayment penalties to the principal-paying bond class even if it does not warrant it. In down interest rate scenarios, IO-C outperforms IO-A because it provides for a fixed 20% of the prepayment penalties to the principal paying bond class even if it deserves more since rates are much lower.

The upside in IO securities is realized when loans prepay with yield maintenance in a favorable interest rate environment. Since most conduit deals are priced at 0% CPR, the benefit comes in the prepayment penalties received on the IO classes.

The analysis shows that even though certain IO securities may appear very similar in terms of average life, WAC, underlying collateral and even call protection, other factors such as structure and allocation of prepayment penalties can dramatically affect the value of the IO security. The simplest way of determining the relative value of IO securities is to isolate the effect of the call protection of the underlying loans by comparing the IO securities under different prepayment scenarios, as shown in Exhibit 7. In addition to the tools described in this article, default and prepayment tables can be used to further evaluate IO securities. Default tables with varying recovery rates allow the comparison of the structure of each IO security because losses and recoveries may have a different impact than prepayments. Also, prepayment scenarios utilizing varying interest rates allow comparison of different types of call protection as well as allocation of prepayment penalties. In this environment of low interest rates, investors are concerned with yield-maintenance penalties

Exhibit 7: Interest Rate Scenarios

Prepayments Applied at End of Lockout – Rates Up 100 bps				
Corporate Bond Equivalent Yield Table				
0% CPR	5% CPR	10% CPR	20% CPR	50% CPR
IO-A 8.429%	8.560%	8.683%	8.899%	9.298%
Avg. Life (years) 9.41	8.54	7.88	6.95	5.60
IO-B 8.356%	10.437%	13.094%	18.768%	40.966%
Avg. Life (years) 5.29	4.36	3.61	2.54	1.08
IO-C 8.405%	8.661%	8.939%	9.448%	10.505%
Avg. Life (years) 8.80	7.88	7.11	5.93	4.08

Prepayments Applied at End of Lockout – Rates Up 200 bps				
Corporate Bond Equivalent Yield Table				
0% CPR	5% CPR	10% CPR	20% CPR	50% CPR
IO-A 8.429%	7.679%	7.030%	5.938%	3.775%
Avg. Life (years) 9.41	8.54	7.88	6.95	5.60
IO-B 8.356%	9.886%	11.884%	15.922%	28.658%
Avg. Life (years) 5.29	4.36	3.61	2.54	1.08
IO-C 8.405%	7.550%	6.744%	5.187%	1.054%
Avg. Life (years) 8.80	7.88	7.11	5.93	4.08

Prepayments Applied at End of Lockout – Rates Up 300 bps				
Corporate Bond Equivalent Yield Table				
0% CPR	5% CPR	10% CPR	20% CPR	50% CPR
IO-A 8.429%	7.116%	5.930%	3.863%	-0.357%
Avg. Life (years) 9.41	8.54	7.88	6.95	5.60
IO-B 8.356%	6.696%	5.170%	0.696%	-16.423%
Avg. Life (years) 5.29	4.36	3.61	2.54	1.08
IO-C 8.405%	6.771%	5.162%	1.947%	-7.319%
Avg. Life (years) 8.80	7.88	7.11	5.93	4.08

Prepayments Applied at End of Lockout – Rates Down 100 bps				
Corporate Bond Equivalent Yield Table				
0% CPR	5% CPR	10% CPR	20% CPR	50% CPR
IO-A 8.429%	9.550%	10.068%	10.789%	11.861%
Avg. Life (years) 9.41	8.54	7.88	6.95	5.60
IO-B 8.356%	10.870%	14.025%	20.844%	47.802%
Avg. Life (years) 5.29	4.36	3.61	2.54	1.08
IO-C 8.405%	11.228%	13.761%	18.018%	26.506%
Avg. Life (years) 8.80	7.88	7.11	5.93	4.08

Prepayments Applied at End of Lockout – Rates Down 200 bps				
Corporate Bond Equivalent Yield Table				
0% CPR	5% CPR	10% CPR	20% CPR	50% CPR
IO-A 8.429%	10.134%	10.905%	11.949%	13.478%
Avg. Life (years) 9.41	8.54	7.88	6.95	5.60
IO-B 8.356%	11.100%	14.520%	21.953%	51.479%
Avg. Life (years) 5.29	4.36	3.61	2.54	1.08
IO-C 8.405%	12.555%	16.157%	22.010%	33.360%
Avg. Life (years) 8.80	7.88	7.11	5.93	4.08

if interest rates go back up dramatically. The tools described in this chapter are meant to be used in evaluating the relative value of different IO securities, not the absolute value of the security. Because the structure and allocation of prepayment penalties are just as important as the quality of the underlying collateral and call protection, it is important to be able to analyze their impact on the IO securities.

Loy Saguil is a vice president in fixed-income research at Prudential Securities, where he is responsible for research and strategy coverage of the commercial mortgage-backed securities sector.

Prior to joining PSI in 1996, Saguil was with Nomura Securities International, where he worked in both sales and research within the mortgage-backed securities division. He also worked at Dean Witter Reynolds Inc. and Institutional Investor Inc.

He is a member of the commercial/multifamily committee of the Bond Market Association and a member of the research committee of the Commercial Real Estate Secondary Market and Securitization Association.

Saguil holds a bachelor of science degree, in finance, from Boston University and a master's degree in business administration, in finance, from the Wharton School of the University of Pennsylvania.

Chapter 11

Weighted-Average Pass-Through Versus Fixed-Rate CMBS: Should They Be Treated Alike?

Loy Saguil
Vice President, Fixed-Income Research
Prudential Securities

C ommercial mortgage-backed securities are often structured with weighted-average pass-through (WAPT) coupons, because of a lack of uniformity in the underlying loan pools with regard to coupons, amortization schedules, and other factors. However, these bonds are often priced identically to fixed-rate structures. In this chapter, we examine WAPT bonds to determine whether these structures should be priced differently from fixed-rate bonds. As a result of our analysis, we will show that, in the presence of default and prepayment risk, WAPT bonds should trade behind fixed-rate CMBS (all other factors being equal).

In a typical CMBS deal consisting of more than one loan, the underlying loan coupons, amortization schedules, maturities, and other factors, can vary widely. For example, coupon dispersion among loans within a typical conduit deal can be as much as 200 basis points or more, while amortization schedules on the underlying loans can range anywhere from fully amortizing to nonamortizing (interest only).

WAPT AND FIXED-RATE PRINCIPAL-PAYING CMBS

As a result, CMBS are normally structured with some combination of fixed-rate coupons or WAPTs applicable to both the principal-paying classes and the IO classes. For example, principal-paying bonds could be structured as fixed-rate bonds, while the IOs would be WAPT bonds in order to absorb the varying WAPT coupon of the underlying loan pool, and vice versa. In addition, some of the principal-paying bonds could have a fixed coupon while others would be WAPTs, and the resulting IO coupon would be some offsetting combination.

Despite this characteristic of WAPT bonds, there is presently very little, if any, price differentiation in the market between fixed-rate and WAPT principal-paying bonds in the CMBS market.

All other factors being equal, a fixed-rate bond from one deal and a WAPT bond from another deal will likely trade at identical or very similar spread levels. An exception may be when the call protection is weak. In this case, a WAPT bond may trade at slightly wider levels to account for the greater risk that the coupon could change dramatically over time as loans prepay. However, even without any prepayments or defaults, a WAPT bond can experience relatively large fluctuations in coupon. A fixed-rate bond priced at par will remain at par when priced any time before maturity, if yield to maturity does not change. A WAPT bond, however, can undergo changes in price, assuming pricing at a constant yield, because the coupon is changing continually.

While these price changes in a constant-yield environment would seem to indicate that fixed-rate and WAPT bonds should be priced differently, they do not play a significant role when evaluating the bonds on a total-return basis, assuming no prepayments or defaults.

Exhibit 1 illustrates two examples of WAPT bonds, the A-2 class from both the Asset Securitization Corporation's ASC 1996-MD6 (a large-loan deal) and ASC 1996-D3 (a conduit deal). These bonds are bulletlike in nature and show a wide variation in the coupons. For example, the ASC 1996-MD6 coupon ranges from 6.496% to 7.644% over its life, and the ASC 1996-D3 coupon ranges from 7.031% to 7.853%.[1] In both cases, the bonds were initially priced at par and the resulting yield was used to price the bonds each month going forward until maturity (the resulting yield to maturity and prices are calculated on a monthly pay structure and have not been converted to the corporate bond equivalent).

As shown by Exhibit 1, both bonds accrete upward in price and ultimately drop to par as they approach maturity, with the ASC 1996-MD6 bond reaching 100 27/32 and the ASC 1996-D3 bond reaching 100 17/32. While these two examples show similar results, the opposite — in which a WAPT's coupon declines over time — also could be the case. For example, if the underlying pool has high-coupon amortizing loans and low-coupon IO loans, the WAPT coupon and the resulting bond price, when priced at the original yield to maturity, should decline over time.

---

[1]While each deal has loans with varying coupons, amortization schedules, etc. that would account for some variability in WAPT coupons, the day count is another factor. The loans from both of these deals are calculated on an actual/360 basis, while the WAPTs are calculated on a 30/360 basis. For example, this results in the downward coupon spikes occurring in February displayed in Exhibit 1, when the interest from the loans is less than the interest in other months.

Exhibit 1: Price Movement in a WAPT-Coupon Bond Assuming Pricing at a Constant Yield

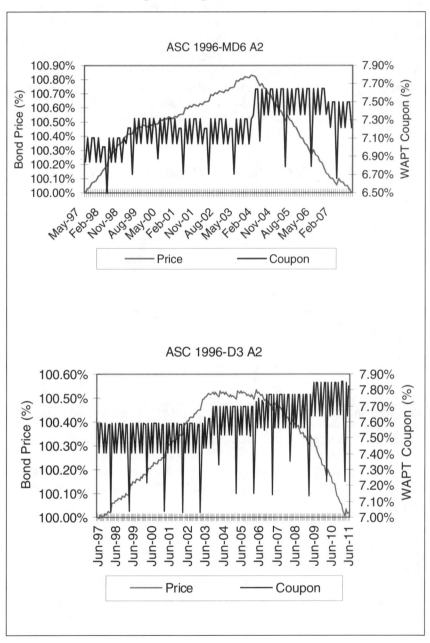

TOTAL-RETURN ANALYSIS

On a total-return basis, there is little difference between fixed-rate and WAPT bonds in a zero-default and zero-prepayment environment. Because future cash flows generated by the bonds, whether fixed or WAPT, are discounted at a constant yield to arrive at the dollar price, the price of each bond over time combined with the interest payments already received should result in similar total-return profiles. Exhibit 2 shows one-year holding-period total returns (assuming reinvestment at yield to maturity) of both a fixed-rate bond (Midland 1996-C2 class C) and the two WAPT bonds. Both the purchase price and sale price assume pricing at a constant yield to maturity.

Exhibit 2: Total Rates of Return on Fixed-Rate and WAPT CMBS

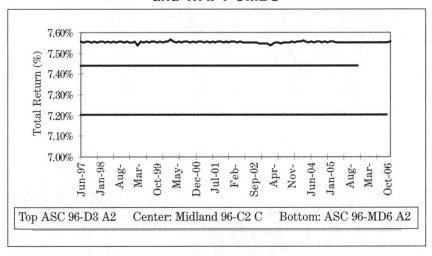

Top ASC 96-D3 A2   Center: Midland 96-C2 C   Bottom: ASC 96-MD6 A2

In Exhibit 2, while it is obvious that the fixed-rate bond will show a total return equal to its yield, the two WAPT bonds also show similar results.

This total-return analysis shows that the wide variance in a WAPT's expected coupon over time still results in similar total-return profiles. But does this imply that fixed-rate bonds and WAPT bonds should be priced similarly?

Not necessarily, since the changes in the WAPT coupons of the two bonds are already known at origination and are thus accounted for in the yield-to-maturity calculation. On the other hand, changes in the

WAPT coupon will likely differ from expectations should unforeseen prepayments[2] and/or defaults occur.

Impact of Defaults and Prepayments

Exhibit 3 illustrates an example of how defaults and prepayments affect a WAPT bond's coupon and ultimately its total-return profile. This example consists of one fixed-rate bond made up of a pool of 8% coupon loans and one WAPT deal. Half of the loans in the WAPT deal have 7% coupons while the other half have 9% coupons, resulting in a WAPT coupon of 8%. For simplicity, all of the loans in both the fixed-rate and WAPT amortize over 10 years and pay interest annually. Recoveries (at 65%) after defaults occur 12 months after losses. Each deal is assumed to be a single bond and the day count on both of the bonds and the underlying loans is 30/360.

The exhibit shows, as expected, that both the fixed-rate and WAPT bond have equal total-return profiles in a zero-loss and zero-prepayment scenario. We then applied default and prepayment rates (assuming no yield maintenance in the first set of examples and yield maintenance at Treasury-flat for life in the next set) to the high-coupon loans of the WAPT deal and applied an equivalent dollar amount of defaults and prepayments on the fixed-rate pool (Note: While we are merely trying to isolate the defaults and prepayments to the high-coupon loans, it would stand to reason that defaults and prepayments are most likely to occur with these loans. Furthermore, a few of the default scenarios are somewhat aggressive and should likely be considered worst-case scenarios.) The resulting total returns are calculated assuming that the bonds are held to maturity.

As the exhibit illustrates, total returns on both the fixed-rate and WAPT bonds drop as losses and prepayments occur, but the impact is greater on the WAPT bonds. The impact is even more pronounced in more severe default and prepayment scenarios as the high-coupon loans

[2]While we would agree to some extent with the argument that stringent prepayment penalties may dissuade a borrower from prepaying, prepayments can and do occur for a number of reasons, such as refinancing property to take out equity. For example, the $1.9 billion SASCO 1996-CFL deal has had 42 loans representing 4.77% of the total balance prepay during a penalty period and pay a weighted-average penalty of 4.95% since issuance (14 months). With the wide availability of real estate debt capital currently, prepayments, especially on higher-coupon loans, could pick up going forward. See Loy Saguil, "SASCO 1996-CFL Prepays" in Prudential Securities' *CMBS Quarterly* (Second Quarter 1997), and "When Does a Loan Become Prepayable," in the *CMBS Quarterly* (Third Quarter 1997).

are removed from the overall pool. With regard to the examples involving yield maintenance, the prepayment of high-coupon loans has no impact on the total return due to the resulting prepayment penalty. However, the WAPT bond still marginally underperforms the fixed-rate bond due to the reduction in the coupon as a result of losses on the high-coupon loans.

Exhibit 3: Total-Return Analysis on Fixed-Rate and WAPT Bonds After Defaults and Prepayments

Assuming default, prepayment, and no yield maintenance				
Constant Default Rate Starting Year 1 (%)	Constant Prepayment Rate Starting Year 1 (%)	Fixed-Rate CMBS Total Return (%)	WAPT CMBS Total Return (%)	Difference (BP)
0	0	8.00	8.01	(1)
1	1	7.81	7.79	2
2	2	7.63	7.58	5
3	3	7.46	7.38	8
4	4	7.30	7.19	11
5	5	7.16	7.02	14

Assuming default, prepayment and yield maintenance at Treasury-flat for life				
Constant Default Rate Starting Year 1 (%)	Constant Prepayment Rate Starting Year 1 (%)	Fixed-Rate CMBS Total Return (%)	WAPT CMBS Total Return (%)	Difference (BP)
0	0	8.00	8.01	(1)
1	1	7.81	7.80	1
2	2	7.62	7.60	2
3	3	7.44	7.40	4
4	4	7.26	7.21	5
5	5	7.09	7.03	6

Source: Prudential Securities IMPACT data base as of June 16, 1997.

WAPT AND FIXED-RATE CMBS IO

While the focus has primarily been on the principal-paying class of a deal, the same principles apply to IO classes. WAPT IO coupons will fluctuate as well, although IO prices on both fixed-rate and WAPT IOs will generally decline over time (assuming pricing at constant yield). As with the principal-paying bonds, both fixed-rate and WAPT IOs will have similar total-return profiles despite the WAPT IO coupon fluctuations over time. Pricing either bond at the horizon date at a constant yield and reinvesting the interest at that same yield will result in a constant total-return profile. Unlike the principal-paying bonds however, assuming all other factors are equal, the market does appear to prefer fixed-rate IOs, leading to some price differentiation versus WAPT IOs. In fact, most recently issued CMBS IOs are fixed-rate structures.

Because IOs are much more levered structures, the effect of defaults and prepayments will likely be much greater on an IO than on the corresponding principal-paying class, as shown in Exhibit 4.

Exhibit 4 uses the same hypothetical fixed-rate and WAPT deals as Exhibit 3 but assumes for simplicity that the entire coupon from both deals is stripped to create an IO. Both IOs were initially priced at an 8% yield, assuming zero prepayments and defaults. The top part of the exhibit shows annual total returns, which were calculated assuming that the IOs were held to maturity and coupon payments were subsequently rein-

Exhibit 4: Total Return and Pricing

Assuming Constant Yield on Fixed-Rate and WAPT IOs				
Constant Default Rate Starting Year 1 (%)	Constant Prepayment Rate Starting Year 1 (%)	Fixed-Rate IO Total Return (%)	WAPT IO Total Return (%)	Difference (BP)
0	0	8.00	8.01	(1)
1	1	7.13	7.02	11
2	2	6.29	6.06	23
3	3	5.50	5.15	35
4	4	4.74	4.28	46
5	5	4.03	3.45	58
Constant Default Rate Starting Year 1 (%)	Constant Prepayment Rate Starting Year 1 (%)	Fixed Rate IO Price At 8% Yield (32^{nds})	WAPT IO Price At 8% Yield (32^{nds})	Difference (32^{nds})
0	0	36 3/32	36 4/32	-1/32
1	1	35	34 29/32	3/32
2	2	34 1/32	33 25/32	8/32
3	3	33 4/32	32 24/32	12/32
4	4	32 9+/32	31 26/32	15+/32
5	5	31 17/32	30 31/32	18/32

Source: Prudential Securities IMPACT data base as of June 16, 1997.

vested at the yield to maturity. The bottom portion of the exhibit shows the resulting price difference between the fixed-rate and WAPT IO assuming that both bonds were priced at a constant 8% yield after defaults and prepayments. As the exhibit shows, defaults and prepayments on the high-coupon loans of the WAPT have a dramatic effect on both total returns and price, more so than on the principal-paying classes. In this exhibit, we do not account for the effect of prepayment penalties because the manner in which prepayment penalties are distributed to the IO holder can vary from deal to deal with regard to how it is shared with the principal-paying classes.

SUMMARY

Although a WAPT's coupon can and will fluctuate over time, this characteristic is meaningless in comparison with fixed-rate CMBS unless losses and prepayments occur. The impact of unexpected prepayments and losses will affect either negatively or positively (depending on the loans involved) the total-return performance of a WAPT bond relative to that of a fixed-rate CMBS.

Because of this uncertainty, WAPT principal-paying and IO bonds should trade behind fixed-rate CMBSs, even on deals with strong yield-maintenance provisions since defaults will have an impact on total returns. As a result, investors should carefully analyze the underlying loan pools to determine the potential for losses and prepayments, especially with regard to high-coupon loans.

Donald G. Carden is a tax partner in the New York office of O'Melveny & Myers LLP, attorneys at law. His practice encompasses all areas of federal and New York State income taxation, with a particular emphasis on structured finance, leveraged leasing, financial products, and real estate investment trusts.

Carden has worked on the tax aspects of securitization transactions involving a wide variety of assets, including commercial and residential mortgages, equipment rentals, railroad car receivables, and revenues from entertainment properties. In the course of these transactions, Carden has addressed various structures affecting holders, issuers, and underwriters.

In the leveraged lease area, Carden has worked on transactions — representing lessors, lessees, and lenders — involving financial leases of airplanes, railroad cars, manufacturing facilities, and automobile manufacturing equipment, including a number of cross-border transactions. Carden has also been involved in a wide variety of real estate investment trust transactions, representing issuers, underwriters, and lenders.

He is the author of "New Developments in Securitization — Tax Legislation and Proposed Treasury Regulations Offer New Structuring Options," published in *New Developments in Securitization 1996* (Practising Law Institute: 1996). Carden also wrote a note, "Availability of Tax-Free Reorganization Treatment for Mergers Involving Hybrid Securities," that appears at 39 *Tax Lawyer* 349 (1986).

Carden holds a bachelor of arts degree from Georgetown University and a law degree from Georgetown University Law Center.

He is admitted to practice law in New York and New Jersey, and is a member of the New York State Bar Association and the Association of the Bar of the City of New York.

Chapter 12

Comparing FASITs with REMICs

Donald G. Carden
Tax Partner
O'Melveny & Myers LLP

Since September 1, 1997, it has been possible to effect commercial mortgage-backed securitization (CMBS) transactions through a brand-new pass-through tax vehicle — the financial asset securitization investment trust (FASIT). This vehicle was created by Congress as a part of the Small Business Jobs Protection Act of 1996, with a delayed effective date that was designed to give Treasury an opportunity to promulgate regulations addressing many of the issues raised by the legislation.

At the time this chapter was prepared, in late 1997, no such regulations had been issued. Therefore, many of the questions relating to how transactions may be structured to take advantage of FASIT remain unanswered. It is nevertheless clear that there will be distinct benefits to structuring CMBS transactions through FASITs, and equally clear that there will be significant costs to utilizing this vehicle. What follows is a brief description of the origins and substance of the FASIT legislation, followed by some simplified examples designed to highlight the major differences between FASIT and its predecessor, the real estate mortgage investment conduit (REMIC).

BACKGROUND

In any securitization transaction, tax lawyers tend to focus on two primary issues: whether the securitization vehicle will be subject to an entity-level tax and whether the securities to be issued will be treated as debt or equity for federal income tax purposes. Making these determinations on a given set of facts involves the application of some rather complex federal income tax principles. Because these principles were not developed with securitization in mind, their application to securitization transactions is often unduly complicated and occasionally produces harsh results.

In an effort to address some of the uncertainties that plagued mortgage securitization transactions, Congress in 1986 passed legislation specifically designed to make it easier to deal with the tax issues associated with those transactions. This legislation created the REMIC, which carries its own set of ambiguities and complex qualification requirements. REMIC structures are only available for securitizing mortgages, leaving those that would securitize other assets with the same set of issues and ambiguities that previously plagued mortgage-backed securities.

In 1996, Congress created the FASIT for the stated purpose of providing tax certainty similar to that available through the use of a REMIC for debt instruments other than mortgages. However, Congress did not prohibit the use of FASITs for mortgage securitization, thus presenting CMBS sponsors with a choice of vehicles. As described in this section, making this choice will in each case involve the weighing of a number of complex factors.

NON-REMIC STRUCTURES

The simplest and most direct way to effect a securitization is to contribute the collateral to a special-purpose vehicle (SPV) which qualifies as a "grantor trust" for tax purposes, and sell certificates of beneficial interest in the trust. A grantor trust, while respected as a separate entity for most legal purposes, is ignored for federal income tax purposes. Instead, the beneficiaries of a grantor trust are treated as the tax owners of the assets held in trust. As a result, the sponsor in such a transaction is deemed to have sold the collateral for tax purposes when the trust certificates are issued, and the status of the certificates for tax purposes (i.e., as representing debt or some other asset) is determined by the nature of the trust collateral itself.

In order to qualify as a grantor trust, however, two significant tax requirements must be met: The trustee must not have the power to reinvest trust assets (that is, the trust corpus must be a static pool of assets); and each certificate — with certain very limited exceptions — must provide the holder with an undivided interest in the income generated by the trust collateral. Unfortunately, these two limitations are often inconsistent with the economic result the parties are attempting to achieve through the securitization.

Specifically, absent a power to reinvest, the certificates will mature earlier than expected if prepayments are received on the underlying collateral. It is often desirable to grant the trustee a power to reinvest prepayments in order to lengthen the weighted average life of some or all of the certificates being issued. In addition, it is often desirable, in order to maximize the proceeds from the sale of trust certificates, to create multiple classes of certificates with differing interest rates and differing priorities as to repayments of principal. In seeking to meet these objectives prior to the enactment of the REMIC provisions, more elaborate structures were developed, which created a certain amount of tax complexity.

Partnership Structures

Prior to the enactment of the REMIC provisions, one technique used to avoid an entity-level tax was to structure the SPV so as to qualify as a partnership for federal income tax purposes. The income of a partnership is taxed to its partners; thus, qualifying the SPV as a partnership had an effect similar to qualifying the SPV as a grantor trust.

However, a partnership is, of course, permitted to have multiple classes of ownership interests and is permitted to engage in a business (and hence may reinvest proceeds from its underlying collateral). For these reasons, partnership structures did not suffer from the same limitations as those based on qualifying as a grantor trust. In order to qualify as a partnership for tax purposes, however, the SPV was required to lack at least two of the four corporate characteristics: continuity of life, centralization of management, free transferability of interests, and limited liability. Although various strategies were developed and employed to satisfy these criteria, none was ideal, in that the parties were often forced to enter into arrangements that they would never have contemplated absent these seemingly arbitrary tax rules.

In addition, in order to effect a CMBS transaction through a partnership structure, it was necessary to identify which of the various interests in the entity were partnership interests, as opposed to debt securities of the partnership. This was necessary in order to determine which interests in the partnership would be subject to the restrictions required to ensure partnership treatment for the SPV. In addition, it was necessary to determine who held equity in the partnership in order to report and allocate the partnership's income accurately.

Determining which of the various parties holding an interest in an SPV is a partner of the SPV involves the application of debt/equity and related principles, and is a notoriously complex and fact-specific analysis. Nevertheless, it was essential to the integrity of the approach to determine which interestholders held debt and which held equity. Each tax lawyer practicing in the area at the time developed his or her own set of criteria for making this determination. However, one common theme was to refuse to opine on the debt characterization of higher-yielding securities, on the theory that the higher yield indicated a level of risk and speculativeness that is inconsistent with true debt characterization.

CMO Structures

As an alternative to the partnership structures, certain transactions were structured by assuming that an entity-level tax would be imposed, and quantifying and reserving for such tax. The advantage of this approach was that there was no need to qualify the SPV as a partnership for tax purposes under the complex and arbitrary rules mentioned earlier.

Under these structures (referred to as collateralized mortgage obligations, or CMOs), like the partnership structures, it was critical for the tax lawyers to conclude that the securities issued were debt, since the interest deductions attributable to such debt were used to minimize the net income of the SPV. Thus, CMO structures created many of the same uncertainties present in partnership structures (but without the need to ensure that the entity would be treated as a partnership for tax purposes). CMO structures also suffered from the uncertainties associated with the tax code itself. Since tax rates and other tax provisions are subject to change, it was impossible to ensure that an adequate reserve had been established within the SPV to pay the tax.

REMIC PROVISIONS

As is readily evident from the foregoing, prior to the Tax Reform Act of 1986 there existed no completely satisfactory way to implement any but the simplest of mortgage securitization transactions. Congress, as a part of the Tax Reform Act of 1986, sought to remedy this problem by creating from scratch a vehicle specifically designed to facilitate mortgage securitization. The result was the real estate mortgage investment conduit, or REMIC. If the REMIC qualification requirements are met and a REMIC election is made, then an entity-level tax will not be imposed, and all securities issued by the REMIC (other than the residual interest of the REMIC) will be treated as debt for federal income tax purposes, regardless of the treatment such instruments would receive in a non-REMIC context.

Qualification Requirements

In order for an entity to qualify as a REMIC, it must meet two principal tests: an asset test and an interests test. Under the asset test, substantially all the assets of a REMIC must consist of "qualified mortgages" and reasonably required reserves. A "qualified mortgage" is defined as an obligation principally secured by an interest in real property, which, with certain very limited exceptions, is transferred to the REMIC upon its formation. Taxpayer-favorable Treasury regulations implementing the REMIC provisions indicate that an obligation will be considered "principally secured by an interest in real property" if, either on the date the loan was originated or on the date it is transferred to the REMIC, the fair market value of the real property securing the obligation is (or was) equal to at least 80% of the principal amount of the obligation. Although this rule is quite liberal, the asset test itself can be problematic in certain circumstances, such as where it is unclear whether the borrower is really the owner of the real property in question.

Under the REMIC "interests" test, a REMIC must issue a single class of residual interests, which represents the equity interest in the REMIC, and may issue one or more classes of regular interests meeting certain specified requirements. The regular interests of a REMIC are required, for the most part, to bear the characteristics that are normally associated with debt instruments: a fixed, noncontingent principal amount and interest payable at a fixed or qualifying variable rate. However, there is no requirement that the REMIC residual interests have any economic value. Indeed, in CMBS transactions, most residual interests have no value. Hence, if a CMBS transaction is effected through a REMIC, all the value of the underlying collateral may be reflected in the regular interests issued, without jeopardizing the treatment of those interests as debt for tax purposes or risking the imposition of an entity-level tax.

In crafting the REMIC legislation, Congress took several steps to ensure that REMICs would be entirely passive entities. First, the REMIC rules require that all REMIC regular and residual interests be issued on a single day (referred to as the startup day), and that, with limited exceptions, all qualified mortgages be transferred to the REMIC on the startup day.

In addition, under the REMIC rules a 100% tax is imposed upon any contributions made to a REMIC more than 90 days after the startup day, and a separate 100% tax is imposed on any net income from prohibited transactions of the REMIC, including any disposition of any mortgage held by the REMIC, with certain very limited exceptions. Thus, it is clear that Congress intended for REMICs to hold static pools of mortgages and, in this sense, to operate essentially in the same way as grantor trusts.

TAXATION OF A REMIC

As noted, a REMIC is not subject to an entity-level tax. Instead, the holder of the residual interest in the REMIC pays tax on the REMIC's income. The income of the REMIC is determined by taking into account interest received on the qualified mortgages (as well as other income of the REMIC), and deducting interest payable on the REMIC regular interests (as well as other expenses of the REMIC).

The net result, in most cases, is the creation of phantom income (in excess of deductions) in the early years of the transaction, offset by phantom losses in the later years of the transaction. Congress was determined to ensure that this phantom income did not escape taxation, which would have created a net tax benefit from the securitization. As a result, the REMIC provisions contain a series of rules designed to ensure that the holder of the residual interest is subject to tax in the United States, and most, if not all, of this phantom income cannot be offset by net operating losses suffered by the residual interestholder as a result of other activities.

No such rules apply to the holders of any REMIC regular interests, regardless of whether those interests would be treated as debt or as equity under common law principles.

The REMIC provisions provide special rules for determining the tax treatment of the formation of a REMIC. Under these rules, the sponsor of the REMIC is treated as having contributed the mortgage pool to the REMIC in exchange for the regular and residual interests. The contribution itself is a tax-free transaction, with the sponsor's tax basis in the mortgages being allocated to the interests received in accordance with their respective fair market values.

As interests are sold, the sponsor recognizes gain or loss based on the tax basis of each interest as so determined. If any interest is retained, the sponsor amortizes any gain or loss attributable to such interest over its weighted average life. The REMIC takes a fair-market-value basis in the mortgages contributed, and recognizes premium or discount on a yield-to-maturity basis. The net result of these rules seems entirely appropriate: The sponsor recognizes income equal to the excess of the amount of cash generated by the transaction over the sponsor's original tax basis in the mortgages contributed to the REMIC.

Taxable Mortgage Pool Provisions

Along with the REMIC provisions, Congress enacted a separate set of provisions which, after 1991, ensure that mortgage securitizations involving the issuance of multiple classes of debt will be affected through an entity that qualifies as a REMIC. Under these rules, any entity which qualifies as a taxable mortgage pool is treated as a separate corporation (regardless of whether it would otherwise qualify for treatment as a partnership or grantor trust). A separate corporation cannot be included in the filing of a consolidated federal income tax return, thereby ensuring that a corporate-level tax will be imposed on the income of any such entity. A taxable mortgage pool is defined as any entity (other than a REMIC) if:

- Substantially all of the assets of such entity consists of debt obligations (or interests therein), and more than 50% of such debt obligations (or interests) consists of real estate mortgages (or interests therein).
- Such entity is the obligor under debt obligations with two or more maturities.
- Payments on such debt obligations "bear a relationship" to payments on the underlying debt obligations owned by the entity.

One unfortunate aspect of the taxable mortgage pool rules is that, while they are designed to ensure that REMICs are used to securitize mortgages, they are actually quite a bit broader than necessary to achieve this result. Thus, for example, if a pool of debt instruments consists principally, but not entirely, of mortgages, the pool would not be eligible for REMIC treatment but would nevertheless meet the requirements for treatment as a taxable mortgage pool. The same horrific result would also apply if the pool could not meet some other REMIC requirement (for example, because a REMIC regular interest was issued other than on the startup day, or a hedging instrument was included in the pool) but the pool nevertheless consists principally of mortgage loans.

FASIT PROVISIONS

On August 20, 1996, Congress enacted the Small Business Jobs Protection Act of 1996, which contains provisions creating a new type of pass-through entity, the financial asset securitization investment trust, or FASIT. The FASIT provisions, which are modeled loosely after the REMIC provisions, are designed to facilitate nonmortgage securitization transactions in the same way that the REMIC provisions have facilitated mortgage securitizations.

Under the FASIT provisions, an entity that qualifies for treatment as a FASIT is not subject to an entity-level tax. Instead, the holder of the ownership interest in the FASIT is treated as the owner of the underlying assets of the FASIT, and recognizes income or loss accordingly. In addition, as is the case with REMIC, the regular interests of a FASIT are treated as debt for federal income tax purposes, regardless of their treatment for other purposes, and regardless of whether they are supported by an economic "ownership interest."

Qualification Requirements

As is the case with REMIC, in order to qualify as a FASIT an entity must satisfy an asset requirement and an interest requirement. Under the FASIT asset requirement, after an initial startup period, substantially all of the assets of the FASIT must consist of:

- Cash or cash equivalents.
- Debt instruments under which interest payments are made either at a fixed or at a qualifying variable rate[1] (other than debt issued by the holder of the ownership interest in the FASIT or any party related thereto).
- Foreclosure property.
- Interest rate or foreign currency swap contracts, insurance, guarantees, and similar instruments which are reasonably required to guarantee or hedge against the FASIT's risks associated with being the obligor on the FASIT regular interests.
- Contractual rights to acquire debt instruments or hedges as described earlier.
- Any regular interest in another FASIT.
- Any regular interest in a REMIC.

Unlike a REMIC, these assets need not be acquired by the FASIT during the startup period, but may be acquired at a later time. Thus, a FASIT need not be a static pool.

The FASIT interests test requires that all interests in the FASIT consist of regular interests and a single ownership interest. Subject to a

---

[1]This requirement, that the debt instruments owned by a FASIT not bear contingent interest, has no corollary in the REMIC provisions, and could prove to be a significant issue. If read literally, for example, this requirement could prevent a FASIT from owning any debt instrument that calls for yield maintenance premiums or gross-ups, since such amounts are analyzed for tax purposes as contingent interest. The prevailing view among tax professionals is that Treasury will take a more liberal approach in regulations, in order to permit the FASIT to develop into a useful securitization tool.

special exception described later, a FASIT regular interest must have the following characteristics:

- Unconditional entitlement of the holder to receive a specified principal amount and interest based on a fixed or qualifying variable rate.
- Stated maturity (including options to renew) no greater than 30 years.
- Issue price that does not exceed 125% of its stated principal amount.
- Yield to maturity that is less than the applicable federal rate (AFR) + 500 basis points.

Notwithstanding these four general requirements, a FASIT can issue what the code refers to as high-yield interests, defined as interest-only regular interests, or interests calling for contingent principal, or interests with an issue price in excess of 125% of their stated principal amount, or interests with a yield to maturity that equals or exceeds the AFR + 500 basis points. Special rules apply to such high-yield interests which ensure that they are held only by taxable domestic corporations, and that the resulting income is not offset by non-FASIT losses. The theory behind these rules, presumably, is that such interests are more like equity than debt, and that steps need to be taken to ensure that they don't escape the imposition of a corporate-level tax. These rules represent a dramatic change from the approach taken in the REMIC provisions, where there are no such restrictions other than for residual interests.

As already noted, a FASIT must also have one, and only one, ownership interest — the interest that corresponds to a REMIC residual interest. As is the case with a REMIC residual interest, a FASIT ownership interest need not have any economic value. The holder of the ownership interest treats the assets, income and deductions of the FASIT as its assets, income, and deductions. The holder of an ownership interest must be a taxable domestic corporation, and special rules ensure that the resulting income from the ownership interest will not be offset by non-FASIT losses.

FASIT 'Prohibited Transactions'

As is the case with a REMIC, a FASIT is subject to a 100% tax on the net income derived from certain prohibited transactions. This tax is imposed upon the holder of the ownership interest (as opposed to a REMIC, where the tax is imposed upon the REMIC itself).

The FASIT provisions define a prohibited transaction as:

- The receipt of any income derived from any asset that is not a permitted asset.
- Except as described below, the disposition of any permitted asset.
- The receipt of any income derived from any loan originated by the FASIT.
- The receipt of any income representing a fee or other compensation for services.

The most important of these categories is likely to be the prohibition on disposing of any permitted asset, which tracks a similar provision in the REMIC rules. However, the FASIT provisions contain an important exception to this rule that is not contained in the REMIC provisions. Specifically, a FASIT is permitted to substitute one debt instrument for another debt instrument which is a permitted asset, and may distribute debt instruments to the holder of the ownership interest to reduce overcollateralization, in each case so long as a principal purpose of acquiring the debt instrument which is disposed of was not the recognition of gain (or the reduction of loss) as a result of an increase in the market value of the debt instrument after its acquisition by the FASIT.

This principal purpose standard appears to have been derived from a Securities and Exchange Commission exemption from 1940 Act treatment. While the substitution exemption generally is intended to permit a broad range of transactions on the part of the FASIT, this principal purpose carveout is designed to prevent FASITs from becoming traders of debt instruments (which is the function of the 1940 Act test as well).

It is quite curious that the FASIT provisions attempt to impose a prohibited transactions tax on distributions of debt instruments to the holder of a FASIT ownership interest. Since such holder is deemed the owner of the assets of the FASIT for tax purposes, such a distribution should be a non-event. Thus, arguably, even if the principal purpose standard is not satisfied with respect to a particular distribution, there should be no confiscatory tax, since there would be no net income resulting from the transaction. Since the statute clearly intends some kind of penalty tax to apply, however, the meaning of this provision is unclear.

Tax Treatment of the FASIT and Its Sponsor

The FASIT rules are quite different from the REMIC rules in their tax treatment of the FASIT and its sponsor. Under the FASIT rules, gain, but not loss, is recognized to the holder of the ownership interest when property is contributed to a FASIT. This contrasts with the REMIC rules, where neither gain nor loss is recognized on a contribution, but gain and loss is subsequently recognized, either on a sale of the regular/residual interests by the sponsor or, with respect to any retained interests, on a constant yield basis over the life of the interest.

Property is deemed contributed to a FASIT, thereby triggering gain, when such property supports a regular interest, even if it is being held outside the FASIT at such time. The Internal Revenue Service is authorized to prescribe regulations which would delay gain recognition on property that has been contributed to a FASIT until such time as such property supports a regular interest.

What may prove to be by far the most important provision contained in FASIT is a special valuation rule utilized to determine the amount of gain, if any, recognized by the sponsor when property is contributed to the FASIT. Under this rule, if such property is nonpublicly traded debt, the fair market value of the debt is determined by discounting the reasonably expected payments to be received under the instrument to present value utilizing a discount rate equal to 120% of the applicable federal rate, or such other rate as may be specified in regulations to be issued by the IRS. The applicable federal rate, or AFR, is an interest rate determined and published monthly by the IRS, based on the then-prevailing yield on Treasuries.[2] As illustrated, this rule results in the sponsor of a FASIT recognizing income for tax purposes which is likely to bear no relationship to the economic gain attributed to the transaction.

A FASIT takes a carryover basis in property contributed to it, increased by any gain recognized by the contribution. If such gain results in a basis that exceeds the stated principal amount of the obligation, the excess gives rise to bond premium that is amortized by the FASIT over the remaining life of the debt instrument. If the FASIT has a basis in an obligation that is less than its stated principal amount (which, in light of the special valuation rule, should be a rare event), the FASIT, like a REMIC, is required to accrue the difference as market discount on a con-

---

[2]There are actually three AFRs: the short-term AFR, which is applicable to instruments with maturities of not more than three years, the mid-term AFR, which is applicable to instruments with maturities over three years but not more than nine years, and the long-term AFR, applicable to all other instruments.

stant yield basis.

Although not stated expressly, since the assets of the FASIT are treated as owned by the holder of the ownership interest, the sale of the regular interests in a FASIT should not give rise to gain or loss. Rather, the holder of the ownership interest should be treated for tax purposes as if it had borrowed against the assets held by the FASIT, a tax-free event. This, as already noted, is a significantly different result than under the REMIC provisions, where the sale of the certificates rather than the contribution of the assets triggers tax.

Effect of FASIT on Other Code Provisions

In addition to enacting the FASIT provisions themselves, Congress in the Small Business Jobs Protection Act amended the following provisions to accommodate the FASIT concept:

- The taxable mortgage pool provisions were amended to exempt FASITs from taxable mortgage pool treatment. (The impact of this change is discussed more fully in a later section.)
- The REMIC provisions were amended to provide that a regular interest in a FASIT is a qualified mortgage if 95% or more of the assets of the FASIT at all times consist of obligations principally secured by real property (which need not be held by the FASIT on the startup day and at all times thereafter).
- The REIT rules were amended to provide that a regular interest in a FASIT is treated as a qualifying REIT asset to the extent that the underlying assets of the FASIT would be so treated, and that the entire interest will be so treated if at least 95% of the underlying assets of the FASIT so qualify.

COMPARISON OF REMIC AND FASIT FOR CMBS TRANSACTIONS

As noted, FASITs are specifically exempted from the taxable mortgage pool rules; thus, beginning September 1, 1997, it is possible to effect a CMBS transaction involving the issuance of securities with multiple maturities through either a REMIC or a FASIT, in each case without incurring an entity-level tax. From an administrative and structuring standpoint, there are a number of clear advantages that FASITs now have over REMICs. The clear advantages of a FASIT include the following:

- Regular interests need not be issued on its startup day, and can be redeemed or refinanced at will.
- Principal payments received on the underlying collateral can

be reinvested, permitting a greater measure of call protection to regular interestholders.

- The FASIT provisions allow for latitude to substitute collateral (although, as noted, a FASIT's right to do so is not limitless).
- The FASIT provisions contain a far more generous asset test, permitting a FASIT to own hedging instruments and any kind of debt instrument, whether or not such instrument qualifies as a mortgage.

Against these benefits, however, sponsors must weigh the following distinct disadvantages of FASIT:

- The inability to sell FASIT high-yield interests, including interest-only (IO) pieces, to anyone other than domestic taxable C corporations.
- The calculation of gain on the formation of a FASIT, based in many cases on an arbitrary formula keyed off the AFR.

It seems likely that these two disadvantages will together constitute a strong disincentive to using FASIT, which in many, if not most, cases will outweigh the substantial additional flexibility offered through the use of FASIT structures.

EXAMPLES COMPARING FASIT WITH REMIC

The following examples are designed to illustrate the different results achieved through use of a FASIT as opposed to a REMIC for a simple multiple-class securitization. The examples are not intended to be realistic, and hence ignore complicating factors such as expenses and initial short-period interest accruals. They also do not illustrate the benefits of using a FASIT, since to introduce an element in the transaction that could not be replicated using a REMIC would prevent an accurate comparison of the relative tax imposed on formation using REMIC and FASIT structures. Nevertheless, these examples are instructive in that they present numerical illustrations of the differences in the tax treatment of REMICs, FASITs and their respective sponsors.

Securitization of a Simple Mortgage

Assume the mortgage pool to be securitized consists of a single $100 million mortgage bearing interest at 10%, compounded annually, and amortizing ratably over a 14-year period. Assume further that the sponsor has a tax basis in such mortgage equal to par. The interest and principal payable with respect to such a mortgage would be as shown in Exhibit 1.

Exhibit 1: Securitization of a Simple Mortgage

COLLATERAL: A single $100,000,000 mortgage loan
Interest rate = 10%, compounded annually
Level payments over 14 years ($13,574,622 per year)
Tax basis = $100,000,000

Year	Beginning Principal	Interest	Amortization	Ending Principal
1	$100,000,000	$10,000,000	$3,574,622	$96,425,378
2	96,425,378	9,642,538	3,932,085	92,493,293
3	92,493,293	9,249,329	4,325,293	88,168,000
4	88,168,000	8,816,800	4,757,822	83,410,178
5	83,410,178	8,341,018	5,233,605	78,176,573
6	78,176,573	7,817,657	5,756,965	72,419,608
7	72,419,608	7,241,961	6,332,661	66,086,947
8	66,086,947	6,608,695	6,965,928	59,121,019
9	59,121,019	5,912,102	7,662,520	51,458,499
10	51,458,499	5,145,850	8,428,772	43,029,726
11	43,029,726	4,302,973	9,271,650	33,758,076
12	33,758,077	3,375,808	10,198,815	23,559,262
13	23,559,262	2,355,926	11,218,696	12,340,566
14	12,340,566	1,234,057	12,340,566	-0-
		$90,044,712	$100,000,000	

Further, assume that this mortgage is to be securitized by issuing the interests shown in Exhibit 2.

Exhibit 2: Interests Issued in Securitization Example

Pieces		Sale Proceeds
A	$70,000,000, 8% interest, sold at par	$70,000,000
A-IO	Excess of 10% over 8%, sold to yield 11%	6,373,623
B	$15,000,000, 10%, sold at par	15,000,000
C	$10,000,000, 10%, sold to yield 15%	7,156,555
D	$5,000,000, 10%, sold to yield 20%	2,694,716
		$101,224,894

The interests to be issued are expected to amortize in accordance with the schedule shown in Exhibit 3.

Exhibit 3: Amortization of Sample Securitization

Year	Principal Payments Received	A	B	C	D
1	3,574,622	3,574,622	- 0 -	- 0 -	- 0 -
2	3,932,085	3,932,085	- 0 -	- 0 -	- 0 -
3	4,325,293	4,325,293	- 0 -	- 0 -	- 0 -
4	4,757,822	4,757,822	- 0 -	- 0 -	- 0 -
5	5,233,605	5,233,605	- 0 -	- 0 -	- 0 -
6	5,756,965	5,756,965	- 0 -	- 0 -	- 0 -
7	6,332,662	6,322,662	- 0 -	- 0 -	- 0 -
8	6,965,928	6,965,928	- 0 -	- 0 -	- 0 -
9	7,662,520	7,662,520	- 0 -	- 0 -	- 0 -
10	8,428,772	8,428,772	- 0 -	- 0 -	- 0 -
11	9,271,650	9,271,650	- 0 -	- 0 -	- 0 -
12	10,198,815	3,758,076	6,440,738	- 0 -	- 0 -
13	11,218,696	- 0 -	8,559,262	2,659,434	- 0 -
14	12,340,566	- 0 -	- 0 -	7,340,566	5,000,000
	$100,000,000	$70,000,000	$15,000,000	$10,000,000	$5,000,000

Taxation If a REMIC Is Utilized

If the securitization described in exhibits 1-3 were effected through a REMIC, the sponsor would be treated as having contributed the mortgage to the REMIC in a tax-free carryover basis transaction in exchange for the REMIC regular and residual interests, then as having sold such interests (other than the residual, which we have assumed will be retained). The sponsor's $100 million tax basis in the mortgage will be allocated to the REMIC interests in accordance with their relative fair

Exhibit 4: Sample Allocation of REMIC Interests

	Issue Price	Tax Basis	Gain on Sale
A	$70,000,000	$69,152,950	$847,050
A-IO	6,373,623	6,296,498	77,125
B	15,000,000	14,818,489	181,511
C	7,156,555	7,069,955	86,600
D	2,694,716	2,662,108	32,608
Residual	-0-	-0-	-0-
	$101,224,894	$100,000,000	$1,224,894

The REMIC's tax basis in the mortgage will equal $101,224,894, which is the aggregate issue price of the REMIC's regular and residual interests. The REMIC will be permitted to amortize $1,224,894 of premium over the life of the mortgage, which will reduce its interest income over such period on a yield to maturity basis.

As can be seen from the foregoing, the sponsor recognized a $1,224,894 gain from the transaction, representing the excess of the amount received on the sale of the securities, $101,224,894, over the sponsor's tax basis of $100 million in the mortgage securitized. Thus, under the REMIC provisions, the sponsor has income on the transaction equal to the amount of excess cash received as a result of the securitization, an entirely sensible result.

Of course, this is not the end of the story. Recall that we have assumed the sponsor will retain the REMIC residual interest, which has no economic value. This interest will, in accordance with the REMIC rules outlined earlier, be allocated net income or loss from the REMIC for the duration of the transaction. As is often the case with securitizations of this type, the residual interestholder will recognize phantom income in the early years of this transaction offset by phantom losses in later years, but resulting in a present-value detriment to the holder. In this case, such amounts would be as shown in Exhibit 5.

Taxation If a FASIT Is Utilized (Based on a 7.75% AFR)

In order to determine the tax results if the transaction described in our example were effected through a FASIT, it is necessary to know one additional fact: the AFR. Assume initially that on the date the transaction is entered into, the AFR is 7.75%. Based on this assumption, the amount deemed received by the sponsor as a result of the securitization is determined by discounting the payments to be received by the sponsor[3] at 120% of the AFR, or 9.30%. This yields the results shown in Exhibit 6.

Based on the foregoing, it appears that if the transaction were effected through a FASIT, the sponsor would recognize gain of $3,933,376 ($103,933,376 less a tax basis of $100 million) notwithstanding that the sponsor only pockets $1,224,894 in pre-tax cash. The difference, $2,708,482, gives rise to additional premium amortization deductions that will reduce income recognized by the sponsor over the life of the transac-

---

[3]As already described, the FASIT provisions require only that reasonably expected payments be discounted for this purpose. However, based on our facts, it seems likely that all payments required under the mortgage should be treated as reasonably expected payments.

will reduce income recognized by the sponsor over the life of the transaction (through the sponsor's ownership of the FASIT ownership interest).

Exhibit 5: Present-Value Detriment
To Residual Interest Holder

Year	Interest Income	Interest Deductions	Net
1	$9,897,184	$9,413,526	$483,658
2	9,537,625	9,069,488	468,137
3	9,142,910	8,699,470	443,440
4	8,709,604	8,301,898	407,706
5	8,233,930	7,875,160	358,770
6	7,711,748	7,417,635	294,114
7	7,138,511	6,927,709	210,802
8	6,509,225	6,403,793	105,432
9	5,818,411	5,844,357	(25,946)
10	5,060,054	5,247,965	(187,911)
11	4,227,549	4,613,320	(385,771)
12	3,313,646	3,939,319	(625,673)
13	2,310,387	3,096,302	(785,915)
14	1,209,036	1,969,879	(760,843)

Exhibit 6: Sample Taxation Based on 7.75% AFR

Year	Payment	PV at 9.3%
1	$13,574,622	$12,419,600
2	13,574,622	11,362,854
3	13,574,622	10,396,024
4	13,574,622	9,511,458
5	13,574,622	8,702,158
6	13,574,622	7,961,718
7	13,574,622	7,284,280
8	13,574,622	6,664,483
9	13,574,622	6,097,423
10	13,574,622	5,578,612
11	13,574,622	5,103,945
12	13,574,622	4,669,666
13	13,574,622	4,272,338
14	13,574,622	3,908,818
		$103,933,376

Exhibit 7: Additional Premium Amortization Deductions

Year	Interest Income	Interest Deductions	Net
1	$9,665,804	$9,413,526	$252,278
2	9,302,284	9,069,488	232,796
3	8,904,956	8,699,470	205,486
4	8,470,677	8,301,898	168,779
5	7,996,011	7,875,160	120,851
6	7,477,199	7,417,635	59,565
7	6,910,140	6,927,709	(17,569)
8	6,290,343	6,403,793	(113,450)
9	5,612,905	5,844,357	(231,452)
10	4,872,465	5,247,965	(375,500)
11	4,063,164	4,613,320	(550,156)
12	3,178,599	3,939,319	(760,720)
13	2,211,768	3,096,302	(884,534)
14	1,155,023	1,969,879	(814,856)
	$86,111,336	$88,819,819	$(2,708,482)

It should be noted that these results are highly sensitive to changes in the AFR. This is significant, since the AFR is set only once a month rather than on a daily basis, and since only very rough adjustments are made to the AFR to account for differing maturities.

Taxation If a FASIT Is Utilized (Based on an 8% AFR)

To illustrate the degree to which small changes in the AFR effect the amount of income realized by the sponsor of the transaction, assume that at the time the transaction occurs the AFR is 8.00%, rather than 7.75%. In such case, 120% of the AFR would be 9.60%, and the amount of gain realized by the sponsor would be determined as shown in Exhibit 8.

The extra amount of gain recognized by the sponsor, in excess of the amount of pre-tax cash pocketed by the sponsor, in this case would be $993,423, and through the ownership interest the sponsor would receive income or loss each year as shown in Exhibit 9.

Securitization of Two Mortgages

As noted earlier, another interesting, and unfortunate, aspect of the taxation of a FASIT transaction is that a sponsor is not entitled to recognize a loss on a transfer of assets to a FASIT. To illustrate the significance of this rule, assume the same facts as in the earlier example, except that instead of one $100 million mortgage, the mortgage pool consists of two

Exhibit 8: Sample Taxation Based on 8% AFR

Year	Payment	PV at 9.6%
1	$13,574,622	$12,385,604
2	13,574,622	11,300,734
3	13,574,622	10,310,889
4	13,574,622	9,407,745
5	13,574,622	8,583,709
6	13,574,622	7,831,851
7	13,574,622	7,145,850
8	13,574,622	6,519,936
9	13,574,622	5,948,847
10	13,574,622	5,427,780
11	13,574,622	4,952,354
12	13,574,622	4,518,571
13	13,574,622	4,122,784
14	13,574,622	3,761,664
		$102,218,316

Exhibit 9: Ownership Interest Gains or Losses

Year	Interest Income	Interest Deductions	Net
1	$9,812,958	$9,413,526	$399,432
2	9,451,839	9,069,488	382,351
3	9,056,051	8,699,470	356,581
4	8,622,269	8,301,898	320,371
5	8,146,843	7,875,160	271,683
6	7,625,775	7,417,635	208,141
7	7,054,687	6,927,709	126,978
8	6,428,773	6,403,793	24,980
9	5,742,771	5,844,357	(101,586)
10	4,990,913	5,247,965	(257,052)
11	4,166,878	4,613,320	(446,442)
12	3,263,734	3,939,319	(675,585)
13	2,273,888	3,096,302	(822,414)
14	1,189,018	1,969,879	(780,861)
	$87,826,395	$88,819,819	($993,423)

$50 million mortgages with identical terms, one with a tax basis of $47 million and the other with a tax basis of $53 million.

Under the REMIC provisions, the results to the sponsor are

Under the REMIC provisions, the results to the sponsor are exactly the same, since the REMIC rules permit sponsors to recognize both gains and losses, which in this case offset each other exactly. Under the FASIT provisions, however, the results are dramatically different, as evidenced by the following (assuming AFR = 7.75%):

Deemed Value
Mortgage 1 = $51,966,688
Mortgage 2 = $51,966,688

Gain on Contribution

Mortgage No. 1	$4,966,688	(51,966,688 - 47,000,000)
Mortgage No. 2	-0-	(deferred loss)
Total	$4,966,688	

Again, this additional income will ultimately be offset through the sponsor's ownership of the ownership interest, but the sponsor suffers a detriment due to the time value of money, as shown in Exhibit 10.

Exhibit 10: Detriment Due to Time Value of Money

Year	Interest Income	Interest Deductions	Net
1	$9,576,088	$9,413,526	$162,562
2	9,211,303	9,069,488	141,815
3	8,813,238	8,699,470	113,768
4	8,378,858	8,301,898	76,960
5	7,904,850	7,875,160	29,690
6	7,387,597	7,417,635	(30,037)
7	6,823,157	6,927,709	(104,552)
8	6,207,222	6,403,793	(196,571)
9	5,535,096	5,844,357	(309,261)
10	4,801,651	5,247,965	(446,314)
11	4,001,295	4,613,320	(612,025)
12	3,127,923	3,939,319	(811,396)
13	2,174,872	3,096,302	(921,430)
14	1,134,876	1,969,879	(835,003)
	$85,078,024	$88,819,819	($3,741,794)

SUMMARY

As these examples illustrate, the FASIT provisions provide flexibility at a price which can fluctuate depending upon seemingly arbitrary variables. Hopefully, Treasury regulations, when issued, will provide for broad exceptions to the general rule that gain is recognized by discounting payments at the statutorily prescribed rate, which is the source of much of this arbitrariness. Otherwise, the FASIT vehicle may prove useful only in circumstances where the underlying collateral has a high basis, or a yield under 120% of the AFR, or otherwise where the sponsor is indifferent to the gain recognized on formation.

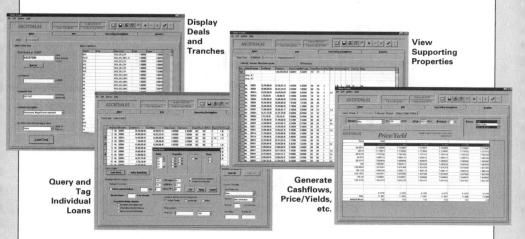

We're Off To A Great Start: $100 Million In Our First 100 Days

Introducing Prudential Mortgage Capital Company, LLC

While we at Prudential are excited about the early success of our new conduit company, our most important message is that we are here for the long term.

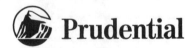

Books available from Frank J. Fabozzi Associates

Bond Portfolio Management
Fixed Income Securities
Managing Fixed Income Portfolios
Selected Topics in Bond Portfolio Management
Valuation of Fixed Income Securities and Derivatives 3rd. Ed.
Valuation of Interest-Sensitive Financial Instruments
Advanced Fixed Income Analytics
Advances in Fixed Income Valuation Modeling and Risk Management
Treasury Securities and Derivatives
Managing MBS Portfolios
The Handbook of Investing in Corporate Debt Instruments
Corporate Bonds: Structures & Analysis
Collateralized Mortgage Obligations: Structures and Analysis
Asset-Backed Securities
The Handbook of Commercial Mortgage-Backed Securities 2nd Ed.
Handbook of Nonagency Mortgage-Backed Securities
Basics of Mortgage-Backed Securities
Inflation Protection Bonds
Perspectives on International Fixed Income Investing
Bank Loans: Secondary Market and Portfolio Management
The Handbook of Stable Value Investments
Handbook of Emerging Fixed Income and Currency Markets
Handbook of Portfolio Management
Introduction to Quantitative Methods For Investment Managers
Measuring and Controlling Interest Rate Risk
Dictionary of Financial Risk Management
Risk Management: Framework, Methods, and Practice
Perspectives on Interest Rate Risk Management for Money Managers and Traders
Essays In Derivatives
Handbook of Equity Style Management – Second Edition
Active Equity Portfolio Management
Selected Topics in Equity Portfolio Management
Foundations of Economic Value-Added
Investing By The Numbers
Professional Perspectives on Indexing
Pension Fund Investment Management – Second Edition
Modeling the Market: New Theories and Techniques
Securities Lending and Repurchase Agreements
Credit Union Investment Management

For more information visit our web site: www.frankfabozzi.com

Article Synopsis: Chapter 16, Measuring Risks in the Whole Loan Commercial Market

Know Thy Collateral!

- Commercial Mortgages are an important ingredient within global asset allocation.
- On a total return basis, multifamily mortgages had a return equivalent to investment grade corporate bonds with half the risk.
- Commercial mortgage performance correlates well with the real estate cycle, not stock and bond market cycles.
- While the attractiveness of commercial mortgage from a yield and diversification perspective is apparent, the level of generally accepted risk analysis has not kept up with the volume and maturity of this market.
- The need for better risk analysis becomes even more magnified with the rapid development of the CMBS market. For CMBS buyers - and especially those who buy the B-pieces - analyzing the default probabilities of the collateral is essential!
- How do you analyze commercial mortgage risk? Modify the contractual cash flow of each loan by the probability of a credit event (delinquency, foreclosure, restructure, sale at discount, etc.) by the probable loss severity of the credit event and by the timing of its occurrence. The difference between the contractual IRR and the risk adjusted IRR = "yield degradation," expressed in basis points.
- Armed with credit risk adjusted cashflows for each loan, better loan pricing should result. Only then can "true portfolio analytics", in the form of a rigorous commercial loan ratings system, be developed. This commercial loan ratings system will lead to a more efficient commercial mortgage capital market.

MORTGAGE ANALYTICS

A DIVISION OF GMAC COMMERCIAL MORTGAGE